M000266545

i-Net+™

The Cram Sheet

This Cram Sheet contains the distilled, key facts about the i-Net+ Exam. Review this information before you enter the test room, paying special attention to those areas where you feel you need the most review. You can transfer any of these facts from your head onto a blank sheet of paper before beginning the exam.

i-NET+ BASICS

1. The Internet depends upon the TCP/IP protocol and its suite of features.

2. Every IP host must have a unique address—a 32-bit binary number. Every IP host must also have a subnet mask and a default gateway setting.

3. Internet Service Providers (ISPs) provide access to the Internet through Network Access Points (NAPs).

4. A Uniform Resource Locator (URL) is used to access resources on the Internet. The URL specifies the protocol used to access the resource (such as http: for a Web page), the name of the server where the resource resides (such as www.domain.com), the port (such as :8080), and the path to the resource (such as /folder/file.htm).

5. Know the common TCP/IP ports:
   - *FTP*—21
   - *Telnet*—23
   - *SMTP*—25
   - *HTTP (WWW)*—80
   - *POP3*—110
   - *NNTP*—119
   - *LDAP*—389

6. Caching allows RAM to be used instead of actual access to speed up operations. Caching can be done on the client or server. A client can also cache Web data, increasing the overall efficiency with which Web pages are retrieved later.

7. To require that a word appear in the results of a keyword search, use a plus sign before the keyword. To ensure that a word does not appear in the results, use a minus sign before the keyword.

i-NET+ CLIENTS

8. TCP/IP is required for a client to access the Internet. Implementations of TCP/IP differ between operating systems. Microsoft implements TCP/IP as a Windows Socket DLL in the Windows operating system.

9. An FTP client can choose to download a file in different formats (binary/ASCII) and use the following commands for interacting with files:
   - **put**—To copy a file to a remote site
   - **get**—To retrieve a file from a remote site
   - **mput**—To copy multiple files to a remote site
   - **mget**—To retrieve multiple files from a remote site

43. The top-level domains include:
    - *com*—Commercial organizations
    - *edu*—Educational organizations
    - *gov*—Government institutions
    - *mil*—Military groups
    - *net*—Internet infrastructure organizations
    - *org*—Non-profit organizations and those not covered above

i-NET+ SECURITY

44. Choose passwords that are alphanumeric and, if possible, use special characters. Never choose a password from a dictionary. Ensure that passwords are at least six to eight characters long.

45. A firewall or a proxy is used to protect a network from external threats by filtering data based upon address or ports. A firewall can be hardware or software implemented.

46. Anti-virus software should be running on all systems on the network, and you should temporarily disable virus protection when installing software.

47. Auditing involves checking log files and using intrusion-detection utilities.

48. SET (Secure Electronic Transactions) is a standard for using digital signatures for credit transactions.

49. Virtual Private Networks (VPNs) use tunneling and encryption, and they are used for creating extranets. VPNs securely connect two or more nodes across a public network.

50. Suspicious activity can include Denial of Service (DoS) attacks and multiple logon failures.

51. A Denial of Service (DoS) attack is typically a deliberate attack to overwhelm the resources on a system so that the system is unable to respond to legitimate requests.

52. SYN floods overwhelm a host with requests for connections at the server entry ports.

53. Spam is the electronic equivalent of junk mail. This includes unsolicited email sent to multiple recipients, or multiple simultaneous postings to newsgroups.

BUSINESS CONCEPTS

54. Copyrights are used to protect Web content. The copyright holder has exclusive access to the content.

55. Copyrights cannot protect items that patents and trademarks were intended to cover.

56. Unicode allows for easy translation of characters into different languages.

57. Pull technology requires a browser to request information from a server. Push technology sends information to a browser before it is requested.

58. Electronic Data Interchange (EDI) allows information to be transferred between dissimilar applications. EDI describes the set of standards for the transfer of business documents between systems.

59. An intranet is a private network that utilizes TCP/IP and Internet technologies, and it is typically used for the management and dissemination of information within an organization.

60. An extranet is created as an extension to the corporate intranet or when two or more intranets are joined. An extranet improves communication and efficiency between an organization and its customers, vendors, and business partners.

i-Net+™

Martin Weiss
Emmett Dulaney

i-Net+™ Exam Cram

Limits Of Liability And Disclaimer Of Warranty

Trademarks

The Coriolis Group, LLC
14455 N. Hayden Road
Suite 220
Scottsdale, Arizona 85260

480/483-0192
FAX 480/483-0193
http://www.coriolis.com

Library of Congress Cataloging-in-Publication Data
Dulaney, Emmett A.
  i-Net+ exam cram/by Emmett Dulaney and Martin Weiss.
    p. cm.
  Includes index.
  ISBN 1-57610-673-X
  1. Electronic data processing personnel--Certification.
2. Internetworking (Telecommunication)--Examinations--Study
guides. I. Weiss, Martin. II. Title.
QA76.3.D8235 2000
004.6--dc21   00-022668
                                               CIP

President, CEO
Keith Weiskamp

Publisher
Steve Sayre

Acquisitions Editor
Shari Jo Hehr

Marketing Specialist
Cynthia Caldwell

Project Editor
Lynette Cox

Technical Reviewer
Andre Paree-Huff

Production Coordinator
Wendy Littley

Cover Designer
Jesse Dunn

Layout Design
April Nielsen

Printed in the United States of America
10 9 8 7 6 5 4 3 2 1

CORIOLIS

14455 North Hayden Road • Suite 220 • Scottsdale, Arizona 85260

Coriolis: The Smartest Way To Get Certified™

To help you reach your goals, we've listened to readers like you, and we've designed our entire product line around you and the way you like to study, learn, and master challenging subjects.

In addition to our highly popular *Exam Cram* and *Exam Prep* books, we offer several other products to help you pass certification exams. Our *Practice Tests* and *Flash Cards* are designed to make your studying fun and productive. Our *Audio Reviews* have received rave reviews from our customers—and they're the perfect way to make the most of your drive time!

The newest way to get certified is the *Exam Cram Personal Trainer*—a highly interactive, personalized self-study course based on the best-selling *Exam Cram* series. It's the first certification-specific product to completely link a customizable learning tool, exclusive *Exam Cram* content, and multiple testing techniques so you can study what, how, and when you want.

Exam Cram Insider—a biweekly newsletter containing the latest in certification news, study tips, and announcements from Certification Insider Press—gives you an ongoing look at the hottest certification programs. (To subscribe, send an email to **eci@coriolis.com** and type "subscribe insider" in the body of the email.) We also sponsor the Certified Crammer Society and the Coriolis Help Center—two other resources that will help you get certified even faster!

Help us continue to provide the very best certification study materials possible. Write us or email us at **cipq@coriolis.com** and let us know how our books have helped you study. Tell us about new features that you'd like us to add. Send us a story about how we've helped you; if we use it in one of our books, we'll send you an official Coriolis shirt!

Good luck with your certification exam and your career. Thank you for allowing us to help you achieve your goals.

Keith Weiskamp
President and CEO

Look For These Other Books From The Coriolis Group:

i-Net+ Exam Prep
Tim Catura-Hauser, Laurel Ann Spivey Dumas, and Matt Simmons

A+ Exam Prep, Adaptive Testing Edition
Jean Andrews

A+ Exam Cram
James G. Jones and Craig Landes

To Kobe John
—Martin

To Lorraine
—Emmett

❧

About The Authors

Martin Weiss, i-Net+, Network+, A+, CCNA, MCSE, MCP+I, CNA, CIP is a Senior Information Management Specialist with ACS GSG providing information technology solutions for client organizations. His other writings include books on the A+ certification, as well as the Windows 2000 operating system. In addition to writing and his career, he attends college online with the University of Maryland.

Marty's personal interests include snowboarding, listening to music, reading, and traveling. Marty currently lives in New England and can be reached via email at **castadream@hotmail.com**.

Emmett Dulaney, i-Net+, Network+, A+, MCSE, CNA is the co-owner of D S Technical Solutions and an instructor for the Continuing Education department of Indiana University/Purdue University of Fort Wayne. The author of over a dozen certification titles, he is a regular contributor to *MCP Magazine*, and he can be reached at **edulaney@iquest.net**.

Acknowledgments

Many thanks to the entire Coriolis team, especially Shari Jo Hehr for getting the project off the ground, as well as Deb Doorley and Lynette Cox for their guidance. Thanks also to Catherine Oliver (a great copyeditor) and André Parre-Huff for his technical review. Special thanks go to Emmett Dulaney for coming aboard this project—it has truly been a pleasure working with you.

Finally, I'd like to thank my family and friends, as they have helped in many ways, both directly and indirectly. First, of course, my mom (hi Mom!) and my dad. I'd also like to thank my wife, Gin, and most of all, my son Kobe (I have a lot of playing catch to catch up on). To my siblings (Tiff, Jay, Mike, Erik, Joanna), thanks for being so proud and supportive. To Paul Calhoun for taking me under his wing (without you I would still be analyzing LESs). To Elisa Giommi for putting up with me. To Victor "sharkbait" Suris for the laughs when I needed them, and to the rest of my friends and family—thank you.

—Martin Weiss

First and foremost, I would like to thank Martin Weiss for bringing me into this project, and I hope we have the opportunity to work together again. At Coriolis, thanks belong to Shari Jo Hehr, Deb Doorley, and Lynette Cox for overseeing the project and transforming rough ideas into polished thoughts.

—Emmett Dulaney

Contents At A Glance

Table Of Contents

. . . .

Introduction

Welcome to *i-Net+ Exam Cram*! This book aims to help you get ready to take—and pass—the CompTIA i-Net+ Certification Exam. This Introduction explains CompTIA's i-Net+ exam in general and talks about how the *Exam Cram* series can help you prepare for the exam.

Exam Cram books help you understand and appreciate the subjects and materials you need to pass CompTIA's i-Net+ Certification Exam. *Exam Crams* are aimed strictly at test preparation and review. They do not teach you everything you need to know about a topic (such as configuring network hardware and software). Instead, we (the authors) present and explain the questions and problems we've found that you're likely to encounter on a test. Our aim is to bring together as much information as possible about the i-Net+ exam.

Nevertheless, to completely prepare yourself for any CompTIA test, we recommend that you begin your studies with some classroom training, or that you pick up and read one of the many available study guides, including The Coriolis Group's *Exam Prep* series. We also strongly recommend that you exercise your knowledge of basic networking and Web principles by putting together a few small networks as well as a Web site. Try building a site utilizing HTML, CGI, Active Server Pages, and other technologies because nothing beats hands-on experience and familiarity when it comes to understanding the questions you're likely to encounter on a certification test. Book learning is essential, but hands-on experience is the best teacher of all!

The i-Net+ Certification Exam

The i-Net+ Certification Exam is designed to certify the knowledge of Internet system administrators, Internet security specialists, Internet application developers, Internet database specialists, e-commerce specialists, network specialists, and site designers with experience in the information technology industry. Ideally, you will have a Network+ certification or equivalent knowledge before you pursue this certification. However, it is not mandatory.

The i-Net+ exam will test your skills and knowledge as they relate to the Internet technology industry. The subject matter is organized into six areas: Internet basics, Internet clients, development, networking, Internet security, and business concepts. Although you will be tested in these six areas, there is only one comprehensive test.

Taking A Certification Exam

Unfortunately, testing is not free. Each computer-based exam costs $185 ($135 if you are a CompTIA member), and if you do not pass, you must pay an additional $185 for a retest. In the U.S. and Canada, the i-Net+ Certification Exam is administered by Sylvan Prometric. Sylvan Prometric can be reached at 887-803-6867, any time from 7:00 AM to 6:00 PM, Central Time, Monday through Friday.

To schedule an exam, call at least one day in advance. To cancel or reschedule an exam, you must call at least 12 hours before the scheduled test time (or you might be charged regardless). When calling Sylvan Prometric, please have the following information ready for the telesales staff member who handles your call:

➤ Your name, organization, and mailing address.

➤ Your Social Security number. Citizens of other nations can use their taxpayer IDs or make other arrangements with the order taker.

➤ The name of the exam you wish to take. (For this book, the exam name is "i-Net+ Certification Exam.")

➤ A method of payment. (The most convenient approach is to supply a valid credit card number with sufficient available credit. Otherwise, payments by check, money order, or purchase order must be received before a test can be scheduled. If the latter methods are required, ask your order taker for more details.)

When you take a test, try to arrive at least 15 minutes before the scheduled time slot. You must bring two forms of identification, one of which must be a photo ID.

All exams are completely closed-book. In fact, you will not be permitted to take anything with you into the testing area, but you will be furnished with a marker board and an erasable marker after you enter. We suggest that you immediately write down all the information you've memorized for the test.

In *Exam Cram* books, the information you should memorize appears on a tear-out sheet inside the front cover of each book. You will have some time to compose yourself, to record this information, and even to take a sample orientation exam before you must begin the real thing. We suggest that you take the orientation test before taking your first exam, but because the tests are all more or less identical in layout, behavior, and controls, you probably won't need to do this more than once.

When you complete a CompTIA certification exam, the software will tell you whether you've passed or failed. All tests are scored on a basis of 100 percent, and results are divided into several topic areas. As of this writing, the percentage needed to pass is 73 percent, but that is subject to change. Even if you fail, we suggest that you ask for—and keep—the detailed report that the test administrator should print for you. You can use this report to help you prepare for another go-round, if needed.

How To Prepare For An Exam

Preparing for the i-Net+ exam requires that you obtain and study materials designed to provide comprehensive information about Internet-related technologies and practices. The following list of materials will help you study and prepare:

➤ *Study guides*—Several publishers—including Certification Insider Press—offer i-Net+ titles. The Certification Insider Press series includes:

  ➤ *The Exam Cram series*—These books give you information about the material you need to know to pass the tests.

  ➤ *The Exam Prep series*—These books provide a greater level of detail than the *Exam Crams* and are designed to teach you everything you need to know from an exam perspective. *i-Net+ Exam Prep* is the perfect learning companion to prepare you for the i-Net+ Certification Exam. Look for this book in your favorite bookstores.

➤ *Multimedia*—These Coriolis Group materials are designed to support learners of all types—whether you learn best by listening, reading, or doing:

  ➤ *The Practice Tests Exam Cram series*—Provides the most valuable test preparation material: practice exams. Each exam is followed by a complete set of answers, as well as explanations of why the right answers are right and the wrong answers are wrong. Each book comes with a CD that contains one or more interactive practice exams.

  ➤ *The Exam Cram Flash Cards series*—Offers practice questions on handy cards you can use anywhere. The question and its possible answers appear on the front of the card, and the answer, explanation, and a valuable reference appear on the back of the card. The set also includes a CD with an electronic practice exam to give you the feel of the actual test—and more practice!

➤ *The Exam Cram Audio Review series*—Offers a concise review of key topics covered on the exam, as well as practice questions.

➤ *Classroom training*—Third-party training companies such as Wave Technologies and American Research Group (now called Global Knowledge Network) now offer, or will soon be offering, classroom training on i-Net+ and Internet technologies. These companies aim to help prepare networking professionals to perform all levels of Internet skills and pass the i-Net+ Certification Exam. While such training runs upwards of $350 per day in class, most individuals find them to be quite worthwhile.

➤ *Other publications*—You'll find direct references to other publications and resources in this text, and there's no shortage of materials available on general Internet-related technologies. To help you sift through some of the publications out there, we end each chapter with a "Need To Know More?" section that provides pointers to more complete and exhaustive resources covering the chapter's information. This section should give you an idea of where we think you should look for further discussion.

This set of recommended materials represents some excellent resources for learning specific technologies and general skills. We anticipate that you'll find that this book belongs in their company. In the section that follows, we explain how this book works, and we give you some good reasons why this book counts as a member of the recommended-materials list.

About This Book

Each topical *Exam Cram* chapter follows a set structure, accompanied by graphical cues about important or useful information. Here's the structure of a typical chapter:

➤ *Opening hotlists*—Each chapter begins with a list of the terms and techniques that you must learn and understand before you can be *fully* conversant with that chapter's subject matter. We follow the hotlists with one or two introductory paragraphs to set the stage for the rest of the chapter.

➤ *Topical coverage*—After the opening hotlists, each chapter covers a series of at least four topics related to the chapter's subject. To highlight topics or concepts likely to appear on a test, we use a special Exam Alert layout, like this:

This is what an Exam Alert looks like. Normally, an Exam Alert stresses concepts, terms, software, or activities that are likely to relate to one or more certification test questions. For that reason, we think any information found offset in Exam Alert format is worthy of unusual attentiveness on your part. Indeed, most of the information that appears on The Cram Sheet appears as Exam Alerts within the text.

Pay close attention to material flagged as an Exam Alert; although all the information in this book pertains to what you need to know to pass the exam, we flag certain items that are really important. You'll find the information that appears in the body of each chapter to be worth knowing, too, when preparing for the test. Because this book's material is very condensed, we recommend that you use this book along with other resources to achieve the maximum benefit.

In addition to the Exam Alerts, we have provided tips that will help you build a better foundation for networking knowledge. Although the information may not be on the exam, it is certainly related and will help you become a better test taker.

This is how tips are formatted. Keep your eyes open for these, and you'll become an Internet guru in no time!

➤ *Practice questions*—Although we talk about test questions and topics throughout each chapter, this section presents a series of mock test questions and explanations of both correct and incorrect answers. We also try to point out especially tricky questions by using a special icon, like this:

Ordinarily, this icon flags the presence of a particularly devious inquiry, if not an outright trick question. Trick questions are designed to be answered incorrectly if not read more than once—and carefully, at that. Although they're not ubiquitous, such questions make regular appearances on the i-Net+ exam. (On the real exam, however, trick questions are not labeled.) That's why we say exam questions are as much about reading comprehension as they are about knowing your material inside out and backwards.

➤ *Details and resources*—Every chapter ends with a section titled "Need To Know More?", which provides direct pointers to CompTIA and third-party resources offering more details on the chapter's subject. If you find a resource you like in this collection, use it, but don't feel compelled to use all the resources. On the other hand, we recommend only resources we use on a regular basis, so none of our recommendations will be a waste of your time or money. (But purchasing them all at once probably represents an expense that many Internet specialists and would-be Internet professionals might find hard to justify.)

The bulk of the book follows this chapter structure slavishly, but there are a few other elements that we'd like to point out. Chapter 16 is a sample test that provides a good review of the material presented throughout the book to ensure that you're ready for the exam. Chapter 17 is an answer key to the sample test that appears in Chapter 16. Additionally, you'll find a glossary that explains terms and an index that you can use to track down terms as they appear in the text.

Finally, the tear-out Cram Sheet attached next to the inside front cover of this *Exam Cram* represents a condensed and compiled collection of facts, figures, and tips that we think you should memorize before taking the test. Because you can dump this information out of your head onto a piece of paper before answering any exam questions, you can master this information by brute force—you need to remember it only long enough to write it down when you walk into the test room. You might even want to look at it in the car or in the lobby of the testing center just before you walk in to take the test.

How To Use This Book

We've structured the topics in this book to build on one another, so some topics in later chapters make more sense after you've read earlier chapters. Therefore, if you're prepping for a first-time test, we suggest that you read this book from front to back for your initial test preparation. If you need to brush up on a topic or you have to bone up for a second try, use the index or table of contents to go straight to the topics and questions that you need to study. Beyond the tests, we think you'll find this book useful as a tightly focused reference for some of the most important aspects of Internet-related practices and skills.

Given all the book's elements and its specialized focus, we've tried to create a tool that will help you prepare for—and pass—the CompTIA i-Net+ Certification Exam. Please share your feedback on the book with us, especially if you have ideas about how we can improve it for future test-takers. We'll carefully consider everything you say, and we'll respond to all suggestions.

Please send your questions or comments to us at **cipq@coriolis.com**. Please remember to include the title of the book in your message; otherwise, we'll be forced to guess which book you're writing about. Also, be sure to check out the Web pages at **www.coriolis.com**, where, for each book, you'll find information updates, commentary, and clarifications in documents that you can either read online or download for use later on.

Thanks, and enjoy the book!

Self-Assessment

We included a self-assessment in this *Exam Cram* to help you evaluate your readiness to tackle i-Net+ certification. The assessment should also help you understand what you need to master the topic of this book—namely the CompTIA i-Net+ Certification Exam. But before you tackle this self-assessment, let's talk about concerns you may face when pursuing the i-Net+ certification and what an ideal i-Net+ candidate might look like.

i-Net+ Engineers In The Real World

In the next section, we describe an ideal i-Net+ candidate, knowing full well that not all candidates will meet this ideal. In fact, our description of that ideal candidate might seem downright scary. But take heart: More than 150,000 CompTIA A+ technicians are already certified, so CompTIA certification is obviously an attainable goal. You can get all the real-world motivation you need from knowing that many others have gone before, so you will be able to follow in their footsteps. If you're willing to tackle the process seriously and do what it takes to obtain the necessary experience and knowledge, you can take—and pass—the i-Net+ certification test. In fact, we've designed this *Exam Cram* and the companion *Exam Prep* to make it as easy as possible to prepare for the exam. But prepare you must!

The same, of course, is true for other CompTIA certifications, which include the following:

➤ *A+ certification*—A testing program that certifies the competency of entry-level service technicians in the computer industry. The A+ testing program consists of a Core exam and a DOS/Windows exam. This testing program is targeted at computer technicians with six months of experience.

➤ *Network+ certification*—A testing program that certifies the knowledge of networking technicians with 18 to 24 months' experience in the information technology industry.

➤ *Certified Document Imaging Architect*—A testing program that is divided into sections that correspond to an imaging professional's areas of responsibility. The technologies include: Input/Capture, Display, Storage, Communications, Output, Standard Computing Environment, Integration, and Management Applications, as well as areas such as preprocessing and paper handling.

The Ideal i-Net+ Candidate

Just to give you some idea of what an ideal i-Net+ candidate is like, here are some relevant statistics about the background and experience such an individual might have. Don't worry if you don't meet these qualifications or don't come that close—this is a far-from-ideal world, and where you fall short is simply where you'll have more work to do. Here are our ideal qualifications:

➤ Academic or professional training in Internet-related theory, concepts, and operations—including everything from networking and internetworking to security and application development

➤ Hands-on experience in implementing and maintaining Internet, intranet, and extranet infrastructure and services

➤ Hands-on experience in developing Internet, intranet, and extranet applications

➤ Experience and knowledge of hardware and software support, like that which is tested with CompTIA's A+ certification, as well as experience and knowledge of networking technologies, like those that are tested with CompTIA's Network+ certification

➤ A thorough understanding of key networking protocols, addressing, and name resolution, primarily involving TCP/IP

➤ A thorough understanding of, as well as experience with supporting, various Internet clients

➤ Familiarity with business issues relating to organizations and the Internet

We believe that well under half of all certification candidates meet these requirements and that most candidates meet fewer than half of these requirements—at least, when they begin the certification process. But because others who have already been certified have survived this ordeal, you can survive it, too—especially if you heed what our self-assessment can tell you about what you already know and what you need to learn.

Put Yourself To The Test

The following series of questions and observations is designed to help you figure out how much work you must do to pursue CompTIA i-Net+ certification and what kinds of resources you may consult on your quest. Be absolutely honest in your answers, or you'll end up wasting money on an exam you're not yet ready to take. There are no right or wrong answers, only steps along the path to certification. Only you can decide where you belong in the broad spectrum of aspiring candidates.

Two things should be clear from the outset, however:

➤ Even a modest background in computer science will be helpful.

➤ Hands-on experience in Internet-related technologies is an essential ingredient of certification success.

Educational Background

Answer the following questions:

1. Have you ever taken any Windows administration, Unix administration, NetWare administration, or general network administration training classes? [Yes or No]

   If Yes, proceed to question 2; if No, consider taking classroom training for these areas or, at the very least, reading up on them. Microsoft provides a self-study system entitled *Microsoft Windows NT Network Administration Training: Hands-On, Self-Paced Training for Administering Version 4.0*, or you can read *Essential Windows NT System Administration*, by Aeleen Frisch (O'Reilly & Associates, 1998, ISBN 1-56-592274-3). Another great book you may want to consider trying is *TCP/IP Network Administration*, by Craig Hunt (O'Reilly & Associates, 1998, ISBN 1-56-592322-7).

2. Have you taken any Internet concepts or technologies classes? [Yes or No]

   If Yes, you will probably be able to handle CompTIA's components addressing your knowledge of Internet basics and client/server technology. If you're rusty, brush up on basic Internet-related concepts. Then proceed to Question 3.

   If No, you might want to read one or two books in this topic area. Try *Computer Networks and Internets* by Douglas E. Comer (Prentice-Hall, 1997, ISBN 0-13-239070-1).

3. Do you have practical Internet-related or development experience in a business environment? [Yes or No]

If Yes, you will probably be able to handle CompTIA's components addressing your knowledge of internetworking, security, development, and business concepts. If you're rusty, brush up on basic networking practices by actually putting together a small network connected to the Internet and running various Internet-related services.

If No, consider some basic reading in this area. We recommend *Information Architecture for the World Wide Web* by Louis Rosenfeld and Peter Morville (O'Reilly & Associates, 1998, ISBN 1-56-592282-4) and *Internet Security: Professional Reference* by Tom Sheldon, et al (New Riders Publishing, 1997, ISBN 1-56-205760-X). If these titles don't appeal to you, check out reviews for other, similar titles at your favorite online bookstore.

Hands-On Experience

The most important key to success on the CompTIA i-Net+ test is hands-on experience. If we leave you with only one realization after you take this self-assessment, it should be that there's no substitute for time spent installing, configuring, developing, and using the various Internet-related technologies on which you'll be tested repeatedly and in depth. If you have never worked with any of the Internet-related technologies mentioned earlier, you would be well advised to visit the CompTIA Web site (**www.comptia.org**), find the nearest authorized training center, and attend classes.

Testing Your Exam-Readiness

Whether you attend a formal class on a specific topic to get ready for an exam or use written materials to study on your own, some preparation for the CompTIA certification exam is essential. At $185 a try ($135 for CompTIA members), pass or fail, you want to do everything you can to pass on your first try. That's where studying comes in.

For any given subject, consider taking a class if you've tackled self-study materials, taken the test, and failed anyway. The opportunity to interact with an instructor and fellow students can make all the difference in the world—if you can afford that privilege. For information about i-Net+ classes, visit **www. comptia.org/certification/inetplus/inetplus.asp** and click on the Training Resources link.

If you can't afford to take a class, visit the Training Resources page anyway for any pointers to free practice exams. And even if you can't afford to spend much at all, you should still invest in some low-cost practice exams from commercial vendors because, more than any other tool, practice exams can help you assess your readiness to pass a test.

We have included practice questions at the end of each chapter, plus a practice exam in Chapter 16 of this book, so if you don't score that well on the chapter tests, you can study more and then tackle the test in Chapter 16.

Have you taken a practice exam? If you have, and you scored 73 percent or better, you're probably ready to tackle the real thing. If your score isn't above that crucial threshold, obtain all the free and low-budget practice tests you can find (this is a new certification so practice tests may be hard to find) and get to work. Keep at it until you can break the passing threshold comfortably.

 When it comes to assessing your test readiness, there is no better way than to take a good practice exam and pass with a score of 73 percent or better. When we're preparing ourselves, we shoot for 80-plus percent, just to leave room for the "weirdness factor" that sometimes shows up on CompTIA exams.

You should also cruise the Web looking for "brain dumps" (recollections of test topics and experiences recorded by others) to help you anticipate topics you're likely to encounter on the test.

 You can't be sure that a brain dump's author can provide correct answers. Therefore, use the questions to guide your studies, but *never* rely on the answers in a brain dump to lead you to the truth. Double-check *everything* you find in any brain dump.

We recommend that you check the Microsoft Knowledge Base—available on its own CD as part of the TechNet collection, or on the Microsoft Web site at **support.microsoft.com/support/**—for meaningful issues relating to the i-Net+ exam topics. We also recommend that you check the Novell Knowledge Base—available on its own CD as part of the Support Connection collection, or on the Novell Web site at **support.novell.com/servlet/knowledgebase**—for issues relating to the i-Net+ exam topics.

You should also check out the Cisco Web site at **www.cisco.com** and the Bay Networks Web site at **www.baynetworks.com** to familiarize yourself with Internet hardware technologies. These sites contain many useful white papers.

i-Net+
Certification Exam

Terms you'll need to understand:

- √ Radio button
- √ Checkbox
- √ Exhibit
- √ Multiple-choice question formats
- √ Careful reading
- √ Process of elimination

Techniques you'll need to master:

- √ Preparing to take a certification exam
- √ Practicing (to make perfect)
- √ Making the best use of the testing software
- √ Budgeting your time
- √ Saving the hardest questions until last
- √ Guessing (as a last resort)

Exam taking is not something that most people anticipate eagerly, no matter how well prepared they may be. In most cases, familiarity helps ameliorate test anxiety. In plain English, this means you probably won't be as nervous when you take your fourth or fifth certification exam as you'll be when you take your first one.

Whether it's your first exam or your tenth, understanding the exam software and the details of exam taking (how much time to spend on questions, the environment you'll be in, and so on) will help you concentrate on the material rather than on the setting. Likewise, mastering a few basic exam-taking skills should help you recognize—and perhaps even outfox—some of the tricks and gotchas you're bound to find in some of the exam questions.

This chapter, besides explaining the exam environment and software, describes some proven exam-taking strategies that you should be able to use to your advantage.

The Exam Situation

When you arrive at the testing center where you scheduled your exam, you'll need to sign in with an exam coordinator. He or she will ask you to show two forms of identification, one of which must be a photo ID. After you've signed in and your time slot arrives, you'll be asked to deposit any books, bags, or other items you've brought with you. Then you'll be escorted into a closed room. Typically, the room will be furnished with anywhere from one to half a dozen computers, and each workstation will be separated from the others by dividers designed to keep you from seeing what's happening on someone else's computer.

You'll be furnished with a pen or pencil and a blank sheet of paper or, in some cases, an erasable plastic sheet and an erasable felt-tip pen. You're allowed to write down any information you want on both sides of this sheet. Before the exam, you should memorize as much as you can of the material that appears on The Cram Sheet (inside the front cover of this book) so you can write that information on the blank sheet as soon as you are seated in front of the computer. You can refer to your rendition of The Cram Sheet anytime you like during the test, but you'll have to surrender the sheet when you leave the room.

Most test rooms feature a wall with a large picture window. This permits the exam coordinator standing behind it to monitor the room, to prevent exam takers from talking to one another, and to observe anything out of the ordinary that might go on. The exam coordinator will have loaded the appropriate CompTIA certification exam—for this book, that's the i-Net+ Certification Exam—and you'll be permitted to start as soon as you're seated in front of the computer.

All CompTIA certification exams allow a certain maximum amount of time in which to complete your work. (This time is indicated on the exam by an onscreen counter or clock, so you can check the time remaining whenever you like.) The i-Net+ exam consists of 72 randomly selected questions. You may take up to 90 minutes to complete the exam.

The CompTIA i-Net+ Certification Exam is computer generated and uses a multiple-choice format. Although this may sound quite simple, not only do the questions check your mastery of basic facts and figures about Internet technologies, but they also require you to evaluate one or more sets of circumstances or requirements. You might be asked to select the best or most effective solution to a problem from a range of choices, all of which technically are correct. Taking the exam is quite an adventure, and it involves real thinking. This book shows you what to expect and how to deal with the potential problems, puzzles, and predicaments.

Exam Layout And Design

Some exam questions require you to select a single answer, whereas others ask you to select multiple correct answers. The following multiple-choice question requires you to select a single correct answer. Following the question is a brief summary of each potential answer and why it is either right or wrong.

Question 1

What layer is routing performed at in the OSI model?

○ a. Application

○ b. Network

○ c. Data Link

○ d. Transport

The correct answer is b. Routing is performed at the Network layer in the OSI model. The Application layer is where programs such as FTP and Telnet operate. Therefore, answer a is incorrect. The Data Link layer is responsible for taking information from the Network layer, generating packets, and sending them via the Physical layer across the network to the address of the destination device. Therefore, answer c is incorrect. The Transport layer manages the end-to-end control and error checking by providing an end-to-end connection between the source and destination nodes to ensure reliable delivery of data. Therefore, answer d is incorrect.

This sample question format corresponds closely to the CompTIA i-Net+ Certification Exam format—the only difference on the exam is that questions are not followed by answer keys. To select an answer, position the cursor over the radio button next to the answer, and click the mouse button.

Let's examine a question that requires choosing multiple answers. This type of question provides checkboxes rather than radio buttons for marking all appropriate selections.

Question 2

A brouter works at which layers of the OSI model? [Choose the two best answers]

❑ a. Network

❑ b. Transport

❑ c. Data Link

❑ d. Application

The correct answers are a and c. A brouter does routing, which is a Network layer function, and it does bridging, which is a Data Link layer function. The Transport layer manages the end-to-end control and error checking by providing an end-to-end connection between the source and destination nodes to ensure reliable delivery of data. Therefore, answer b is incorrect. The Application layer is where programs such as FTP and Telnet operate. Therefore, answer d is incorrect.

For this type of question, more than one answer is required. Such questions are scored as wrong unless *all* the required selections are chosen. In other words, a partially correct answer does not result in partial credit when the test is scored. If you are required to provide multiple answers and you do not provide the number of answers that the question asks for, it will mark the question for you and indicate at the end of the test that you did not complete that question. For Question 2, you have to check the boxes next to items a and c to obtain credit for a correct answer. Notice that picking the right answers also means knowing why the other answers are wrong.

Although these two basic types of questions can appear in many forms, they constitute the foundation on which all the i-Net+ Certification Exam questions rest. At any time, CompTIA can choose to include other questions involving exhibits, charts, or network diagrams to help document an Internet-related scenario that you'll be asked to troubleshoot or configure. Careful attention to such exhibits is the key to success.

Using CompTIA's Exam Software Effectively

A well-known principle when taking exams is to first read the entire exam from start to finish while answering only those questions you feel absolutely sure of. On subsequent passes, you can dive into more complex questions more deeply, knowing how many such questions you have left.

Fortunately, CompTIA exam software makes this approach easy to implement. At the top-left corner of each question is a checkbox that permits you to mark that question for a later visit. (Note: Marking questions makes review easier, but you can return to any question if you are willing to click the Forward or Back buttons repeatedly.) As you read all the questions, if you answer only those you're sure of and mark for review those you're not sure of, you can keep working through a decreasing list of questions as you answer the trickier ones in order.

There's at least one potential benefit to reading the exam completely before answering the trickier questions: Sometimes, information supplied in later questions will shed more light on earlier questions. Other times, information you read in later questions might jog your memory about Internet facts, figures, or behavior that also will help with earlier questions. Either way, you'll come out ahead if you defer those questions about which you're not absolutely sure.

Keep working on the questions until you're certain of all your answers or until you know you'll run out of time. If questions remain unanswered, you'll want to zip through them and guess. Not answering a question guarantees that you won't receive credit for it, and a guess has at least a chance of being correct.

At the very end of your exam period, you're better off guessing than leaving questions unanswered.

Exam-Taking Basics

The most important advice about taking any exam is this: Read each question carefully. Some questions are deliberately ambiguous, some use double negatives, and others use terminology in incredibly precise ways. The authors have taken numerous exams—both practice and live—and in nearly every one have missed at least one question because they didn't read it carefully enough.

Here are some suggestions on how to deal with the tendency to jump to an answer too quickly:

➤ Make sure you read every word in the question. If you find yourself jumping ahead impatiently, go back and start over.

➤ As you read, try to restate the question in your own terms. If you can do this, you should be able to pick the correct answer(s) much more easily.

➤ When returning to a question after your initial read-through, read every word again—otherwise, your mind can fall quickly into a rut. Sometimes, revisiting a question after turning your attention elsewhere lets you see something you missed, but the strong tendency is to see what you've seen before. Try to avoid that tendency at all costs.

➤ If you return to a question more than twice, try to articulate to yourself what you don't understand about the question, why the answers don't appear to make sense, or what appears to be missing. If you chew on the subject for awhile, your subconscious might provide the details that are lacking, or you might notice a "trick" that will point to the right answer.

Above all, try to deal with each question by thinking through what you know about Internet technologies—the characteristics, behaviors, facts, and figures involved. By reviewing what you know (and what you've written down on your information sheet), you'll often recall or understand things sufficiently to determine the answer to the question.

Question-Handling Strategies

Based on exams the authors have taken, some interesting trends have become apparent. For those questions that take only a single answer, usually two or three of the answers will be obviously incorrect, and two of the answers will be plausible—of course, only one can be correct. Unless the answer leaps out at you, begin the process of answering by eliminating those answers that are most obviously wrong. (If an answer does leap out at you, reread the question to look for a trick; sometimes, those questions are the ones you're most likely to get wrong.)

Things to look for in obviously wrong answers include nonexistent commands, incorrect utility names, inconsistent conditions, and terminology you've never seen. If you've done your homework for an exam, no valid information should be completely new to you. In that case, unfamiliar or bizarre terminology probably indicates a totally bogus answer.

Numerous questions assume that you understand internetworking structures and client/server environments inside and out. If your knowledge in these areas is well grounded, it will help you cut through many otherwise confusing questions.

As you work your way through the exam, another counter that CompTIA provides will come in handy—the number of questions completed and the number of questions outstanding. Budget your time by making sure that you've completed one-quarter of the questions by one-quarter of the way through the exam period, and three-quarters of them by three-quarters of the way through.

If you're not finished when 85 minutes have elapsed, use the last 5 minutes to guess your way through the remaining questions. Remember, guessing is potentially more valuable than not answering, because blank answers are always wrong, but a guess may turn out to be right. If you don't have a clue about any of the remaining questions, pick answers at random, or choose all a's, b's, and so on. The important thing is to submit an exam for scoring that has an answer for every question.

Mastering The Inner Game

In the final analysis, knowledge breeds confidence, and confidence breeds success. If you study the materials in this book carefully and review all the practice questions at the end of each chapter, you should become aware of those areas where additional learning and study are required.

Next, follow up by reading some or all of the materials recommended in the "Need To Know More?" section at the end of each chapter. The idea is to become familiar enough with the concepts and situations you find in the sample questions that you can reason your way through similar situations on a real exam. If you know the material, you have every right to be confident that you can pass the exam.

After you've worked your way through the book, take the practice exam in Chapter 16. This will provide a reality check and help you identify areas you need to study further. Before scheduling a real exam, make sure you follow up and review materials related to the questions you missed on the practice exam. Only when you've covered all the ground and feel comfortable with the whole scope of the practice exam should you take a real one.

 If you take the practice exam and don't score at least 73 percent correct, you'll want to practice further. If you need more practice, you might want to purchase additional test materials or download the self-study software from **www.CertificationCorner.com**.

Armed with the information in this book and with the determination to aug-
ment your knowledge, you should be able to pass the certification exam. You
need to work at it, however, or you'll spend the exam fee more than once before
you finally pass. If you prepare seriously, you should do well. Good luck!

Additional Resources

A good source of information about CompTIA certification exams comes from
CompTIA itself, and the best place to go for exam-related information is online.
If you haven't already visited the CompTIA Web site, do so right now. The
i-Net+ page can be found by linking from the CompTIA home page, which
resides at **www.comptia.org**. Alternatively, you can link directly to the i-Net+
page, located at **www.comptia.org/certification/inetplus/inetplus.asp** (see
Figure 1.1).

> *Note: Web pages mentioned in this book might not be there by the time
> you read this or might have been replaced by something new. Should this
> happen, please read the section titled "Coping With Change On The Web."*

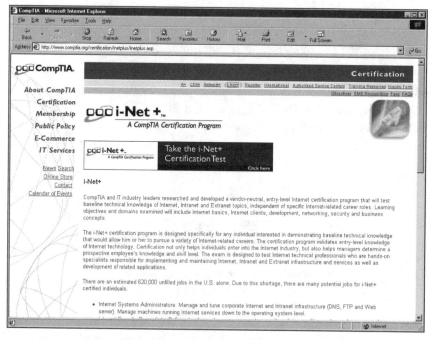

Figure 1.1   The CompTIA i-Net+ home page.

The menu options at the top of the i-Net+ home page point to the most important sources of information in the CompTIA i-Net+ pages. Here's what to check out:

➤ *Objectives*—Use this menu option to review the skills and knowledge that will be tested on the i-Net+ exam, as well as the weighted percentile average of each area of questioning.

➤ *FAQs*—This area discusses the most frequently asked questions about the i-Net+ Certification Exam.

➤ *Training Resources*—This page lists the computer-based training materials that are endorsed by CompTIA.

These are just the high points of what's available in the CompTIA i-Net+ pages. As you browse through them—and we strongly recommend that you do—you'll probably find other informational tidbits mentioned that are every bit as interesting.

Coping With Change On The Web

Sooner or later, all the information we've shared with you about the CompTIA i-Net+ pages and the other Web-based resources mentioned throughout this book will go stale or be replaced by newer information. In some cases, the URLs you find here might lead you to their replacements; in other cases, the URLs will go nowhere, leaving you with the dreaded "404 File not found" error message. When that happens, don't give up.

There's always a way to find what you want on the Web if you're willing to invest some time and energy. CompTIA's site has a site map to help you find your way around. Most large or complex Web sites offer a search engine. Finally, feel free to use general search tools—such as **www.search.com**, **www.altavista.com**, and **www.excite.com**—to search for related information. Although CompTIA offers the best information about its certification exams online, there are plenty of third-party sources of information, training, and assistance in this area. The bottom line is this: If you can't find something where the book says it lives, start looking around. If worse comes to worst, you can always email us. We just might have a clue.

Internet Structure

Terms you'll need to understand:

√ Hubs

√ Bridges

√ Routers

√ Gateways

√ Internet Service Provider (ISP)

√ Network Access Points (NAPs)

√ T1

√ E1

√ T3

Techniques you'll need to master:

√ Recognizing which connectivity device is best for a given scenario

√ Understanding the basics of wide-area-network access methods

In this chapter, you'll learn about the basics of Internet structure and about the hardware used to connect to the Internet and other networks. You'll learn the access speeds available through different technologies, and you'll be introduced to the organizations behind different aspects of the Internet.

A Brief History Of Networking And The Internet

The Internet is one of the first wide area networks ever created, and it is currently the largest network in the world. The underlying protocol that the Internet relies upon is Transmission Control Protocol/Internet Protocol (TCP/IP).

TCP/IP was originally designed as a set of wide area network (WAN) protocols for the express purpose of maintaining communication links and data transfer between sites in the event of an atomic or nuclear war. Since those early days, development of the protocols has passed from the hands of the government and has been the responsibility of the Internet community.

The evolution of these protocols from a small, four-site project into the foundation of the worldwide Internet has been more than 25 years in the works. Yet, despite numerous modifications to the protocol suite, the inherent spirit of the original specifications is still intact. In the 1970s, the Department of Defense (DoD) was a major purchaser of computers and associated items. The DoD decided that it wanted to standardize on an operating system to use on the majority of its computers, rather than having a plethora of operating systems to support. The DoD sent out word that it would standardize on an operating system that allowed two or more computers to talk to each other—in other words, an operating system that had the ability to build a network.

One of the major operating systems at the time in government and academia was Unix, and there were a number of versions, vendors, flavors, and variants available. A number of companies, universities, and individuals took it upon themselves to work with Unix and find a means by which it could network. To make a long story short, the DoD decided to use two protocols—TCP, the Transmission Control Protocol, and IP, the Internet Protocol.

TCP/IP came about as a solution to a need and quickly became ingrained in almost every version of Unix from that day on. No one patented it or claimed it as proprietary—instead it became an open standard that everyone could write to.

In the early nineties, the following two remarkable things happened that made this protocol, which had been around for so long, suddenly leap to the limelight:

➤ As personal computers began to get networked, every vendor started using proprietary protocols (NetWare used IPX/SPX, Microsoft used

NetBEUI, etc.). This made it very hard for heterogeneous systems to communicate. TCP/IP, however, was free for anyone to use, so if every vendor included support for it, suddenly all of your machines could communicate regardless of the OS they were running.

➤ The Internet, which had been around for years in various forms, suddenly got a graphical user interface with the World Wide Web and sparked the interest of millions. The Internet, in the early nineties, consisted of hosts running Unix; Unix meant TCP/IP. Today, there are hosts running NT, Linux, and other OSs, but they still do so by using TCP/IP.

It is imperative that when you think of the Internet, you think of TCP/IP and put into perspective the time frame through which all of this came to be.

Networking Devices

A network can be as small as two computers talking together in a peer-to-peer relationship, or as large as the Internet—with unlimited possibilities between the two ends of the spectrum. All networks, regardless of size, have the following items in common:

➤ An operating system on the client or host that allows for the use of networking redirectors

➤ A networking protocol—a common language—through which communication can take place. Every workstation must run its own stack or use the stack of a server (as in a proxy server) to be able to communicate.

➤ Applications that utilize the network—email, FTP, etc.

➤ Network interface cards (NICs) installed in each machine

➤ Cabling

The cabling can be of various types, or even wireless. Cable types are tested heavily in the Network+ exam. The i-Net+ exam picks up in content where Network+ leaves off and looks at the connectivity devices used between the hosts to build the network. In particular, you must know four connectivity devices—hubs, bridges, routers, and gateways—each of which is examined in the following sections.

Hubs

Hubs are devices used to build networks utilizing a star topology, as shown in Figure 2.1. Hubs make it easy to add workstations to the network and to reconfigure the network at any time by simply unplugging and plugging in patch cables.

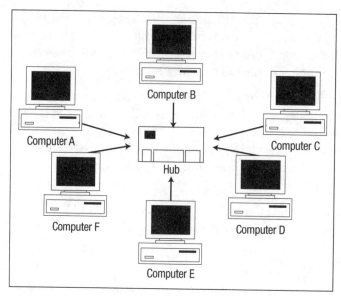

Figure 2.1   With a star topology, all devices run to a central device—a hub.

The three hub types are passive, active, and intelligent. *Passive* hubs allow for connections and central wiring only. *Active* hubs amplify the signals coming in and filter out noise. *Intelligent* hubs provide either switching capabilities or management features.

Switching hubs provide quick routing of signals between hub ports in order to direct data where it needs to go and reduce the bandwidth of sending the data to all locations. Switching hubs are always intelligent hubs, but intelligent hubs are not always switching hubs.

 In the absence of switching, a hub sends all traffic it receives to all ports.

Hubs are occasionally known as *concentrators* and range in size from 4 ports to 16 ports or more. Cascading allows numerous hubs to be connected to form larger networks. Where switching is employed, it is possible for a hub to perform some of the functions of a bridge—but this is typical only if multiple networks are within a limited geographic scope.

Bridges

While hubs are used to build a network at a single site, bridges are used to build a network at two sites—or to join two networks . A bridge operates by looking at the header of the data that comes to it. If the data is for the network on which the bridge resides, the bridge leaves the data alone. If the data is for another network, the bridge gets rid of the data by sending it to a predefined location. An example would be two networks, one in New York and the other in Chicago, that have a bridge at each location (on each network). If a user sends a message in New York and it is not for another user in New York, it must be for a user in Chicago, so it is sent there. Likewise, if a user in Chicago sends a message and it is not for another user in Chicago, it must be for a user in New York.

 A bridge can never be used with more than two sites. If San Francisco were added into the mix, the bridge at Chicago could not determine whether to send the message to San Francisco or to Chicago and could send it to only one location.

The biggest advantages to bridges are that they are reasonably cheap, and they work with all protocols by dropping down to and concentrating on the physical addresses of devices. Physical addresses give bridges the ability to work with NetBEUI (NetBIOS Extended User Interface) and non-routable protocols as easily as they work with TCP/IP. *Remote bridges* are nothing more than bridges that connect two LANs into a WAN and filter signals.

It is important to understand that a bridge—like a hub—receives every data packet sent on the network. The bridge then looks at the header and at an internal table (known as the forwarding database, or *routing table*) and determines if it should leave the packet alone or send the packet out to the address it has. In this capacity, a bridge is used to expand the geographic scope of the network to another location. The opposite could also be true in that a bridge could be used to divide one network into two segments to reduce traffic throughout the whole network.

To visualize the latter situation, suppose that a company has two large departments: Manufacturing and Sales. Every piece of data generated by Manufacturing is sent throughout the network, as is every piece of data generated by Sales. If the network could be divided into two segments with a bridge between Sales and Manufacturing, the network traffic could arguably be cut in half. All the Manufacturing traffic would stay on the Manufacturing segment, and all the Sales traffic would stay on the Sales segment. Data would cross over through the bridge only when Sales requested data from or sent data to Manufacturing, or vice versa.

Routers

Routers are one step above bridges in every way (including cost). Routers can be used to establish pathways between any number of networks. In the earlier example of the New York/Chicago network, assume that the company goes on a buying spree and opens offices (separate networks) in Indianapolis and Los Angeles, while keeping the headquarters in New York. Routers can be placed on each network, as shown in Figure 2.2.

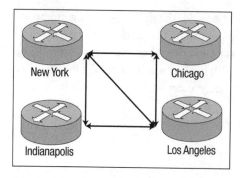

Figure 2.2 Routers allow an unlimited number of networks to be connected to each other.

Now, suppose that the header of data on the New York network shows that the data is not intended for a user on the New York network. Rather than just dumping the data in a predefined location, the router can determine which network it is for and send it to the appropriate location—likewise for routers at all other locations. Notice that there is not a direct connection between Indianapolis and Chicago—there need not be. Data originating in Chicago can get to Indianapolis in a number of ways through varying numbers of *hops*:

➤ *To New York, to Indianapolis*—two hops

➤ *To Los Angeles, to Indianapolis*—two hops

➤ *To New York, to Los Angeles, to Indianapolis*—three hops

➤ *To Los Angeles, to New York, to Indianapolis*—three hops

The biggest problem with a router is that it depends upon the protocol in question to be routable. Routers cannot work with non-routable protocols—typically those that rely on broadcasts and are intended to stay within the confines of the LAN. With the vast number of network protocols in use, it is easier to remember the small number of non-routable protocols than the large number of routable protocols. Non-routable protocols include NetBEUI, DLC (Data Link Control), and LAT (Local Area Transport—a protocol from Digital Equipment Corporation, or DEC).

If your network must use routable and non-routable protocols—for example, say that the newly acquired Indianapolis network is running Windows for Workgroups, which uses NetBEUI—then you can use a *brouter,* which combines the features of a router with those of a bridge. What you are really combining is the MAC (Media Access Control) subcomponent functionality from the Data Link layer with the functionality of the Network layer.

On another note, just as bridges can be used to divide a single network into two segments, a router can divide it into multiple segments—instead of dividing the network into Sales and Manufacturing, you can divide it into Sales, Marketing, Accounting, and so on. The advantages of using a router in this sense are many. Instead of broadcasting into Sales everything coming from Manufacturing that is not for Manufacturing, now traffic can be far more directed. Additionally, the routing table can be far more complex and can even build itself through the use of a number of algorithms. These algorithms can identify multiple paths to a location and determine the best one to use.

> *Note: Routers can also be used to join disparate network types such as Ethernet and Token Ring.*

Gateways

In network terminology, the term *gateway* can have two meanings. In TCP/IP, a gateway is the address of the machine to which data is sent when it is not intended for a host on the network. (In other words, in this context, a gateway is a router and not really a gateway at all.) A gateway is also an application or physical device that operates between the Transmission and Application layers of the OSI model and that can send data between dissimilar systems. The best example of the latter is a mail (SMTP) gateway—no matter which two networks are communicating, the gateway allows them to exchange email.

Other examples of gateways can include proxies, filters, and—to some extent—firewalls. While gateways operate at all upper layers of the networking protocols, they most often work at the Application layer.

Packets from different types of networks can have different data in their headers, and the information can be in different formats. A gateway provides a sophisticated connection between networks and can translate information from one type to another. The gateway can take a packet from one network, read the header, and encapsulate the entire packet into a new one, adding a header that is understood by the second network.

Table 2.1 summarizes the networking devices discussed.

Backbone Issues

Building a private network by using network connectivity devices is one issue, but connecting to the Internet is quite another. Internet Service Providers and connectivity issues are explored in the next few sections.

Table 2.1   Networking devices.

Hardware Device	OSI Layer It Operates With	Protocols And Services At That Layer
Gateway	Application	SMB, NCP, NFS, SNMP, Telnet
Gateway	Presentation	NCP, NFS, SNMP
Gateway	Session	NFS, SNMP, RPC
Gateway	Transport	TCP, UDP, SPX, NetBEUI
Router or Brouter	Network	IP, IPX, NetBEUI, ICMP, ARP, RARP, RIP, OSPF, DLC, DecNET
Bridge or Brouter	Data Link	LLC, MAC
Hub	Physical	None

Internet Service Providers

The vast majority of users access the Internet through ISPs (Internet Service Providers)—companies that provide access to the Internet for a fee. Although ISPs most often provide dial-up access (complete with a username and password), they can also offer Web hosting, email services, e-commerce, direct connections, and more. ISPs can be local or national, with the best example of the latter being America Online. ISP servers traditionally run Unix, but Linux and Windows NT are catching up, and there are a handful of other operating-system options.

ISPs can bill for their services under one of two types of plans: by usage, or unlimited. As the name implies, in an unlimited arrangement, you pay a set fee each month regardless of the amount of bandwidth consumed. Under a "by usage" agreement, you pay a fee based upon the number of hits you receive or the amount of bandwidth you generate, or based upon some other measurable item.

The ISPs access the Internet through Network Access Points (NAPs), which act like point-to-point connections (known as *peering*) and effectively create the Internet backbone. The ISP backbone interconnects the servers (and their services and accounts) to one another, with each NAP representing a large-capacity exchange point. NAPs are overseen by the National Science Foundation (NSF) and other overseeing committees, as well as by commercial companies. Asynchronous Transfer Mode (ATM) technology is often utilized between the exchange points.

Note: Prior to the implementation of NAPs, the Internet backbone depended upon NSFNet for a backbone—entirely overseen by the National Science Foundation. Prior to NSFNet, the backbone was ARPANET (Advanced Research Projects Agency Network).

Connectivity

Whereas the NAPs are used between ISPs, the speed by which you can reach your ISP, and thus reach the Internet, is most often the determining factor in how responsive your online sessions are. The most common access outside of the workplace is through the use of analog modems and POTS (Plain Old Telephone Service).

Dial-up speeds are based upon the modem in use, and the speed is relatively slow because digital signals are converted to analog signals before and after transmission. In its MOdulation phase, the modem turns the computer's digital signals into analog signals, and in the DEModulation phase, the reverse takes place, converting analog signals into digital signals.

 The only way to exceed the speed of an analog modem using POTS is to employ multilink technology. With multilink, you combine the speed of a number of modem connections into a single session; thus, by using four phone lines and four 14.4Kbps modems, you can run a session at 56Kbps. Multilink requires an operating system and applications that can work with the technology. Although it's not always required, it's highly recommended that all modems used in the session be of the same speed.

When the speed of modem lines is not sufficient, which is almost always the case in the business world, alternatives include point-to-point leased lines (T1 through T4), X.25, Frame Relay, ATM, and DSL (Digital Subscriber Line).

Tx Connections

A T1 line is a dedicated line that operates across 24 channels at 1.544Mbps. The European counterpart to this is E1, which uses 32 channels and can run at 2.048Mbps. A T2 connection (rarely used) adds more channels (96) and can operate at 6.312Mbps. A T3 line (E3 being the European equivalent) is a dedicated line of 672 channels able to run at speeds of 43Mbps. A T4 line jumps to 4,032 channels and speeds of over 274Mbps. Of the dedicated-phone-line options, T1 and T3 are the most commonly implemented. Very few private networks require the capacity of a T3 line, and many do not even need the full capacity of a T1. The channels of a T1 or T3 line thus can be subdivided or combined for fractional or multiple levels of service. For instance, one channel of a T1 line's 24-channel bandwidth can transmit at 64Kbps. This single-channel service is called DS-0. DS-1 service is a full T1 line. DS-1C is two T1 lines, DS-2 is four T1 lines, and DS-3 is a full T3 line (equivalent to 28 T1 lines).

X.25

X.25 is a packet-switching standard widely used in WANs. The X.25 standard was developed by the International Telegraph and Telephone Consultative Committee (CCITT), which has been renamed the International Telecommunications Union (ITU). The standard, referred to as Recommendation X.25, was first introduced in 1974, and it provides to networks the options of permanent or switched virtual circuits. X.25 is required to provide reliable service and end-to-end flow control. Because each device on a network can operate more than one virtual circuit, X.25 must provide error and flow control for each virtual circuit.

A big advantage of X.25 is that it is used internationally, while the major drawback is that error checking and flow control slow down X.25. Traditionally, networks utilizing it are implemented with line speeds of up to 64Kbps. These speeds are inadequate to provide most LAN services, which typically require speeds of 10Mbps or better. X.25 networks, therefore, are poor choices for providing LAN application services in a WAN environment.

Frame Relay

Frame Relay, a packet-switching protocol supporting T1 and T3, was designed to support the Broadband Integrated Services Digital Network (B-ISDN). The specifications for Frame Relay address some of the limitations of X.25. As with X.25, Frame Relay is a packet-switching network service, but Frame Relay was designed around newer, faster fiber-optic networks. Unlike X.25, Frame Relay assumes a more reliable network. This enables Frame Relay to eliminate much of the X.25 overhead required to provide reliable service on less reliable networks. Frame Relay relies on higher-level network protocol layers to provide flow and error control. To use Frame Relay, you must have special Frame-Relay-compatible connectivity devices (such as Frame-Relay-compatible routers and bridges).

Frame Relay typically is implemented as a public data network and therefore is regarded as a WAN protocol. Frame Relay provides permanent virtual circuits, which supply permanent virtual pathways for WAN connections. Frame Relay services typically are implemented at line speeds from 56Kbps up to 1.544Mbps (T1). Customers typically purchase access to a specific amount of bandwidth on a Frame Relay service, for which the customer is guaranteed access.

ATM

ATM, Asynchronous Transfer Mode, is a high-bandwidth switching technology developed by the ITU Telecommunications Standards Sector (ITU-TSS). ATM uses 53-byte cells for all transmissions. Because ATM cells are uniform in length, switching mechanisms can operate with a high level of efficiency. This high efficiency results in high data-transfer rates. Some ATM systems can operate at 622Mbps; a typical working speed for an ATM, however, is around 155Mbps.

The unit of transmission for ATM is called a *cell*. All cells are 53 bytes long and consist of a 5-byte header and 48 bytes of data. The "Asynchronous" aspect refers to the fact that transmission time slots don't occur periodically but are granted at irregular intervals. Traffic that is time-critical, such as voice or video, can be given priority over data traffic that can be delayed slightly with no ill effect. Devices communicate on ATM networks by establishing a virtual path, within which virtual circuits can be established.

 ATM is considered an excellent way to combine voice, data, and video transmission on the same high-bandwidth network. As a result, it is one of the most widely used industry buzzwords.

DSL

DSL, Digital Subscriber Line, uses existing copper phone lines. DSL is available only in certain areas, and you must be within a short distance of a switching station. Speeds can vary based upon type of DSL but are typically around 9Mbps (the theoretical maximum is 52Mbps). DSL is typically less expensive than even ISDN in terms of hardware, setup, and service costs, yet the need to be within a few miles of a switching station is a big deterrent.

There are several types of DSL to choose from, and not all types are available in all markets. The types available include:

➤ *Asymmetric DSL (ADSL)*—uses existing copper phone lines

➤ *High-bit-rate DSL (HDSL)*—requires two wire pairs

➤ *ISDN DSL (IDSL)*—uses existing ISDN facilities

➤ *Rate Adaptive DSL (RADSL)*—adjusts the speed based on signal quality

➤ *Symmetric DSL (SDSL)*—a version of HDSL using a single pair of wires (and providing slower rates)

➤ *Very-high-bit-rate DSL (VDSL)*—transmits over short distances; the connection rate increases as the distance decreases

Table 2.2   DSL transmission specs.

Type Of Service	Upstream Speed	Downstream Speed	Wire Pairs	Maximum Distance From Switch (In Feet)
ADSL	1Mbps	8Mbps	1	12,000
HDSL	1.544Mbps	1.544Mbps	2	12,000
HDSL	2.048Mbps	2.048Mbps	3	12,000
IDSL	128Kbps	128Kbps	1	18,000
RADSL	90Kbps	610Kbps	1	18,000
RADSL	1.088Mbps	7.168Mbps	1	25,000
SDSL	1.544Mbps	1.544Mbps	1	10,000
VDSL	1.6Mbps	12.96Mbps	1	3,000
VDSL	2.3Mbps	25.82Mbps	1	3,000

To illustrate the performance possible with the different types and the way it varies, Table 2.2 shows the transmission rates and distances for various DSL implementations.

Other Alternatives

For dial-in access, DSL is an alternative to the traditional analog modem discussed earlier. Other modem alternatives include ISDN (Integrated Services Digital Network) and cable modems.

ISDN requires two phone lines and can reach a speed of around 128,000bps. As the "Digital" portion implies, ISDN replaces all analog services with digital services and is appropriately known as Basic Rate Interface ISDN (BRI). Basic Rate Interface ISDN uses two data channels (carrying voice or data) simultaneously, thus allowing you to transmit data and voice at the same time on the same line. Primary Rate Interface ISDN (PRI) is the same as T1 service and is a higher level of ISDN.

Cable modems work with the coaxial from the cable TV company. Under the best of conditions, cable modems can achieve downstream speeds of about 27Mbps, but the speed is reduced with the increase in the number of users on the line and is usually around 2Mbps in actual implementations. The decrease in speed as subscribers use the technology constitutes the biggest disadvantage, while the fact that the cable can be run for miles (using amplifiers along the way) constitutes its greatest advantage over other technologies.

Table 2.3 summarizes some of these technologies and compares features.

Table 2.3	Connectivity technologies.	
Technology	**Name**	**Feature**
ATM	Asynchronous Transfer Mode	155Mbps to 622Mbps packet switching with all data being packaged in 53-byte cells
DSL	Digital Subscriber Line	Uses existing phone lines for access speeds of up to 9Mbps but is available only in certain areas
Frame Relay	N/A	A point-to-point system across leased lines through the use of a bridge or router
Tx	N/A	Leased phone lines that operate between speeds of 1.544Mbps (T1) and 274.176Mbps (T4)
X.25	N/A	Connects at low-cost remote terminals to mainframe hosts through Public Data Networks (PDNs) and does error-checking (which slows it down)

Organizations Shaping The Internet

When you're dealing with the Internet structure, it is important to know of the agencies involved in it. The following lists many of those organizations, in alphabetical order, and their primary roles.

➤ *Internet Architecture Board (IAB)*—the organization of the Internet Society that oversees the physical architecture, guides the Internet Engineering Task Force (IETF), and handles complaints. The IAB approves appointments to the Internet Engineering Steering Group (IESG) from nominees coming from IETF.

➤ *Internet Assigned Numbers Authority (IANA)*—an organization under the IAB that assigns IP addresses and ensures that unique values are issued. Rather than handling the tasks themselves, IANA now contracts to ICANN.

➤ *Internet Corporation of Assigned Names and Numbers (ICANN)*—a new not-for-profit organization that now issues IP addresses for IANA.

➤ *Internet Engineering Steering Group (IESG)*—the group to which all Area Directors of the IETF belong. A part of the Internet Society (ISOC), it ensures that rules passed by the ISOC are carried out and moves Internet proposals along the path needed to become standards.

➤ *Internet Engineering Task Force (IETF)*—the organization overseeing standards, which are typically drafted first as Requests For Comments (RFCs). The IETF is divided into numerous subcommittees (called working groups) managed by Area Directors. It is composed of volunteers who meet three times a year—anyone may attend and participate (no membership is required). There are currently eight working groups, though the number can change at any time.

➤ *Internet Society (ISOC)*—A board of overseers that primarily focuses on policy issues. The Internet Society approves appointments to the IAB from nominees submitted by the IETF.

➤ *Internet Network Information Center (InterNIC)*—a collaboration between Network Solutions, Inc. (NSI) and AT&T that oversees domain name and IP address assignments, support services, publications, and database services. InterNIC is a registered trademark of the U.S. Department of Commerce.

➤ *National Science Foundation (NSF)*—a not-for-profit organization that was helpful in funding many of the early Internet needs.

➤ *Network Solutions, Inc. (NSI)*—a for-profit corporation that has been instrumental in many aspects of the Internet's growth and in the administration of domain names.

 Know that the ISOC oversees other organizations and focuses mainly on policies. The IETF, on the other hand, is divided into working groups and was initially created by the IAB.

Practice Questions

Question 1

> The operating system with which the TCP/IP networking protocol suite was first associated is:
>
> ○ a. Windows NT
>
> ○ b. Windows 95
>
> ○ c. Unix
>
> ○ d. Linux

The correct answer is c. When the Department of Defense was looking for an operating system to standardize upon, it wanted one that could offer networking capabilities. None of the other listed operating systems existed during this time period, and TCP/IP was formulated for, and associated with, Unix.

Question 2

> A networking device that passes all incoming traffic out to all attached ports is a(n):
>
> ○ a. Gateway
>
> ○ b. Hub
>
> ○ c. Router
>
> ○ d. Switch

The correct answer is b. A hub, in the absence of switching, passes all incoming data out to all attached ports. Through the use of switching, only those ports for which the data is intended receive the transmissions. Answer a is incorrect because a gateway sends messages between upper layer applications. Answers c and d are incorrect because routers can route data to specific addresses, and a switch is a hub that can direct data to specific ports.

Question 3

Your network is running NetBEUI and TCP/IP protocols, and you want to connect your network to two other locations. One of those locations is using only
NetBEUI, and the other is using only TCP/IP. What connectivity device should
you add to your site to connect to the other two?

○ a. Router

○ b. Hub

○ c. Bridge

○ d. Brouter

The correct answer is d. A brouter combines the functionality of a bridge and
a router and allows routable (TCP/IP) and non-routable protocols to be used
together. Answer a is incorrect because a router cannot work with non-routable
protocols (such as NetBEUI). Answer b is incorrect because a hub cannot be
used to combine multiple networks. Answer c is incorrect because a bridge will
use non-routable protocols but only between two locations.

Question 4

To transfer email between networks, what hardware connectivity device should
you use between them?

○ a. Gateway

○ b. Bridge

○ c. Router

○ d. Hub

The correct answer is a. A gateway is an upper-layer device that can work
between applications, such as email, and send data between networks. The
other devices given are not capable of working at the application layer: Bridges
work at the Data Link layer, routers at the Network layer, and hubs at the
Physical layer.

Question 5

> The number of channels in a T1 connection is:
>
> ○ a. 4
> ○ b. 8
> ○ c. 16
> ○ d. 24

The correct answer is d. A T1 connection has 24 channels and can operate at speeds of up to 1.544Mbps. The other answers are incorrect, as they do not represent the correct number of channels available.

Question 6

> A packet-switching technology that requires flow control and error detection for each circuit would be considered:
>
> ○ a. Frame Relay
> ○ b. X.25
> ○ c. ATM
> ○ d. E1

The correct answer is b. X.25 is the oldest of the technologies listed. It requires flow control and error detection because these features were assumed to be needed on all circuits when X.25 was created. Answers a and c are incorrect because Frame Relay and ATM can operate faster by avoiding these steps. Answer d is incorrect because E1 is not a valid choice; it is not a packet-switching technology but the European equivalent of a T1 (dedicated connection).

Question 7

> ISPs connect to the Internet through:
>
> ○ a. Multilink
> ○ b. CCITTs
> ○ c. NAPs
> ○ d. DS-0

The correct answer is c. Network Access Points (NAPs) are used by Internet Service Providers to connect to the Internet and form the backbone. Answer a is incorrect because multilink is used by users to combine the speed of a number of modems into a single connection. Answer b is incorrect because CCITT is the committee behind the X.25 standard. Answer d is incorrect because DS-0 is a single channel within a T1.

Question 8

The organization behind the physical architecture of the Internet is:

○ a. IETF

○ b. ISOC

○ c. ICANN

○ d. IAB

The correct answer is d. The Internet Architecture Board (IAB) oversees the physical architecture of the Internet. The other answer choices are incorrect because the scope of their missions does not include the Internet's physical architecture.

Question 9

The technology that allows access speeds of up to 9Mbps and uses the existing phone lines is:

○ a. DSL

○ b. ISDN

○ c. Cable modems

○ d. Analog modems

The correct answer is a. DSL allows access speeds of up to 9Mbps and uses the existing phone lines. Answer b is incorrect because ISDN requires two phone lines and can reach a speed of around 128,000bps. Answer c is incorrect because cable modems do not use existing phone lines. Answer d is incorrect because the analog modem, the slowest item in the list, is the traditional dial-up method for reaching speeds of around 56Kbps.

Question 10

The speed at which a T3 connection could operate if all channels were used is:

○ a. 1.544Mbps

○ b. 2.048Mbps

○ c. 12.678Mbps

○ d. 43Mbps

The correct answer is d. A T3 line offers 672 channels, and each operates at approximately 64K. With all channels combined, this line offers an operating speed of 43Mbps. The other choices are incorrect as they understate the possible speed of a T3 connection.

Need To Know More?

 Dulaney, Emmett. *MCSE Fast Track: Networking Essentials*. New Riders Publishing, Indianapolis, IN, 1998. ISBN: 1-56205-939-4. Chapter 2 discusses WAN technologies.

 ftp://ftpeng.cisco.com/fred/rfc-index/rfc.html is a site where you can find an index of all Requests For Comments and links to them.

 http://navigators.com/internet_architecture.html—"The Big Picture," "What are the major pieces of the Internet, and who are the major players in each segment?" Details Internet interactions from the user PC through the ISP and into online content, including market leaders in each category.

 www.icann.org is the home page for The Internet Corporation for Assigned Names and Numbers, describes its purpose, and contains links to the FAQs, notes, and minutes of meetings.

 www.ietf.org/tao.html—*The Tao of IETF—A Guide for New Attendees of the Internet Engineering Task Force.* Contains a description of the IETF and its beginnings.

 www.pacbell.com offers an excellent description of Pacific Bell's Network Access Point and how the structure is built.

TCP/IP

Terms you'll need to understand:

√ Transmission Control Protocol/ Internet Protocol (TCP/IP)

√ Request for Comments (RFCs)

√ Open Systems Interconnection (OSI)

√ Flow control

√ Internet Control Message Protocol (ICMP)

√ IP address

√ Address classes

√ Subnet mask

√ Default gateway

√ Windows Internet Name Service (WINS)

√ Dynamic Host Configuration Protocol (DHCP)

Techniques you'll need to master:

√ Understanding the layers of the OSI model

√ Understanding the layers of the TCP/IP reference model

√ Knowing the common TCP/IP port numbers

√ Familiarizing yourself with the operational essentials of TCP/IP

√ Understanding the difference between a connection-oriented protocol and a connectionless protocol

√ Converting decimal and binary numbers back and forth

√ Identifying Class A, B, and C IP addresses

√ Identifying and understanding the difference between private and public IP addresses

√ Determining the number of usable subnets and hosts per subnet given an IP address

√ Familiarizing yourself with the configuration of TCP/IP

√ Understanding the operational essentials of DHCP

The previous chapter introduced TCP/IP (Transmission Control Protocol/ Internet Protocol) and discussed the importance of TCP/IP and the Internet. This chapter will explore the components of TCP/IP in more depth. Additionally, you will be introduced to TCP/IP configuration and to the way TCP/IP uses IP addressing to send information from network to network. Most importantly, you need to understand the relationship between the Internet and TCP/IP. Because the i-Net+ exam is an Internet/intranet certification exam and because the Internet and a growing number of local networks use TCP/IP to a great extent, you will find that most of this book is in fact dealing with TCP/IP in one aspect or another.

TCP/IP Background

The TCP/IP protocol is often referred to as the *language* or *protocol* of the Internet and also as the *architecture* of the Internet. These descriptions provide a quick and concise description of TCP/IP, but TCP/IP is actually more than a single protocol or even a pair of protocols. In fact, TCP/IP is actually a suite of protocols and a set of services, which provide connectivity and management of IP-based networks.

The Department of Defense Advanced Research Projects Agency (DARPA) developed TCP/IP for the Advanced Research Projects Agency Network (ARPANET). TCP/IP replaced the Network Control Protocol (NCP), which at the time provided the basic services for ARPANET. Initially, the two primary design goals of TCP/IP were to provide:

➤ Universal connectivity between networks

➤ Hardware and software independence

TCP/IP is a non-proprietary protocol, and its development is actually quite amazing considering the proprietary nature of most systems during its time of development. From its inception onward, TCP/IP continued to gain broader acceptance, especially as the Department of Defense started requiring contracts to recognize TCP/IP as a military standard. Furthermore, in the early 1980s, a version of Unix was made publicly available that had incorporated TCP/IP into the operating system.

The success of TCP/IP continues to grow even today. While TCP/IP has been the communication protocol for Unix systems and the Internet, it has only been recently that operating systems from Novell, as well as Microsoft's Windows 2000, have incorporated TCP/IP as native networking protocol. Without a doubt, TCP/IP has become the *de facto* standard not only for the Internet but also for data communication within individual networks.

Request For Comments (RFCs)

TCP/IP and other Internet-related technologies are covered under Request for Comments (RFCs) and are freely available to all on the Internet. RFCs are by the Internet Architecture Board (IAB) and can be viewed by visiting the Internet Engineering Task Force (IETF) at **www.ietf.org**. An RFC proposal can be written by anyone. The Internet Engineering Steering Group (IESG) reviews each comment document to determine whether it will ultimately be assigned a number.

RFCs are issued a sequential number and can never be reused or updated. Any changes that need to be made to the original RFC will require a new number. Although you are not likely to be tested on the numbers of the many RFCs that are related to TCP/IP, it is important that you are aware of their existence and understand that all TCP/IP standards are published as RFCs.

> *Note: Although the standards for TCP/IP will always be published in an RFC, not all RFCs specify standards. RFCs are given various status assignments. For example, an RFC may be given a status assignment of Required, Recommended, Elective, Limited Use, or Not Recommended. Additionally, a document being considered for a standard will go through a couple of stages, or maturity levels, before being labeled an Internet Standard. These other levels include Proposed Standard and Draft Standard.*

Comparing The OSI Model And TCP/IP

As I mentioned earlier, TCP/IP is actually made up of more than just one or two protocols—it comprises a suite of protocols. These protocols map to a conceptual four-layer model much like that of the Open Systems Interconnection (OSI) reference model (see Figure 3.1).

Although the OSI and TCP/IP models are not incompatible, they are also not exactly compatible either. The TCP/IP stack's model does, however, map very closely to the OSI model. They both use a layered model approach, but the OSI model's layers are more independent, whereas the TCP/IP model combines layers from the OSI model into single layers. These differences are a result of the requirements of TCP/IP. For example, TCP/IP combines the OSI model's Physical and Data Link layers into one network interface layer because of the need for a connectionless protocol.

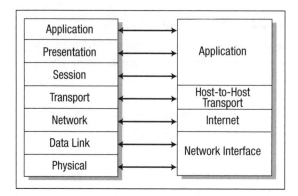

Figure 3.1 The seven-layer OSI model compared to the four-layer TCP/IP protocol stack.

Note: The TCP/IP reference model is also referred to as the Internet reference model and the DARPA model.

The OSI Model

The OSI model is a seven-layer model that serves as the framework for internetworking applications and protocols. Before examining the layers of the TCP/IP model, let's briefly examine the seven OSI layers and their functions:

➤ *Application*—This top layer provides network services to user applications.

➤ *Presentation*—This layer works closely with the Application layer to provide data representation and formatting so that the data being passed up to the next layer will be understood. Examples of Presentation Layer standards include ASCII, TIFF, and encryption.

➤ *Session*—The Session layer's responsibilities include establishing, maintaining, and managing the sessions between applications.

➤ *Transport*—This layer transmits messages from sender to receiver by segmenting and reassembling data into a data stream.

➤ *Network*—The Network layer determines the best way to move data from one network to another by managing device locations and addresses. Routers work at this layer.

➤ *Data Link*—This layer is actually composed of two sublayers, which include the Logical Link Control (LLC) sublayer and the Media Access Control (MAC) sublayer. The Data Link layer is primarily responsible for the physical transmission of packets across the network media.

➤ *Physical*—This bottom layer is hardware-oriented, so it's concerned with the physical method by which bits are sent and received across the network.

Data transmission through the model is actually vertical—that is, the Application layer attaches an application header and passes the frame to the Presentation layer. Next, the Presentation layer does its part, and this process continues until the data is received at the receiving end. At this time, the process is reversed, starting with the Physical layer and working its way vertically up the layers. Each layer, however, behaves as if the transmission were horizontal. For example, the Session layer on the sending end communicates with the Session layer on the receiving end, and is not concerned that the actual transmission must first traverse various other layers.

To better understand this layered and modular approach, think in terms of the various functions within a corporation. For example, imagine that you work in a marketing department of a giant publishing company, and at the end of every month, you need to ship promotional copies of books to certain businesses. You simply package the book, address it, and hand it to the shipping department. From this point, your job is done, and any changes that occur in the shipping department should operate independently of your department. For example, if the shipping department decides to change carriers from FedEx to UPS, it can do so without "rewriting" the entire process and affecting the way the department does business.

The TCP/IP Reference Model

Now that you are familiar with the OSI model, let's take a closer look at the TCP/IP stack. Figure 3.1, shown earlier, illustrates how the TCP/IP model maps out to the OSI model. The process of one layer passing data to the next in the OSI model also applies to the TCP/IP model.

Within each layer of the TCP/IP stack are additional protocols, and each protocol functions independently of other protocols. Using our earlier analogy, the marketing department expects that the shipping department will accept outgoing mail and ensure that it is delivered to the specified destination, just as each protocol expects services from the protocol underneath it. Discussed next are the four layers of the TCP/IP model as well as the common protocols within each layer.

The TCP/IP reference model is made up of the following four layers: Application, Transport, Internet, and Network Interface.

Application Layer

The Application layer provides network access to applications and services. From this layer, sockets provide access to the transport protocols. A *socket* is an identifier for a particular service on a particular system on the network.

Some of the most-used Application-layer protocols include the following:

➤ *HTTP (Hypertext Transfer Protocol)*—HTTP is used to transfer Webpage data that makes up the World Wide Web.

➤ *FTP (File Transfer Protocol)*—This protocol provides file transfer service. The process of uploading and downloading files often uses FTP. Although support for FTP is built into most Web browsers, FTP client software, such as the popular WS_FTP program, is still used to provide file transfer functionality.

➤ *SMTP (Simple Mail Transfer Protocol)*—The SMTP protocol provides basic services for the transfer of email. SMTP actually uses TCP and IP to route the messages across the Internet.

➤ *SNMP (Simple Network Management Protocol)*—This protocol is used for monitoring networks and providing network device statistics.

➤ *Telnet*—This protocol is commonly used for providing connectivity between dissimilar systems and for providing connectivity for the management of routers. Windows operating systems include a Telnet program with which you may already be familiar.

Transport Layer

The Transport layer primarily provides flow control, as well as reliability, by using sequence numbers and acknowledgments. The TCP/IP protocol derives part of its name from this layer.

This layer consists of the following two protocols:

➤ *TCP (Transmission Control Protocol)*—TCP breaks messages into segments and vice versa. TCP is a reliable and connection-oriented protocol. This concept is important and differs greatly from UDP, discussed next. The fact that TCP is connection-oriented means that two nodes may send and receive data only after they have established a viable connection. Additionally, TCP provides reliability by using a sequence number for each packet. This numbering ensures that the receiving node receives all the packets and that they are processed in the proper order. In addition, the receiving end will return an acknowledgment for the segments received.

➤ *UDP (User Datagram Protocol)*—UDP, on the other hand, is a connectionless and unreliable protocol. You are not required to make a connection beforehand to send and receive data, and delivery of information is not guaranteed. UDP usually relies upon the application to perform the various functions that TCP provides.

Although it may initially appear that UDP is inferior to TCP, UDP does have its benefits. Because UDP does not use acknowledgments, it is fast and efficient. Suppose, for example, that you pop into a co-worker's office, say, "Don't forget about the meeting at noon," and walk out immediately. Although this method might be faster than waiting for a reply such as, "Okay, I will be there at noon," it does not guarantee that the co-worker properly understood what you said. Thus, UDP is the protocol of choice when speed is important or when you wish to limit the amount of chatter traversing the network.

Know the differences between TCP and UDP, and be sure you understand the advantages and disadvantages of connection-oriented and connectionless protocols.

Flow Control

Flow control is the process by which a transmitting node avoids flooding a receiving node with data faster than that node can receive it. For example, we humans experience flow control on the telephone when speaking with a customer service representative who's asking for personal information. If you are telling the receiving party your address, telephone number, and so on, and you are talking faster than he or she can type and remember, you will most likely be asked to wait.

TCP And UDP Ports

The Transport layer uses port numbers to transfer data to the Application layer. These ports allow a system to support and keep track of simultaneous sessions with other computers on the network. Table 3.1 lists many of the common port assignments.

You should memorize the port assignments listed in Table 3.1. It's not likely that you could feasibly memorize every available port, but you should memorize at least the ports listed here.

Table 3.1   Well-known ports.

Port Number	Protocol	Service	Description
21	TCP	FTP	File Transfer Protocol
23	TCP	Telnet	Telnet
25	TCP	SMTP	Simple Mail Transfer Protocol
53	TCP	DNS	Domain Name System
69	UDP	TFTP	Trivial File Transfer Protocol
80	TCP	HTTP	World Wide Web
110	TCP, UDP	POP3	Post Office Protocol 3
119	TCP, UDP	NNTP	Network News Transfer Protocol
161	UDP	SNMP	Simple Network Management Protocol

There are actually over 65,000 available ports, but the most common services use ports only up to 1,023 (called *well-known ports*). A port must be used to access a particular application. For example, when you are browsing the Web and connecting to a Web page on a server, you are most likely connecting to port 80 on the server. Normally, this port assignment is transparent to the user; however, there may be instances when a port needs to be specified. It is possible, for example, to connect to a Web page or other service using a different port assignment. For example, perhaps you have seen some Web pages that specify the port in the Uniform Resource Locator (URL), such as **http://www.domain.com:8080**. The 8080 specifies to connect to port 8080 on domain.com. URLs, also known simply as addresses, are discussed more later in the book.

Well-known port numbers are defined in RFC 1700.

Internet Layer

The Internet layer is responsible for routing packets throughout the network. Naturally, routers operate at this layer. The two most common protocols at this layer are:

➤ *IP (Internet Protocol)*—This is a connectionless protocol that uses units of information called datagrams to deliver data. IP is primarily concerned with getting these datagrams to the destination network. Like UDP, IP does not provide error checking or flow control. IP does, however, provide the IP address of the source and destination network.

➤ *ICMP (Internet Control Message Protocol)*—ICMP is used by IP and other protocols and is best known for the status and error messages it provides. ICMP messages are carried within IP datagrams. Internet utilities such as PING and TRACERT rely upon ICMP. These utilities are often used for troubleshooting networks and are discussed in detail in Chapter 15.

Network Interface Layer

One of the design goals of TCP/IP was to provide a communication connection that would operate independently of the physical media. As its name implies, the Network Interface layer provides an interface between the upper layers and the actual physical network. Regardless of the type of network, this layer will create a compatible frame for the datagram from the previous layer in order to send the data on to the network.

IP Addressing

An IP address identifies a host on a network. IP uses this address to route data across the Internet and TCP/IP networks.

Most often, IP addresses are displayed as four decimal numbers separated by periods, a format referred to as *dotted decimal notation*; for example:

```
192.168.56.1
```

Of those four decimal numbers, one or more of the numbers from the left will designate a network identifier, and one or more numbers from the right will designate a host identifier. If we take the IP address from above and convert it to binary, it looks like this:

```
11000000.10101000.00111000.00000001
```

Given this information, keep the following points in mind when dealing with IP addresses:

➤ IP addresses often appear as four decimal numbers separated by periods.

➤ Each number consists of 8 bits for a total of 32 bits.

➤ Each set of 8 bits is called an *octet*.

➤ Each octet in the decimal format can range from 0 to 255 and in binary from 00000000 to 11111111.

➤ An IP address contains a network and a host portion.

To determine which part of an IP address is the network identifier and which part is the host identifier, you must know the class of the IP address and the subnet mask.

Remember that the network ID portion specifies the network, whereas the host ID portion identifies the specific host. This is analogous to a house address. For example, a postal address for a home identifies the street address as well as the house number. Just as many nodes may reside to one network ID, many homes may exist on a single street. However, each house on the street will have a unique house address, just as each node will have a unique host ID.

Binary 101

Before we go any further with IP addressing, you should first understand binary. Binary is the base-2 numbering system in which values are expressed as combinations of two digits, 0 and 1. For those not already familiar with this numbering system, binary may seem a bit overwhelming. As you will soon see, however, it is quite simple.

If you read the heading "Binary 101" as "Binary 5," you may already speak binary; otherwise, let's examine how we get 5 from 101.

Raising the number 2 to varying powers creates binary numbers. Start with 2 to the 0 power on the far right, and continue raising a power as you move left. Table 3.2 illustrates the powers of two.

Table 3.2 Decimal-value equivalents for the powers of two.	
2^n	Decimal Value
2^0	1
2^1	2
2^2	4
2^3	8
2^4	16
2^5	32
2^6	64
2^7	128

Alternatively, another way to think about it is to start with the number 1, double it and continue to double each succeeding number from right to left:

128	64	32	16	8	4	2	1

In order to determine the decimal value of a binary number, simply take the binary number and plug it beneath the corresponding value starting on the right side. Thus, the binary number 101 equals decimal value 5. Table 3.3 shows how this method is used to derive this answer.

Add the numbers in the top row wherever the number 1 is present from the binary number you plug in. Therefore, 4+1=5. Table 3.4 shows various binary numbers and their resulting decimal values. Using the method just discussed, you should be able to see how you can easily arrive at a binary number without having to memorize a huge table.

Address Classes

The Internet Network Information Center (InterNIC) is responsible for allocating IP addresses to organizations that want to connect their networks to the Internet. The InterNIC was formed in 1983 as a consortium between the National Science Foundation (NSF), AT&T, General Atomics, and Network

Table 3.3   Decimal and binary conversion.

128	64	32	16	8	4	2	1
0	0	0	0	0	1	0	1

Table 3.4   Binary numbers and their corresponding decimal values.

Binary	Bit Value	Decimal
00000000	0	0
10000000	128	128
11000000	128+64	192
11100000	128+64+32	224
11110000	128+64+32+16	240
11111000	128+64+32+16+8	248
11111100	128+64+32+16+8+4	252
11111110	128+64+32+16+8+4+2	254
11111111	128+64+32+16+8+4+2+1	255

Solutions Inc. When assigning addresses, the InterNIC uses *classes* to assign an organization a network ID, and the organization receiving the class address is responsible for assigning the host portion of the address (the host ID).

There are five classes of IP addresses, labeled with the letters A to E. Classes A, B, and C are most common, whereas classes D and E are not generally used except for special purposes. Each class of IP address can be identified by its first octet. Table 3.5 shows the first three common address classes and the networks and hosts available to each.

 Know the information presented in Table 3.5. In addition, you should know that the first octet range for a Class D address is 224 through 239, and the first octet range for a Class E address is 240 through 247.

Class A Addresses

Class A addresses are used for very large networks. The first octet in a Class A address identifies the network ID, and the last three octets represent the host ID. The first octet of a Class A address ranges from 1 to 127. This class of address has a *high-order bit* of zero. This simply means that the bit furthest to the left is always zero. Thus, if we use the chart we used earlier, we see that if the high-order bit is set to zero, the highest possible number we can obtain is 127 (Table 3.6). Thus, if we use the methodology described earlier, 64+32+16+8+4+2+1=127. Although the result of 127 can be obtained, you must remember that 127 is reserved for loopback testing and cannot be used.

Note: The use of 127 in the first octet is reserved for loopback and cannot be used as a valid node address. In addition, keep in mind that a network address consisting of all binary ones or zeros cannot be used because these are considered special addresses.

Table 3.5   Class A, B, and C addresses.

Class	First Octet Range	Networks Available	Hosts Available
A	1-127	127	16,777,214
B	128-191	16,384	65,534
C	192-223	2,097,152	254

Table 3.6   Class A address (127) with high-order bit of 0.

128	64	32	16	8	4	2	1
0	1	1	1	1	1	1	1

Class B Addresses

Class B addresses are used for mid-sized networks. The first two octets are used to identify the network ID, and the remaining two octets represent the host ID. The first octet of a Class B address ranges from 128 to 191. A Class B address has a high-order bit of 10, as shown in Table 3.7. The maximum number that can be obtained is 191 (128+32+16+8+4+2+1=191).

Class C Addresses

Class C addresses are used for smaller networks. The first three octets are used to identify the network ID, and the last octet represents the host ID. The first octet of a Class C address ranges from 192 to 223. The high-order bit for a Class C address is always set to 110, as shown in Table 3.8. The maximum number that can be obtained is 223 (128+64+16+8+4+2+1=223).

Class D And E Addresses

Class D networks are used for multicasting and do not contain network or host IDs. *Multicasting* is the process of sending a message simultaneously to more than one destination on a network. The first octet of a Class D address ranges from 224 to 239.

 Multicasting is often used to send information simultaneously to several registered hosts. A computer will register itself using a Class D address.

Class E addresses fall into the range of 240 to 247 for the first octet, and this address class is reserved for future use.

Table 3.7	Class B address (191) with high-order bit of 10.						
128	64	32	16	8	4	2	1
1	0	1	1	1	1	1	1

Table 3.8	Class C address (223) with high-order bit of 110.						
128	64	32	16	8	4	2	1
1	1	0	1	1	1	1	1

Private Vs. Public Addresses

Usually a network address is assigned to an organization from an Internet Service Provider (ISP). Most ISPs have obtained their network class from the InterNIC, and unfortunately, the number of available networks is limited.

> *Note: IP version 6 (IPv6) is the next generation of IP addressing. It will have a larger address range, thus increasing the number of available network addresses.*

The Internet Assigned Numbers Authority (IANA) has reserved three blocks of IP addresses for private use on a network that will not be connected to the Internet. These blocks include:

➤ 10.0.0.0 through 10.255.255.255

➤ 172.16.0.0 through 172.31.255.255

➤ 192.168.0.0 through 192.168.255.255

Any organization may use addresses from these assigned ranges without prior coordination, as long as the addresses will be used privately. Likewise, any organization that needs IP addresses for a network connected to the Internet will never be assigned addresses from these three private blocks.

Memorize the three blocks of private IP addresses, and be sure you can distinguish a private IP address from a public address. Do not make the mistake, for example, of agreeing that the address 172.16.45.1 is a valid Class A network for a node connected to the Internet.

An address of 172.16.45.1 does fall within the Class A range; however, it belongs to one of the private IP address blocks and cannot be used for a node connected to the Internet.

An excellent resource for learning more about private IP addresses is RFC 1918. This memo also specifies many Internet Best Current Practices for implementing private IP addresses. RFC 1918 also provides several excellent examples of organizations that could benefit from the use of private IP addresses. One such example is an airport that relies on TCP/IP to network its many arrival and departure displays via IP addressing.

Where Internet connectivity is not a concern, using a private IP address not only conserves the limited globally unique addresses available, but it also provides an organization with added network flexibility. On the other hand, a disadvantage to using private IP addresses is that an organization might be faced with a renumbering nightmare should it later decide to connect to the Internet or merge more than one private network.

Subnets And Masks

Earlier it was mentioned that an IP address contains two parts—a network ID and a host ID. In order to determine which part is which, a subnet mask is used. The purpose of the mask, besides distinguishing between the network ID and the host ID, is to determine whether data belongs on the local network or to another network.

Note: Subnet masks do not apply to Class D or E addresses.

Each of the first three classes of IP addresses has a default subnet mask. Table 3.5 listed these three classes, along with the default number of networks and hosts available. These numbers apply when you're utilizing the default mask; however, they can be manipulated by applying a subnet mask. Now take a look at Table 3.9, which identifies the default subnet masks for Class A, B, and C networks.

Memorize the default subnet masks for Class A, B, and C networks, listed in Table 3.9.

Looking at the subnet masks reveals the network portion and the host portion. A portion containing all ones specifies the network addresses—this portion cannot be manipulated. The host portion is represented by all zeros, and this portion can be manipulated.

Table 3.9 Default subnet masks for Class A, B, and C networks.		
IP Address Class	**Subnet Mask (Decimal)**	**Subnet Mask (Binary)**
Class A	255.0.0.0	11111111.00000000.00000000.00000000
Class B	255.255.0.0	11111111.11111111.00000000.00000000
Class C	255.255.255.0	11111111.11111111.11111111.00000000

Using Subnetting

Subnetting means that you take an existing network ID and subdivide it, thus creating subnets. Reasons you may want to consider subnetting include the following:

➤ To accommodate multiple physical networks; for example, if you are assigned a Class C address range but have multiple networks

➤ To reduce network traffic and provide increased network performance

➤ To simplify network management

To create these additional subnets, you must first create a *custom subnet mask*. Creating a subnet mask involves "borrowing" bits from the host ID portion of an IP address. Remember, you can't mess with the network portion—you can, however, manipulate and administer the host ID portion in any way you see fit.

Let's begin by using a Class B network as an example. First, here are some things we already know about the Class B network's default subnet mask:

➤ The default subnet mask is 255.255.0.0.

➤ This default mask allows for 65,534 hosts.

➤ This default mask uses the first 16 bits (255.255) and leaves the remaining 16 bits for the host (0.0).

Next, we need to borrow bits from the host portion (16 available) to create our custom mask. Table 3.10 lists the various subnets and shows how they are used to create a certain number of subnets and hosts.

It is clear that a maximum number of usable subnets and hosts can be assigned to each subnet mask. Many people seem to be unclear, however, on the masked-

Table 3.10   Creating Class B subnet masks.

Subnet Mask	Masked Bits	Usable Subnets	Hosts Per Subnet
255.255.0.0	16	1	65,534
255.255.192.0	18	2	16,382
255.255.240.0	20	14	4,094
255.255.255.0	24	254	254
255.255.255.240	28	4,094	14
255.255.255.252	30	16,382	2

bits portion. To make this point more clear, you must think in binary. Now, looking at the Class B subnet mask of 255.255.0.0, you should be able to see that there are 16 bits in the mask. Thus, by converting this mask to binary, we can derive the following:

```
255.255.0.0 = 11111111.11111111.00000000.00000000
```

(Count the ones as a masked bit.)

Now, if we convert 255.255.192.0 to binary, we get the following:

```
11111111.11111111.11000000.00000000
```

(The original 16 bits in the mask plus the two borrowed from the host portion equals 18 bits in the mask.)

Once you have mastered this idea, you can figure out the number of usable subnets and hosts per subnet mask. Given a Class B subnet mask of 255.255.240.0, we should first do two things.

1. Determine the default subnet mask for the given class.

2. Convert the custom and default subnet masks to binary.

The default mask for a Class B address is 255.255.0.0. Converted to binary, it is:

```
11111111.11111111.00000000.00000000
```

The custom mask, 255.255.240.0, converted to binary is:

```
11111111.11111111.11110000.00000000
```

We can see that four bits were borrowed from the host, leaving 12 bits available. To determine the number of subnets and hosts per subnet, use the following formula: 2^n-2, where n equals the number of borrowed bits or the number of bits leftover. As a result:

➤ $2^4-2 = 14$ subnets (4 represents the number of borrowed bits)

➤ $2^{12}-2 = 4,094$ hosts per subnet (12 represents the number of available bits left over)

> *Note: You must always remember to subtract two. This takes into account the fact that you can never use all ones or all zeros.*

The methods presented are the same regardless of whether you are using a Class A, B, or C network. The trick to subnetting is determining an adequate subnet mask that will provide you with an acceptable number of hosts per needed subnet, while at the same time leaving room for growth.

Although the i-Net+ exam will not provide you with a subnet calculator program, there are many programs out there (most of them free) that can perform advanced subnet calculations. Additionally, the Calculator program included with the Windows operating system can be used to convert back and forth between decimal and binary. To convert a decimal number to binary, for example, enter the number you wish to convert and select the *Bin* option button, also called a radio button.

Configuring TCP/IP

Before a client can obtain access to a TCP/IP network or the Internet, TCP/IP will need to be properly configured (after it has been installed, of course, if it is not already present). To successfully configure TCP/IP, you should configure the client with an IP address and a subnet mask (at a minimum) and possibly with a default gateway.

TCP/IP is required for a client to access the Internet. TCP/IP may be implemented differently depending upon the operating system being used. Microsoft Windows operating systems implement TCP/IP as a Winsock (Windows Socket) DLL (Dynamic Link Library).

Several parameters can be configured for TCP/IP. Each operating system differs on the method of configuration. The i-Net+ exam is not likely to expect you to be able to configure TCP/IP step-by-step for various operating systems, but you do need to be aware of the following configuration parameters:

➤ *IP address*—On a TCP/IP network, every node must possess a unique IP address.

➤ *Subnet mask*—Unless the network employs subnetting, the default subnet mask for the corresponding class network will suffice.

➤ *Gateway*—The gateway is an address that specifies the default route for forwarding packets that are destined outside of the network. This gateway is also often referred to as the *default gateway* or the *default router*.

➤ *Domain Name System (DNS)*—An address of one or more DNS servers will be required for the client to be able to resolve easier-to-remember host names to IP addresses.

➤ *Windows Internet Name Service (WINS)*—WINS is strictly a Microsoft technology. WINS resolves NetBIOS computer names in a Windows network to IP addresses.

Note: WINS is slowly going away. With the introduction of Windows 2000, Microsoft has abandoned WINS for the Internet-standard DNS naming convention.

DHCP

The Dynamic Host Configuration Protocol (DHCP) is an open standard designed by the IETF (Internet Engineering Task Force) that provides automatic client configuration for TCP/IP parameters.

 RFC 2131 provides detailed information on DHCP.

DHCP is based on the client/server model. A client will initiate a broadcast request with the intent of reaching a DHCP server to receive the needed configuration parameters. On a network such as a local area network, DHCP provides a simple, centralized, and "hands-free" method of configuring client workstations. Home users who connect to the Internet most often are set up for DHCP, and, after connecting to the Internet Service Provider, they will be issued the required parameters. This makes the job of the Internet Service Provider easier by decreasing the number of tech support calls; in addition, the end user has less to worry about as far as inputting a bunch of dotted numbers.

DHCP can be used to dynamically assign an IP address, a subnet mask, a default gateway, a DNS server, and a WINS server. These parameters are dynamically assigned and are not meant to be permanent. The network administrator has the option to configure the specific length of the assignment. IP address assignments are called *leases*, and, just like a car or an apartment lease, they expire and will have to be renewed. A common default lease duration is three days.

Using DHCP is definitely a convenient way to manage remote access connections. Although DHCP may sound like a panacea for curing the IP address nightmares that plague so many administrators, there are times when assigning static IP addresses may be appropriate.

DHCP Vs. Static IP

DHCP provides many benefits. The centralized and automatic configuration of client IP addresses has proven to be the largest benefit. DHCP also provides a means of powerful control via a scope. A *scope* defines the range of IP addresses that can be dynamically assigned; furthermore, an *exclusion scope* can be set to allow some clients to have static IP addresses while other clients still use dynamic assignments.

There are many instances when certain clients must be statically assigned an IP address. In these cases, DHCP can be set to exclude a certain range of IP addresses that will not be dynamically assigned. For example, IP addresses assigned to routers, print servers, DNS servers, and a client operating through a firewall are likely to be included in the exclusion scope.

In addition to specifying exclusion lists for specific clients that will be assigned static addresses, assigning static IP addresses to every client may be the way to go for some networks. An example includes a very small network with few nodes. As a network becomes larger, however, or if there just aren't enough IP addresses to be statically assigned to all systems, then DHCP becomes an obvious choice.

Despite all the benefits of DHCP, it can also create some problems. Because a client is dynamically assigned an IP address on a temporary basis, tracking an address's owner can become difficult. This has the potential to make auditing and security more difficult. Additionally, although DHCP generally results in fewer configuration errors, there is the possibility that a client will be reconfigured with a static IP address, which creates the possibility of an IP address conflict.

Remember that DHCP provides dynamic TCP/IP configuration for the host, and be sure that you understand the advantages of DHCP over static addressing.

Practice Questions

Question 1

What does the abbreviation TCP/IP stand for?

○ a. Transfer Control Protocol/Internet Protocol

○ b. Transfer Control Protocol/Internetwork Protocol

○ c. Transmission Control Protocol/Internet Protocol

○ d. Transmission Control Protocol/Internetwork Protocol

The correct answer is c. TCP/IP is the abbreviation for Transmission Control Protocol/Internet Protocol.

Question 2

How many layers does the TCP/IP reference model have?

○ a. Three

○ b. Four

○ c. Six

○ d. Seven

The correct answer is b. The TCP/IP reference model consists of four layers: the Network Interface layer, the Internet layer, the Transport layer, and the Application layer. Do not confuse the TCP/IP reference model with the OSI reference model, which consists of seven layers.

Question 3

Which of the following pairs of protocols resides at the Transport layer of TCP/IP?

○ a. TCP and UDP

○ b. TCP and HTTP

○ c. UDP and HTTP

○ d. FTP and HTTP

○ e. UDP and FTP

The correct answer is a. Both TCP (Transmission Control Protocol) and UDP (User Datagram Protocol) reside at the Transport layer. HTTP (Hypertext Transfer Protocol) and FTP (File Transfer Protocol) are application protocols that reside at the Application layer; therefore, answers b, c, d, and e are incorrect.

Question 4

Which of the following best describes a connectionless protocol?

O a. Reliable and guaranteed delivery

O b. Reliable with best-effort delivery

O c. Unreliable and does not guarantee delivery

O d. Unreliable with guaranteed delivery

The correct answer is c. A connectionless protocol such as UDP is unreliable and does not provide guaranteed delivery. Such protocols usually depend upon the application to perform the functions that a reliable connection-oriented protocol would perform. Although a connectionless protocol is unreliable and not guaranteed, it is best used when speed and efficiency are most important. A connection-oriented protocol provides reliable and guaranteed delivery; therefore, answer a is incorrect. Answers b and d are also incorrect, as they describe neither a connectionless nor even a connection-oriented protocol.

Question 5

What is the well-known port for NNTP?

O a. 21

O b. 25

O c. 80

O d. 119

The correct answer is d. The Network News Transfer Protocol (NNTP) uses well-known port 119. Port 21 is used by FTP; therefore, answer a is incorrect. Port 25 is used by SMTP; therefore, answer b is incorrect. Port 80 is used by HTTP; therefore, answer c is incorrect.

Question 6

> What is the well-known port for HTTP?
>
> O a. 21
>
> O b. 25
>
> O c. 80
>
> O d. 119

The correct answer is c. The Hypertext Transfer Protocol uses well-known port 80. Port 21 is used by FTP; therefore, answer a is incorrect. Port 25 is used by SMTP; therefore, answer b is incorrect. Port 119 is used by NNTP; therefore, answer d is incorrect.

Question 7

> Which of the following IP addresses is an address that is valid for assignment to a host?
>
> O a. 207.133.76.1
>
> O b. 127.0.0.1
>
> O c. 201.56.42.257
>
> O d. 256.133.76.1
>
> O e. Both a and c
>
> O f. All of the above

The correct answer is a. 207.133.76.1 is a valid Class C address. 127.0.0.1 is the address for the loopback; therefore, answer b is incorrect. 201.56.42.257 exceeds the maximum numerical value possible in the last octet; therefore, answer c is incorrect. 256.133.76.1 is not a proper class address and exceeds the maximum numerical value allowed in the first octet; therefore, answer d is incorrect. Because only answer a is correct, answers e and f are both incorrect. Be sure to carefully examine each octet when answering questions asking for a valid IP address, and remember that 127.0.0.1 is reserved for loopback.

Question 8

> What is the default subnet mask for a network beginning with 164?
>
> ○ a. 255.0.0.0
>
> ○ b. 255.255.0.0
>
> ○ c. 255.255.255.0
>
> ○ d. 127.0.0.1

The correct answer is b. To answer this question correctly, you must know the address ranges of the various classes and the corresponding default subnet masks. 164 falls into the Class B address range of 128 to 191 and has a default subnet mask of 255.255.0.0. 255.0.0.0 is the default subnet mask for a Class A address; therefore, answer a is incorrect. 255.255.255.0 is the default subnet mask for a Class C address; therefore, answer c is incorrect. 127.0.0.1 is the loopback address; therefore, answer d is incorrect.

Question 9

> What address class is used for multicasting?
>
> ○ a. Class A
>
> ○ b. Class B
>
> ○ c. Class C
>
> ○ d. Class D
>
> ○ e. Class E

The correct answer is d. Hosts that are subscribed to a multicast will use a Class D address. Classes A, B, and C are used on most networks. Addressees assigned to hosts from these classes must be globally unique; therefore, answers a, b, and c are incorrect. Class E is reserved for future use; therefore, answer e is incorrect.

Question 10

Which of the following addresses is one of the reserved addresses set aside by the IANA for use on private networks?

○ a. 164.216.54.100

○ b. 127.0.0.1

○ c. 192.168.54.1

○ d. 45.56.168.100

The correct answer is c. 192.168.54.1 falls into the 192.168.0.0-to-192.168.255.255 block range set aside for use by private networks. The other two blocks set aside for private use are 10.0.0.0 to 10.255.255.255 and 172.16.0.0 to 172.31.255.255. 164.216.54.100 is a Class B public address; therefore, answer a is incorrect. 127.0.0.1 is the loopback address; therefore, answer b is incorrect. 45.56.168.100 is a Class A public address; therefore, answer d is incorrect.

Question 11

What is the maximum number of hosts allowed for a class C network?

○ a. 254

○ b. 2,097,152

○ c. 65,534

○ d. 16,777,214

The correct answer is a. Only the last octet is available for assignment to hosts on a Class C network; therefore, 11111111 converted to decimal is 256; and 256 minus 2 equals 254. 2,097,152 is the number of networks available for a Class C network; therefore, answer b is incorrect. 65,534 is the number of hosts available for a Class B network; therefore, answer c is incorrect. 16,777,214 is the number of hosts available for a Class A address; therefore, answer d is incorrect.

Question 12

An address of 206.156.58.12 uses what default subnet mask?

○ a. 255.0.0.0

○ b. 255.255.0.0

○ c. 255.255.255.0

○ d. 255.255.255.255

The correct answer is c. An address of 206.156.58.12 belongs to a Class C network, and the default subnet mask for a Class C network is 255.255.255.0. A Class A network's default subnet mask is 255.0.0.0; therefore, answer a is incorrect. The default subnet mask for a Class B network is 255.255.0.0; therefore, answer b is incorrect. 255.255.255.255 is not a default subnet mask—it is actually a broadcast address; therefore, answer d is incorrect.

Question 13

An address of 5.156.73.2 uses what default subnet mask?

○ a. 255.0.0.0

○ b. 255.255.0.0

○ c. 255.255.255.0

○ d. 255.255.255.255

The correct answer is a. An address of 5.156.73.2 belongs to a Class A network, and the default subnet mask for a Class A network is 255.0.0.0. A Class B network's default subnet mask is 255.255.0.0; therefore, answer b is incorrect. The default subnet mask for a Class C network is 255.255.255.0; therefore, answer c is incorrect. 255.255.255.255 is not a default subnet mask—it is actually a broadcast address; therefore, answer d is incorrect.

Question 14

> Microsoft operating systems implement TCP/IP as a(n):
>
> O a. DLL
> O b. INI
> O c. IRQ
> O d. DMA

The correct answer is a. Microsoft uses a Winsock DLL for TCP/IP. An INI refers to an initilization file used in legacy operating systems; therefore, answer b is incorrect. An IRQ is a hardware interrupt; therefore, answer c is incorrect. DMA involves memory access that bypasses the microprocessor; therefore, answer d is incorrect.

Question 15

> In order for an Internet client to gain access to the Internet, the computer must be configured with which of the following? [Choose the two best answers]
>
> ❑ a. IP address
> ❑ b. Subnet mask
> ❑ c. DNS address
> ❑ d. Windows 98

The correct answers are a and b. An Internet client will require an IP address (answer a) and a subnet mask (answer b), as well as possibly a default gateway address. A client should usually be configured with a DNS address; however, it is not necessary for Internet access. DNS resolves host names to IP addresses. This is typically the method used for clients to access Web sites, but it is not necessary—a client could feasibly access Internet resources by using only the IP address. Answer d is incorrect because the type of operating system does not limit Internet access.

Question 16

Which of the following Class B subnet masks will provide three subnets with at least 2,000 hosts per subnet?

○ a. 255.255.0.0

○ b. 255.255.192.0

○ c. 255.255.240.0

○ d. 255.255.255.0

The correct answer is c. The decimal value 240, in the third octet, equals 11110000 when converted to binary. Each "1" represents a power of 2; thus, 2^4 equals 16, and we must always subtract two, which gives us 14 usable subnets. Left over for the host addresses are 12 bits; thus, 2^{12}-2 equals 4,094 hosts per subnet. Although this gives us more subnets and hosts than required, if we tried to use 255.255.192.0, this would give us only 2 subnets; therefore, answer b is incorrect. 255.255.0.0 allows 1 subnet with 65,534 hosts; therefore, answer a is incorrect. 255.255.255.0 allows 254 subnets with 254 hosts per subnet; therefore, answer d is incorrect.

Question 17

What protocol provides automatic client configuration for IP addresses?

○ a. DHCP

○ b. HTTP

○ c. WINS

○ d. DNS

The correct answer is a. Dynamic Host Configuration Protocol (DHCP) is used to facilitate central control of TCP/IP properties. DHCP is commonly used to dynamically assign IP addresses as well as subnet masks, default gateways, and DNS servers. HTTP is a TCP/IP application protocol used for Web access; therefore, answer b is incorrect. WINS is used in Windows environments to resolve computer names to IP addresses; therefore, answer c is incorrect. DNS is an Internet standard used to resolve computer names to IP addresses; therefore, answer d is incorrect.

Question 18

Which of the following statements best describe DHCP and static IP addresses? [Choose the two best answers]

- ❑ a. DHCP is best used only on small networks where the number of nodes is not expected to exceed 50.
- ❑ b. Although a network uses DHCP, some systems may still require configuration with a static IP address.
- ❑ c. Using static IP addresses provides for centralized and automatic client TCP/IP configuration.
- ❑ d. DHCP can provide a client with an IP address, a subnet mask, a gateway address, and a DNS server.

The correct answers are b and d. DHCP allows for address exclusions, taking into account that some computers may require a static IP address. This exclusion prevents DHCP from issuing an IP address that may conflict with one already statically assigned. DHCP cannot only provide a client with an IP address and a subnet mask, but it can also provide the address for the default gateway, the DNS server, and the WINS server. Although DHCP is suitable for networks of all sizes, a small network may prefer to use static IP addresses; therefore, answer a is incorrect. DHCP provides centralized and automatic TCP/IP configuration; therefore, answer c is incorrect.

Question 19

An Internet Service Provider that wants to provide its customers with automatic TCP/IP configuration should use which of the following?

- ○ a. AOL
- ○ b. Static IP addresses
- ○ c. Instructions for inputting IP and DNS addresses
- ○ d. DHCP

The correct answer is d. Most ISPs use DHCP to automate the TCP/IP configuration for the client. Some ISPs require the customer to input the DNS server address but still use DHCP for IP address assignment. AOL is a popular online service; therefore, answer a is incorrect. Static IP addresses would not be used if automation were needed; therefore, answer b is incorrect. Using DHCP prevents the customer from having to manually wade through the properties of TCP/IP, trying to figure out where to enter the address information; therefore, answer c is incorrect.

Need To Know More?

 Stevens, Richard. *TCP/IP Illustrated, Volume 1: The Protocols.* Addison-Wesley Publishing Co., Reading, MA, 1994. ISBN 0-2016-3346-9. A great book for everything TCP/IP-related.

 Microsoft offers a CD subscription as well as an online version of TechNet (**www.microsoft.com/technet/default.asp**) that covers various TCP/IP technologies. Search TechNet for "TCP/IP."

 www.ietf.org offers complete information on RFCs and provides several methods for searching the database. Search for "TCP/IP," "RFC 1880," "RFC 1541," "RFC 1180," and "RFC 2151."

Remote Connectivity

Terms you'll need to understand:

√ Serial Line Internet Protocol (SLIP)

√ Point-to-Point Protocol (PPP)

√ Link Control Protocol (LCP)

√ Network Control Protocol (NCP)

√ Point-to-Point/Multilink (MP)

√ Point-to-Point Tunneling Protocol (PPTP)

√ Layer 2 Forwarding (L2F)

√ Layer 2 Tunneling Protocol (L2TP)

√ Public Switched Telephone Network (PSTN)

√ Modem

√ Integrated Services Digital Network (ISDN)

√ Basic Rate Interface (BRI) ISDN

√ Primary Rate Interface (PRI) ISDN

√ Digital Subscriber Line (DSL)

Techniques you'll need to master:

√ Understanding the basics of remote connectivity

√ Understanding the purpose of serial line protocols

√ Recognizing the differences between SLIP and PPP

√ Knowing the types of tunneling protocols

√ Explaining the attributes of PSTN, ISDN, cable modem service, and xDSL

√ Using the basic modem commands

Imagine a network where all of the computers are physically connected in a small room. Now imagine a computer thousands of miles away that requires the ability to attach to this small network. In order to provide this remote access, you need some sort of connectivity.

Regardless of whether you are accessing the Internet or the corporate office from your home, the principles are the same. Remote connectivity is required in order to gain access to a network from a distant location. This chapter discusses the equipment needed to establish a remote connection, as well as the protocols and services that enable this equipment to communicate with other systems over the Internet.

Although the term *remote access* is usually used to refer to dialing in to the Internet or a remote network, many networks themselves utilize remote access technology to connect to the Internet. In comparison, computers on a network access the network resources directly via a network interface card (NIC), which connects the computer to the physical networking media. Dial-up remote access for a network is usually implemented only when a low-cost solution is most important; otherwise, dedicated leased lines such as a T1 offer greater speed at a higher cost.

Remote Access Protocols

Serial Line Internet Protocol (SLIP) and Point-to-Point Protocol (PPP) are communication protocols that operate at the Data Link layer of the OSI model, and they are implemented by software that allows a computer to make a connection to an ISP (Internet Service Provider). Both SLIP and PPP are *encapsulation protocols* in that they encapsulate other Network-layer protocols to be put onto the actual communication lines.

> *Note: It seems that after years of use, acronyms related to computers and networking often become misinterpreted. For example, SLIP is often referred to as Serial Line Interface Protocol; however, it is actually the acronym for Serial Line IP (Internet Protocol).*

SLIP and PPP are similar; however, there are many important differences between the two. SLIP was introduced in the early 1980s and quickly became the *de facto* standard. It was originally designed to be simple, but unfortunately this led to many shortcomings. PPP was introduced in the early 1980s and compensated for the shortcomings of SLIP; soon it replaced SLIP and became the emerging standard. One of the most important differences—and one that you must know for the i-Net+ exam—is that SLIP supports only TCP/IP, whereas

PPP supports multiple protocols and can transport IP, AppleTalk, and DECnet traffic. The following sections discuss each of these protocols in depth and elaborate on the differences between the two.

Serial Line Internet Protocol (SLIP)

SLIP was implemented in 1984 as a serial line protocol to encapsulate IP packets. At the time of its development, many standard encapsulation types for TCP/IP were running over various types of networks, such as token ring and Ethernet, but there was really no standard for serial lines. At the time, SLIP provided an easy way to connect to the Internet and other point-to-point serial connections utilizing TCP/IP. SLIP was a simple protocol that appeared to be a viable solution; however, as the Internet grew, so did SLIP's shortcomings. The following list describes some of these shortcomings, which were the reasons that SLIP was soon succeeded by PPP:

➤ SLIP supports only TCP/IP and cannot transport more than one protocol at a time. (Although the term TCP/IP is used, SLIP can actually transport only IP traffic.)

➤ SLIP does not provide error correction, so it relies on TCP/IP and the hardware for this function. This makes SLIP highly susceptible to noisy lines.

➤ SLIP does not support compression. (Compressed SLIP—or CSLIP—does provide compression by compressing header information, but its capabilities are still limited.)

➤ SLIP does not allow hosts to communicate addressing information; therefore, SLIP is difficult to use where dynamic IP addresses are being utilized.

➤ SLIP does not support synchronous links.

 SLIP was one of the first protocols designed to carry TCP/IP traffic. SLIP cannot differentiate between different protocols, so it supports only TCP/IP.

The one advantage that SLIP does have over PPP is that it's quicker. Keep in mind, however, that it's faster by only a minor margin, so speed is not a reason to choose SLIP over PPP. SLIP is rarely used anymore, except in a few special circumstances. PPP is now accepted as the current standard and is being actively developed.

Point-To-Point Protocol (PPP)

PPP was implemented in 1990 and was designed to address the limitations of SLIP. PPP provides multi-protocol support for transporting data over point-to-point links; it also provides error correction, compression, and support for both asynchronous and synchronous connections. Again, although SLIP may be technically faster than PPP, PPP's use of error correction and compression provide added reliability and increased efficiency, thus negating the fact that SLIP is marginally faster. The primary improvements of PPP are a result of the three main components of PPP as described in RFC 1771. These components are:

➤ A method for encapsulating multiprotocol datagrams

➤ A Link Control Protocol (LCP) for establishing, configuring, and testing the data-link connections

➤ A family of Network Control Protocols (NCPs) for establishing and configuring different Network-layer protocols

Unlike SLIP, with PPP you can choose from multiple protocols, as shown in Figure 4.1, if a dial-up server supports them. These options will be negotiated during the second phase of the PPP connection. Additionally, it is primarily these added components of PPP that allow it to overcome many of the limitations of SLIP.

PPP is based upon both LCP and NCP. LCP sets up the links between two nodes, and NCP negotiates the Network-layer protocol configuration related to the transmission between the nodes.

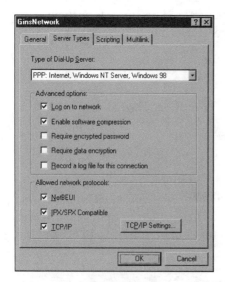

Figure 4.1   PPP provides many features, including the ability to use multiple protocols.

Utilizing LCP and NCP, PPP operates in the following stages:

1. Each end of a PPP link sends LCP packets to configure and test the data link before establishing communications.

2. Next, the originating PPP link sends NCP frames to configure one or more Network-layer protocols.

3. After the Network-layer protocols have been configured, packets from each of the protocols are sent over the link.

4. LCP or NCP packets close the link. Another event, such as a loss of carrier or an inactivity timer, can also close the link.

 In addition to being able to support any protocol by itself, PPP can support multiple network protocols simultaneously.

Point-To-Point/Multilink (MP)

Because PPP can handle only one link at a time, Point-to-Point Multilink Protocol (MP) was developed to allow multiple Network-layer protocols to be combined into one logical connection called a *bundle*. Unique to MP is the ability to allow physical links to be dynamically added or removed from the logical bundle as needed; this feature is called *rubber bandwidth*.

> *Note: The Multilink Protocol is referred to by many different forms, including "Point-to-Point/Multilink," "Multilink Point-to-Point," "Multilink PPP," "PPP Multilink," "Multilink," and just "MP."*

Originally MP was developed to take advantage of the multiple channels in ISDN, thus providing even more bandwidth. Today, however, MP is also used over various services where multiple PPP links connect two nodes. Using LCP, MP can indicate to a peer its ability to combine multiple physical links into a bundle. These bundled links do not need to be of the same type. For example, various physical links—such as dial-up synchronous links, asynchronous links, and the multiple channels provided by ISDN—can all be combined.

 Point-to-Point/Multilink (MP) is similar to PPP, but MP provides the ability for Network-layer protocols to be multi-plexed over a PPP link. The combined connections form a virtual bundle and provide greater bandwidth than a single physical connection provides.

Tunneling Protocols

Three tunneling protocols support dial-up access and help establish Virtual Private Network (VPN) tunnels. A VPN consists of two or more nodes that communicate via a public network, such as the Internet, yet use encryption technology to create a *virtual* network that acts as if the nodes were connected via private lines. VPNs are discussed further in Chapter 13, but for now, let's focus on the three tunneling protocols. These three tunneling protocols, which are actually extensions of PPP, are:

➤ Point-to-Point Tunneling Protocol (PPTP)

➤ Layer 2 Forwarding (L2F)

➤ Layer 2 Tunneling Protocol (L2TP)

 There is also a fourth tunneling protocol called IP Security (IPSec), but this protocol is a Layer 3 protocol, which supports only IP. The IPSec protocol does not provide PPP user authentication; thus, it is primarily used between routers and firewalls.

These three tunneling protocols operate at the Data Link layer (Layer 2 of the OSI model) and create a virtual tunnel to connect a dial-up user to a private network via an ISP. Although this tunnel goes through an ISP for the connection, the tunnel creates a virtual link from the dial-up user to the remote network as though it were direct. In contrast, a PPP session without a tunnel connects a dial-up user directly to a private modem pool or to an ISP.

 PPTP, L2F, and L2TP are tunneling protocols that are extensions of PPP used for creating VPNs. Although IPSec is a tunneling protocol, it is not an extension of PPP.

Point-To-Point Tunneling Protocol (PPTP)

The Point-to-Point Tunneling Protocol (PPTP) is a proprietary tunneling protocol developed by Microsoft and other networking vendors to support secure connections to a VPN utilizing TCP. PPTP encapsulates secure packets inside an IP packet. PPTP is designed only for IP networks, but it does support encapsulation for other protocols besides IP, such as NetBEUI (NetBIOS Enhanced User Interface) and IPX (Internetwork Packet Exchange).

Layer 2 Forwarding

Layer 2 Forwarding (L2F) is another proprietary tunneling protocol, which was developed by Cisco Systems. Although it is similar to PPTP in function, it does have several distinct differences. For example, L2F provides protocol independence in that it can run over various types of networks; in addition, it uses UDP (User Datagram Protocol) instead of TCP for Internet tunneling.

Layer 2 Tunneling Protocol

Layer 2 Tunneling Protocol (L2TP) combines the best of PPTP and L2F. L2TP is currently supported by many vendors, continues to gain support, and can be expected to become the predominant tunneling protocol. Rather than rely on the encryption provided by PPP, L2TP uses IP Security (IPSec) for encryption; however, it will resort to PPP for encryption should the remote node not support IPSec.

Public Switched Telephone Network (PSTN)

The Public Switched Telephone Network is a circuit-switched network that has been around a long time. In fact, PSTN is basically the same system many of us have been using our entire lives to make telephone calls. Homes and businesses are connected to a telephone company's central office by twisted-pair copper wires. By itself, PSTN has been providing remote connectivity for computers with a modem.

> *Note: The Public Switched Telephone Network—also commonly referred to as Plain Old Telephone Service (POTS)—usually does not provide the bandwidth needed for today's remote acccess applications. POTS is being replaced by PANS (Pretty Amazing New Stuff—or Services).*

The modem (modulator/demodulator) modulates the digital data received from the computer to an analog signal to be sent across the PSTN, and the process is reversed at the receiving node. Most modems in use today support transfer rates of 28.8Kbps to 56.6Kbps. To achieve faster data transfer, you may want to consider one of the newer technologies discussed later in this chapter.

Modem Setup And Commands

Most modern modems are easily detected and configured by plug-and-play operating systems, such as Windows 98, and require little or no configuring.

Although modems are available in various speeds, most modems are either one of two types: internal or external. An external modem uses an external serial port, so the modem does not need to tie up another scarce interrupt request (IRQ) in the system.

After the modem has been properly installed and configured, various commands known as *AT commands* are used to control the modem. AT commands are usually issued and controlled by the communications software, but they can also be manually manipulated. For example, a modem's AT commands can be manipulated from the Advanced Properties dialog box in a Windows operating system. Before issuing any AT commands, you should first always check with the provided documentation because each chip set varies from others. For the most part, however, you will find that many of the basic commands are standard.

The prefix AT, also known as the Attention Code, must start each command line. For example, the command to dial the telephone number 555-1212 is ATDT5551212. Using *AT*, this string first alerts the modem that it is going to be sent a command. Next, *D* tells the modem to dial the numbers that follow, and the *T* (a subcommand of *D*) tells the modem to dial in touch-tone mode. Finally, the telephone number *5551212* is dialed. Table 4.1 lists many of the common commands.

Be sure you can recognize the various commands listed in Table 4.1.

Table 4.1 Common modem AT commands.	
AT Command	**Description**
AT	Alerts the modem to expect commands. AT must precede each command line. By itself, this command should result in a modem response of "OK," indicating that the modem is properly configured.
D	Instructs the modem to dial the numbers that follow.
T	As a subcommand of *D*, it instructs the modem to dial in touch-tone mode.
P	As a subcommand of *D*, it instructs the modem to dial in pulse-mode.
H	Instructs the modem to hang up.

(continued)

Table 4.1 Common modem AT commands (continued).	
AT Command	**Description**
Z	Instructs the modem to reset and load the default configuration.
M0	Instructs the modem to leave the speaker off.
M1	Instructs the modem to leave the speaker on only during a connection.
M2	Instructs the modem to leave the speaker on.
*70	Turns off the call-waiting feature.
, (comma)	Issues a pause.

Integrated Services Digital Network (ISDN)

Integrated Services Digital Network (ISDN) is a switched digital communications network originally designed to replace the current telephone network. More accurately considered an upgrade to PSTN, ISDN uses the existing copper wires to provide digital connectivity and services. Thus, ISDN provides a quick connection from a computer to the network. In contrast, an analog modem used over PSTN is required to first convert the computer's digital signals to analog signals and then reverse the process on the other end of the connection.

Advantages of ISDN include the following:

➤ Data speeds up to four times faster than PSTN

➤ Cost effectiveness when used for dial-up non-dedicated service

➤ Availability from many ISPs on a per-usage basis

➤ Near-perfect line quality because it is a digital service

➤ Simultaneous voice and data transfer over ISDN's multiple channels

ISDN has multiple channels and uses multiplexing technology in order to combine these channels. For example, Multilink PPP, discussed previously, and a method called *Bonding* (Bandwidth On Demand Interoperability Group) allow multiple channels to be combined and released as necessary. The standard channel types for ISDN include the following:

➤ *A*—4kHz analog

➤ *B*—64Kbps digital

➤ *C*—16Kbps digital

➤ *D*—16Kbps or 64Kbps digital for out-of-band signaling

➤ *E*—64Kbps digital for internal ISDN signaling

➤ *H*—384, 1536, or 1920Kbps digital

Several channel combinations have been defined; two of these include the Basic Rate Interface (BRI) ISDN and Primary Rate Interface (PRI) ISDN.

Basic Rate Interface (BRI) ISDN

BRI is most commonly installed for home users connecting to the Internet or a remote access server, and it consists of two 64Kbps B channels and one 16Kbps D channel. You can combine both B channels to get higher speeds, up to 128Kbps, or you can use one channel at 64Kbps, which leaves the other channel available for other uses, such as voice transfer. If both B channels are being used for Internet access and the phone is picked up, some ISDN configurations can automatically adjust and drop one B channel from the Internet connection for use with the telephone.

 BRI is 2B + 1D (two 64Kbps B channels and one 16Kbps D channel). The two B channels can be combined to achieve data speeds of 128Kbps.

Note: The D channel is used for out-of-band signaling. For example, it may be used to indicate that the line is busy. A newer use for the D channel—called Always On/Dynamic ISDN (AO/DI)—provides a constant 9.6Kbps Internet connection. Like a modem and POTS, ISDN is not meant to be connected all day; however, AO/DI provides this functionality and is great for receiving computer calls, receiving streaming stock quotes, and being notified immediatley of incoming email.

BRI ISDN has actually been around for many years but has only recently been seen as a viable solution for providing Internet access for home users. In fact, Windows 98 even includes support for ISDN adapters via the ISDN Configuration Wizard to assist in a trouble-free setup.

Primary Rate Interface (PRI) ISDN

PRI is usually found in organizations that require more bandwidth to access remote networks. PRI supports 23 64Kbps B channels and 1 64Kbps D channel. PRI can provide a total bandwidth equivalent to a T1 line or 1.544Mbps.

PRI is 23B + 1D, or 23 64Kbps B channels and 1 64Kbps D channel. PRI can use all channels to achieve data speeds of 1.544Mbps—the equivalent of a T1 line. In Europe and Australia, ISDN provides 30 B channels rather than the 23 B channels available in the USA, Canada, and Japan.

Digital Subscriber Line

Chapter 2 discusses Digital Subscriber Lines (DSL) and introduces you to the large family of DSL technologies. This family is collectively known as *xDSL*. DSL is a relatively new digital technology that uses the existing copper telephone lines for high-speed access. Besides providing Internet access, DSL is commonly used for various broadband services because of its high bandwidth rates.

DSL has been divided into two main categories:

➤ *Asymmetric Digital Subscriber Line (ADSL)*—Asymmetric means that more data flows in one direction than in the other.

➤ *Symmetric Digital Subscriber Line (SDSL)*—Symmetric means that data flows equally in both directions, as is the case with ISDN.

The i-Net+ exam is not likely to test you on the many types of DSL lines, but you should be familiar with those available, which are listed in Chapter 2. You must know that ADSL and SDSL are the two main categories of xDSL.

Of the various types of DSL, currently Asymmetric DSL (ADSL) is the most common for providing remote access. It is gaining momentum as the preferred method for home dial-up users.

Asymmetric Digital Subscriber Line (ADSL)

ADSL is like ISDN in that it provides a completely digital solution over upgraded telephone lines and supports simultaneous data and voice transfer. Taking advantage of the fact that most users do more downloading than uploading, ADSL provides an asymmetric data transfer rate that is greater downstream than upstream. Unfortunately, however, ADSL greatly depends upon the distance from the telephone company's central office (CO). Upstream rates can go as high as 1Mbps, whereas downstream rates typically range from 1Mbps to over 8Mbps. Table 4.2 describes some of the major differences between ADSL and ISDN.

> *Note: ADSL modems come in pairs. One is located at the central office, and the other is located in the customer's residence. These modems are also referred to as ADSL transmission units (ATUs).*

Table 4.2   Differences between ADSL and ISDN.

ADSL	ISDN
Provides a permanent packet-switched connection.	Provides a circuit-switched service.
Provides for one voice transmission and one data transmission simultaneously.	Provides multiple voice and data transmissions simultaneously.
Provides asymmetric but consistently faster data transfers.	Provides symmetric but consistently slower data transfers.
Is meant to be always on.	Is not meant to be always on.

Symmetric Digital Subscriber Line (SDSL)

Like ADSL, a Symmetric Digital Subscriber Line (SDSL) provides high-speed access. SDSL, however, uses only one pair of copper wires rather than two pairs and provides symmetrical data transfer: 768Kbps upstream and 768Kbps downstream.

Cable Modem Service

Yes, the same people who deliver dozens of channels to your television set now bring the Internet to your computer. If you think about the coaxial cable provided for your television set, you can probably imagine what's unique about cable modem service. First, cable modem service does not affect the phone lines in any way. Also, there is no need to dial-up the cable provider to gain access—just like cable television programming, cable modem service is always on, providing constant connectivity. Because cable was designed to deliver cable television programming, there was no initial need to be concerned with data going upstream. As a result, many cable companies are forced to upgrade their networks to *hybrid fiber-coax (HFC)*, which assists in handling the data going upstream.

Thus, cable modem service is asymmetric. Depending upon whether the provider has optimized its network to support two-way traffic, and depending upon the number of neighbors you have, data transfer rates can vary greatly. Although cable modem service can provide extremely high transfer rates (faster than an ordinary computer can handle), everyone connected to the same cable must share this bandwidth.

Note: Most cable modems are usually external devices that connect the customer's computer via a 10BaseT Ethernet network adapter card.

Practice Questions

Question 1

Which of the following protocols lacks error correction and can encapsulate only TCP/IP?

○ a. PPP

○ b. SLIP

○ c. POTS

○ d. PPTP

The correct answer is b. SLIP is a line protocol that supports only TCP/IP. SLIP is an older protocol, which has been replaced by PPP and which lacks many features that PPP supports, such as error correction and multi-protocol support. Therefore a is incorrect. Answer c is incorrect because POTS is the circuit-switched telephone system used for most dial-up connections. Answer d is incorrect because PPTP is a tunneling protocol that is an extension of PPP.

Question 2

Which of the following are Layer 2 tunneling protocols? [Choose the three best answers]

❏ a. L2F

❏ b. L2TP

❏ c. PPTP

❏ d. IPSec

❏ e. PPP

❏ f. SLIP

The correct answers are a, b, and c. L2F, L2TP, and PPTP are all Layer 2 tunneling protocols used to create a VPN. IPSec is not a Layer 2 tunneling protocol. It is a set of protocols that operates at Layer 3 of the OSI model and supports the secure exchange of packets; therefore, answer d is incorrect. Both PPP and SLIP are data-link line protocols and not tunneling protocols; therefore, answers e and f are incorrect.

Question 3

> What technology does PPP use to establish, configure, and test the data-link connection?
>
> ○ a. LLC
>
> ○ b. PPTP
>
> ○ c. LCP
>
> ○ d. PLTP

The correct answer is c. PPP is based upon the Link Control Protocol, which is responsible for setting up a computer-to-computer link. One of the first steps performed by LCP is configuring and testing the link. Answer a is incorrect because LLC, Logical Link Control, is a sublayer of the Data Link layer of the OSI model. Although the LLC sublayer is responsible for managing communication links, it is not the best answer to this question. Answer b is incorrect because PPTP is an extension of PPP used as a tunneling protocol for supporting VPNs. Answer d is incorrect because PLTP does not exist.

Question 4

> Which of the following is the command string used to dial the telephone number 555-1212?
>
> ○ a. *ATDL5551212
>
> ○ b. ATT5551212
>
> ○ c. ATDT5551212
>
> ○ d. *AT5551212

The correct answer is c. AT prepares the modem to receive commands, and DT dials using touch-tone. Finally, 5551212 is the phone number to be dialed. A command string is always preceded by the AT command. Review Table 4.1 for a listing of common AT commands. Because answer c is correct, answers a, b, and d are incorrect.

Question 5

Which of the following commands will cause the modem's speaker to be on during the connection phase? [Choose the two best answers]

- ❑ a. M0
- ❑ b. M1
- ❑ c. M2
- ❑ d. M01
- ❑ e. M02

The correct answers are b and c. Both M1 and M2 are on during the connection phase. M2, however, is on only during the connection process, while M1 is on all the time, which includes during the connection. M0 instructs the modem to leave the speaker off; therefore, answer a is incorrect. Answers d and e are incorrect because these do not exist.

Question 6

Which of the following does BRI ISDN provide?

- ○ a. 23 B channels and 1 D channel
- ○ b. 2 B channels and 23 D channels
- ○ c. 23 D channels and 1 B channel
- ○ d. 2 B channels and 1 D channel

The correct answer is d. BRI ISDN is the most common ISDN type for accessing remote networks. BRI ISDN supports two B channels at 64Kbps each and one D channel that carries control and signal information at 16Kbps. PRI ISDN has twenty-three B channels and one D channel, which all operate at 64Kbps; therefore, answer a is incorrect. Answers b and c are also incorrect.

Question 7

> What is the combined transfer rate of the two B channels in Basic Rate Interface ISDN?
>
> ○ a. 144Kbps
>
> ○ b. 128Kbps
>
> ○ c. 144Mbps
>
> ○ d. 64Kbps
>
> ○ e. 128Mbps
>
> ○ f. 64Kbps

The correct answer is b. BRI ISDN consists of two B channels and one D channel. The two B channels provide 64Kbps for a combined total of 128Kbps; therefore, answers a, c, d, e, and f are incorrect.

Question 8

> What are the two main categories of DSL?
>
> ○ a. ADSL and BDSL
>
> ○ b. HDSL and VDSL
>
> ○ c. ADSL and VDSL
>
> ○ d. ADSL and SDSL

The correct answer is d. There are several types of DSL technologies within the xDSL family. The two main categories are Asymmetric DSL (ADSL) and Symmetric DSL (SDSL). BDSL is not a valid type within the xDSL family; therefore, answer a is incorrect. High-bit-rate Digital Subscriber Line (HDSL) and Very-high-bit-rate Digital Subscriber Line (VDSL) are part of the xDSL communication technologies but are not the main categories; therefore, answers b and c are incorrect.

Question 9

Which of the following does DSL operate over?

○ a. Satellite communications

○ b. Telephone lines

○ c. Fiber optic cable

○ d. Coaxial cable

The correct answer is b. DSL operates over upgraded telephone lines and provides high-speed access. Although satellites are being used for remote communications, DSL does not operate over these links; therefore, answer a is incorrect. Fiber-optic cable transmits signals optically, instead of electrically as with coaxial and twisted-pair cable. Because DSL operates over twisted-pair telephone lines, answer c is incorrect. Coaxial cable is commonly used for cable modem service and does not support DSL; therefore, answer d is incorrect.

Question 10

Which one of the following is used to route IP over ISDN and multiplexes several physical connections across one logical connection?

○ a. Binding

○ b. Multithreaded PPP

○ c. BinHex

○ d. Multilink PPP

The correct answer is d. Multilink PPP was originally developed to combine the multiple channels of ISDN but is now used in many different areas as well. Answer a is incorrect because binding describes protocols associated with each other and a network adapter. Answer b is incorrect because multithreading refers to running multiple processes within a single program and is not related to PPP. Answer c is incorrect because BinHex is short for binary-to-hexadecimal and represents a type of conversion scheme.

Need To Know More?

 Ibe, Oliver C. *Remote Access Networks and Services.* John Wiley & Sons Inc., New York, NY, 1999. ISBN 0-471-34820-1. A complete book describing the technologies, services, and protocols related to remote access.

 Stevens, Richard. *TCP/IP Illustrated, Volume 1: The Protocols.* Addison-Wesley Publishing Co., Reading, MA, 1994. ISBN 0-2016-3346-9. A great book for everything TCP/IP related.

 Microsoft offers a CD subscription as well as an online version of TechNet (**www.microsoft.com/technet/default.asp**) that covers various TCP/IP technologies. Search TechNet for "PPP," "PPTP," "IPSec," and "Remote Access."

 www.3com.com provides both introductory and in-depth white papers discussing many of the technologies covered in this chapter.

 www.computingcentral.com/topics/bandwidth/ provides a great forum that discusses various bandwidth technologies. There is even a link that will test and report your current connection speed.

 www.ietf.org offers complete information on RFCs and provides several methods for searching the database. Search for "PPP," "SLIP," "RFC 1661," "RFC 1990," and "RFC 1055."

 www.microsoft.com/isn/ is Microsoft's Internet Services Network, which provides great information designed for ISPs, telecommunications companies, cable companies, and enhanced service providers offering Internet access, Web hosting, or network services.

Name Resolution

Terms you'll need to understand:

√ HOSTS file

√ Domain Name Service (DNS)

√ Fully Qualified Domain Name (FQDN)

√ LMHOSTS file

√ Windows Internet Name Service (WINS)

√ Address Resolution Protocol (ARP)

Techniques you'll need to master:

√ Understanding the fundamentals of name resolution

√ Determining which name resolution method is best for a given scenario

In this chapter, you'll learn the basics of name resolution, including why it is such an important component of any network—not just the Internet—using TCP/IP. You'll also be introduced to the methods of name resolution and the concepts in play behind each method.

Why Name Resolution

Without meaning to generate an argument from any members of Mensa, it is probably safe to say that it is difficult for most people to remember a large number of 32-bit binary numbers. This is unfortunate, for it is by utilizing unique 32-bit binary numbers that all hosts on the Internet can differentiate themselves one from another.

As a merchant doing business on the Internet, when I set up a machine to host a Web site, I assign the IP address 11010001001000111011101011011010. To make this number a bit easier to write, memorize, work with, and relay to others, it is converted into four octets equaling 209.35.188.218. Both of these values are identical, but the latter is a bit easier to work with—a bit, but not a great bit.

If the name of my company is D S Technical Solutions, hoping that you will memorize 209.35.186.218 and equate it with the company is a stretch. You may be able to memorize one IP address in this fashion—you may even be able to memorize ten—but memorizing dozens would be beyond the ability of most people. To simplify the IP address even further, a hostname of plain text is used for the site. Instead of telling you to go to 209.35.186.218, I'll simply say **www.ds-technical.com**. Because the hostname closely resembles the company name, the odds are much better that you will be able to memorize this entity.

Likewise, suppose that you want to find information about the home where the President of the United States lives, but you have no idea of the site's address. The odds are much better that you will be able to think up **www.whitehouse.gov** and stumble upon the correct hostname faster than you will be able to randomly enter octet values and come across 198.137.241.30.

There are a number of ways of resolving hostnames like "Mickey," "Server9," "whitehouse.gov," etc., to IP addresses. The one issue you must keep in mind is that in all cases, the resolution is to IP addresses because they are the unique values that identify the site/host. Regardless of the resolution method implemented, all resolution is done by applications and occurs at the seventh layer (Application) of the OSI model.

In this chapter, the methods of resolution—simple and advanced—will be examined.

Working With HOSTS Files

Many years ago (when TCP/IP was new), networks were small, consisting of only a handful of hosts at each site. There may have been dozens of users accessing the network, but they were doing so as dumb terminals connected to a host. The majority of the user's work would be done on one host, with an occasional need to interact with another host by sending email to another user, opening a file, and so on.

In those days—and in that environment if it still exists today—the usage of HOSTS files is ideal for name resolution. HOSTS files are static, ASCII text files that must reside on each host and that hold the information needed to resolve names in the form of columns. An example of a HOSTS file from a host would be:

```
#This is an example to show how the HOSTS file works
#the name of this host is Muncie, and need not be listed here
192.168.14.10 Yorktown
192.168.14.11 Daleville Chesterfield
192.168.14.12 Anderson
192.168.14.13 Lapel #Pendleton
192.168.14.14 Noblesville Westfield Carmel
192.168.14.15 Rosston
192.168.14.16 Lebanon
```

Being ASCII text files, HOSTS files can be created and edited with any text editor, including the simplest ones offered by each operating system. The pound sign (#) is used as a comment character and causes the line to be ignored from the location of the character to the remainder of the line. In the example just given, the first two lines are all comment and are ignored for purposes of resolution; in the sixth line, the name Pendleton is also ignored.

 Whether the entries in the HOSTS file are case-sensitive or not depends upon the operating system in use. On Unix systems, the entries are case-sensitive, but on Windows NT 4 and Windows 2000 systems, the entries are not case-sensitive.

Each line of the file can contain up to 255 characters, and the file can contain an unlimited number of lines. The first column of each line is the IP address of the host. White space must follow that to separate the columns; this white space can be either a space character or a tab. Whichever delimiter is used must be used to separate subsequent columns as well. The second column and all subsequent columns are text names (hostnames) associated with that IP address.

On the host in our example, users could specify that they want to Telnet to 192.168.14.10 by using that IP address or by specifying "Yorktown." The HOSTS file would be used to translate the text name "Yorktown" into 192.168.14.10, and the connection results would be the same: this is the only hostname associated with this host. The host 192.168.14.14 can be referred to by three names—"Noblesville," "Westfield," and "Carmel."

Because the HOSTS file must reside on every host, the file on each host should be slightly different. In the above example, the file is from the host Muncie and need not contain a reference to itself (though the existence of such would do no real harm). On host Anderson, it need not have a reference to itself, but must have a reference to Muncie, as the following shows:

```
#This is an example to show how the HOSTS file works
#the name of this host is Anderson, and need not be listed here
192.168.14.9 Muncie
192.168.14.10 Yorktown
192.168.14.11 Daleville Chesterfield
192.168.14.13 Lapel #Pendleton
192.168.14.14 Noblesville Westfield Carmel
192.168.14.15 Rosston
192.168.14.16 Lebanon
```

Every time a new host is added to the network, you must update the HOSTS file on each host, or the hosts will not be able to access the new system. This restriction severely limits the usage of this method of name resolution to small networks that do not change often. On the positive side, this implementation is accepted by every operating system capable of running TCP/IP.

Also worthy of note: The file is always read sequentially from the top to the bottom or until a resolution is found. To speed up resolution, do the following:

1. Move comment lines to the bottom of the file to prevent their being in the way each time the file is read.

2. Place the most commonly accessed hosts at the top of the file so their matches are found quickly.

It is also extremely important that duplicate hostnames *not* appear within the file. Consider the following file:

```
#This is an example to show how the HOSTS file works
#the name of this host is Muncie, and need not be listed here
192.168.14.10 Yorktown
192.168.14.11 Daleville Chesterfield
192.168.14.12 Anderson
```

```
192.168.14.13 Lapel #Pendleton
192.168.14.14 Noblesville Westfield Carmel
192.168.14.15 Rosston
192.168.14.16 Lebanon
192.168.14.17 Carmel
```

Because the file is read sequentially from top to bottom, all attempts to access the host named "Carmel" will always take the user to 192.168.14.14 and never to 192.168.14.17. If the order of the lines is reversed on another host, then a user will always get to the latter host there and not the former. This can cause havoc in a great many ways, so care must always be taken to avoid duplicate name entries.

DNS: A Superset Of HOSTS

In the early days of the Internet, a single HOSTS file was routinely updated and downloaded to all hosts for name resolution. The major problem with the HOSTS file method of resolution, though, is that it must exist on every host, so changes must be made in every copy to take effect.

DNS, Domain Name Service or Server, solves this problem for large networks. Instead of having each host use an ASCII file locally, the hosts access a server to do the name resolution for them. First introduced in 1984, this method allows the hostnames to reside in a database that can be distributed among multiple servers. The distribution decreases the load on any one server and allows for more than one point of administration. It also allows the database size to be virtually unlimited because more servers can be added to handle additional parts of the database.

> Note: In Windows 2000, Microsoft made a revolutionary departure from the security database used in previous versions of Windows NT. The new database is called Active Directory, and it is dependent upon DNS to exist, working in conjunction with it to resolve addresses. Whereas DNS was always an option in Windows NT, its implementation is a requirement in Windows 2000.

Configuring a client to use DNS is simply a matter of supplying it with the IP address of the server offering this service, as shown in Figure 5.1. The example shown here is on a Windows 2000 Professional client.

 On operating systems that lack a graphical environment, such as Unix, the DNS server can be specified in the ASCII file resolv.conf, found in the /etc directory.

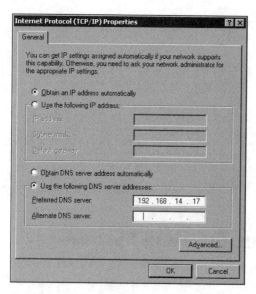

Figure 5.1   Configuring a client to use a DNS server for name resolution requires only the IP address of the server providing the service.

DNS Structure

The name system is based on hierarchical names in a tree-type directory structure that closely resembles a directory structure like you would see with files and folders. To use an analogy, you can have a file called warranty.doc in c:\ and have another file called warranty.doc in c:\docs\refrigerator. With a non-tree structure, you could have only one file by that name, whereas the tree structure allows you to have multiples and to interpret each one as existing on its own. In a network using DNS, you can have more than one server with the same name, as long as each server is located in a different path.

> *Note: For contrast with DNS, consider a flat database like the one that NetBIOS uses for hostnames. With a flat database, all names exist at the same level (no tree), so there can't be any duplicate names. The names must now be unique regardless of the size of your system. Another example of a flat database is the set of Social Security numbers, a national system that encompasses all workers in the United States: Every participant in the Social Security program must have a unique number.*

Resolution is done through the use of a combination of domains and hostnames into Fully Qualified Domain Names (FQDNs). The domain can be one of several possibilities, the most common of which are:

➤ *com*—commercial enterprise

➤ *edu*—educational institution

➤ *gov*—government

➤ *mil*—military

➤ *net*—network provider

➤ *org*—organization/original/not-for-profit

All of these domains represent entities within the United States. If the entity resides outside the United States, then the domain becomes an abbreviation (typically two letters) for the host country. Some of those most used include:

➤ *au*—Australia

➤ *de*—Germany (Deutschland)

➤ *es*—Spain (España)

➤ *fr*—France

➤ *il*—Israel

➤ *pr*—Puerto Rico

➤ *uk*—United Kingdom

The hostname can be just the name of the host to contact or can include subdomains as well. For example, **www.ds-technical.com** is considered a Fully Qualified Domain Name for it includes the domain (**com**), and the hostname (**ds-technical**).

Note: The www portion merely indicates what service to utilize.

An FQDN of **kristin.ds-technical.com** contains additional information. Although the domain stays the same (**com**), it must now find the network **ds-technical** and then find the host **kristin** beneath that.

 Always read an FQDN from right to left when breaking it into components.

DNS Zones

With the enormous number of hosts and sites on the Internet, it is not possible for a single server to hold all the address resolutions needed, regardless of the capabilities of the database. Instead of a single server, DNS resolution for the Internet is performed by a number of servers, each responsible for a zone.

By using multiple servers and multiple zones, the load and the administrative burden of managing the database are dispersed. Administrators manage only the DNS database records stored in their zones, which can be any portion of the domain name space. Each zone has a primary server, responsible for all updates, and one or more secondary servers. Any changes made to the zone file must be made on the primary server because the zone file on the secondary server(s) is a read-only copy. Zones are copied from the primary to the secondary name servers through replication (also known as *zone transfer*).

 Another benefit of multiple zones is that smaller amounts of information are replicated than would be necessary if the domain records were located in only one zone file.

In addition to primary and secondary servers, there are also servers known as *caching-only servers*. A caching-only DNS server doesn't have a zone file; its only function is to make DNS queries, return the results, and cache the results. Primary and secondary servers always have a file locally, but when a caching-only server first starts, it has no stored DNS information. It builds this information over time when it caches results of queries made after the server starts.

> *Note: Because entire zone files don't need to be transferred, a caching-only server is best used where there is a slow WAN link. When a query is made, only one record is sent and not the full zone file. All future queries for the same information are resolved locally from the cache, eliminating the need to go across the WAN link.*

DNS Records

Each record within the DNS zone file consists of a number of entries. The entries are also known as resource records. They can vary slightly, but the following sections examine the most common record types.

SOA Records

Every database file starts with an SOA (Start Of Authority) record. This record identifies the zone and contains a number of other parameters, including:

➤ *Source host*—the name of the primary server (with the read/write copy of the file)

➤ *Contact email*—the email address for the administrator of the file

➤ *Serial number*—the incrementing version number of the database

➤ *Refresh time*—the delay in seconds that secondary servers wait before checking for changes in the database file

➤ *Retry time*—the time in seconds that a secondary server waits before another attempt if replication fails

➤ *Expiration time*—the number of seconds on secondary servers before the old zone information is deleted

➤ *Time To Live (TTL)*—the number of seconds that a caching-only server can cache resource records from this database file before discarding them and performing another query

NS Records
The Name Server (NS) record specifies the other name servers for the domain or maps a domain name to that of the primary server for the zone.

A Records
The Address record holds the IP address of the name.

CNAME Records
The Canonical Name (CNAME) record is an alias field allowing you to specify more than one name for each TCP/IP address. For example, the CNAME record for **ftp.ds-technical.com** would indicate that it is an alias for **kristin.ds-technical.com**.

 Using CNAME records, you can combine an FTP server and a Web server on the same host.

MX Records
The Mail Exchanger (MX) record specifies the name of the host that processes mail for this domain.

HINFO Records
The Host (HINFO) record is the record that actually specifies the TCP/IP address for a certain host. All hosts that have static TCP/IP addresses should have an entry in this record.

PTR Records

Pointer (PTR) records are used for reverse lookup entries. They specify the IP address in reverse order—that is, the octets of the IP address are reversed—and the corresponding hostname.

Utilities To Use With DNS

Any application—Telnet, PING, etc.—can resolve addresses for hostnames simply by querying the address of the DNS server specified on the client. If the DNS server specified does not have a resolution for the address, then it will query another DNS server based upon the specified domain given in the FQDN. Applications that are capable of this silent resolution are known as *resolvers*.

The **hostname** command returns the name of the current host. The **nslookup** command is used to query DNS and find IP resolution. When first issued, the **nslookup** command begins an interactive session and shows the DNS server's name and IP address. Commands that can be given are shown below.

```
NAME               - print info about the host/domain NAME
  using default server
NAME1 NAME2        - as above, but use NAME2 as server
help or ?          - print info on common commands
set OPTION         - set an option
  all                    - print options, current server, and host
  [no]debug              - print debugging information
  [no]d2                 - print exhaustive debugging information
  [no]defname            - append domain name to each query
  [no]recurse            - ask for recursive answer to query
  [no]search             - use domain search list
  [no]vc                 - always use a virtual circuit
  domain=NAME            - set default domain name to NAME
  srchlist=N1[/N2/.../N6] - set domain to N1 and set
search list to N1,N2, etc.
  root=NAME              - set root server to NAME
  retry=X                - set number of retries to X
  timeout=X              - set initial time-out interval to X
seconds
  type=X                 - set query type (e.g., A, ANY, CNAME,
MX, NS, PTR, SOA, SRV)
  querytype=X            - same as type
  class=X                - set query class (e.g., IN (Internet), ANY)
  [no]msxfr              - use MS fast zone transfer
  ixfrver=X              - current version to use in IXFR transfer
  request
server NAME        - set default server to NAME, using current
  default server
```

```
lserver NAME    - set default server to NAME, using initial server
finger [USER]   - finger the optional NAME at the current
 default host
root            - set current default server to the root
ls [opt] DOMAIN [> FILE] - list addresses in
DOMAIN (optional: output to FILE)
  -a            - list canonical names and aliases
  -d            - list all records
  -t TYPE       - list records of the given type (e.g., A,
CNAME, MX, NS, PTR, etc.)
view FILE       - sort an 'ls' output file and view it with pg
exit            - exit the program
```

Besides using the utility in interactive mode, you can issue a parameter with it, and have it automatically return the result. For example, if you enter an FQDN, the IP address of the given site or host is returned.

In addition to resolving a hostname to an IP address, you can also resolve an IP address to a hostname through a process known as *reverse lookup*. Whereas an FQDN starts with the specific host and then the domain, an IP address starts with the network ID and then the host ID. Because you want to use DNS to handle the mapping, both must go the same way, so the octets of the IP address are reversed. That is, 148.53.66.7 in the inverse address resolution is 7.66.53.148.

Now that the IP address is reversed, it is going the same way as an FQDN, and you can use DNS to resolve the address. To do so, you need to create a zone based upon address class. For example, in the address 148.53.66.7, the portion that was assigned to the site by the governing committee is 148.53 (and for 204.12.25.3, it is 204.12.25). Given this information, simply create a zone in which these numbers are reversed and to which you add the records in-addr.arpa—that is, 53.148.in-addr.arpa or 25.12.204.in-addr.arpa, respectively. These zones can be copied from their respective primary servers.

LMHOSTS And Microsoft

Similar to HOSTS files, LMHOSTS files are static ASCII text files. Whereas the HOSTS file contains the mappings of IP addresses to hostnames, the LMHOSTS file contains the mappings of IP addresses to NetBIOS names (known as "computer names").

All operating systems using TCP/IP utilize hostnames, but only Microsoft operating systems utilize NetBIOS names. This limitation restricts the scope of LMHOSTS files to the workplaces dependent upon Windows 9x or Windows NT.

In the LMHOSTS file, the pound sign (#) indicates comments. The file is read sequentially on each lookup, thus limiting the size of the comment lines at the beginning of the file is highly recommended.

A number of special commands can be used in the file to load entries into a name cache, which is scanned on each lookup before referring to the file. (By default, entries are not preloaded, but are parsed only after dynamic name resolution fails.) Using these commands will decrease your lookup time and increase system efficiency.

The biggest advantage of LMHOSTS files is that resolution from NetBIOS entries to TCP/IP hostnames can be accomplished. The biggest disadvantages are that they work only in Microsoft operating systems and—like HOSTS— are static files that must be kept updated. Incidentally, the LM stands for LAN Manager, the predecessor to Windows NT.

WINS: A Superset Of LMHOSTS

If your network grows too large to resolve IP addresses by using the HOSTS files, you can implement DNS. By the same token, if your network is too large for you to continuously update and administer LMHOSTS files, you can implement a WINS server on Windows NT or Windows 2000 Server. In fact, the configuration parameters on the WINS server include an option to incorporate existing LMHOSTS files into the WINS database.

WINS, Windows Internet Name Service, provides a centralized method of name management that is both flexible and dynamic. A WINS server automatically collects entries whenever a client is configured with that WINS server's address. An example of this for Windows 98 is shown in Figure 5.2.

 All of the burden is on the client—when the client starts up, it sends a registration request to the WINS server, and it is the client's responsibility to renew that registration. The WINS server does not initiate any registration renewals with clients. The registration is released if it's not renewed by the time the TTL (time to live) expires.

WINS writes error messages to the Windows NT/2000 Event Log and writes messages about its status (started, stopped, etc.) to the System log.

By default, non-WINS clients cannot directly communicate with a WINS server to resolve a name, but resolution can be done if you install a *WINS proxy agent*, which works by using broadcasts. If they are not locally cached, the proxy agent forwards broadcasts for name resolution to the WINS server and gets the resolution. The proxy agent does not send the resolution back to the

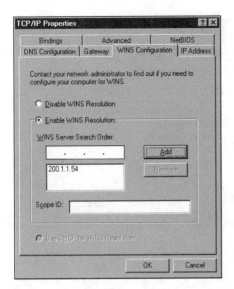

Figure 5.2   Configuring a Microsoft client to use a WINS server for name resolution requires the IP address of the server.

requester, but instead waits for it to request it again, at which time it finds the cached entry and responds. The proxy agent must be located on the same subnet as non-WINS clients so the proxy agent receives the broadcasts for name resolution (broadcasts don't go through routers).

Any Windows-based WINS client can be a WINS proxy agent, but a client cannot be a WINS server. After you configure a WINS client to be a proxy agent, you must reboot the machine for this change to take effect. No other configuration is needed for this proxy agent. This WINS client remains a proxy agent until you turn off the proxy agent parameter and reboot the computer.

Comparing The Options

All four of the name resolution methods discussed work by resolving names into IP addresses. Each is ideal for a given situation, and Table 5.1 compares these methods.

In all cases, after the IP address has been found, the Address Resolution Protocol (ARP) is used to convert the IP address into a physical address. If ARP does not have a map in memory, it has to go find one on the network. ARP uses local broadcasts to find physical addresses of machines, and it maintains a cache of IP addresses recently mapped to physical addresses. Although this cache does not last indefinitely, it enables ARP to not have to broadcast every time IP needs a physical address.

Table 5.1 Name resolution methods.

Method	Works With	Biggest Advantage	Ideal For
HOSTS file	Hostnames—all operating systems	Simple to start with	Small network of hosts of any type
DNS server	Hostnames—all operating systems into zones	Unlimited size; database divided	Large network, Internet
LMHOSTS file	NetBIOS names— Microsoft operating systems	Allows entries to be preloaded into cache for quick resolution	Small Microsoft-based network
WINS server	NetBIOS names— Microsoft operating systems	Dynamic once	Large Microsoft-based network

ARP works only locally and cannot work across a router (again, ARP works by using broadcasts). If the data is being sent outside the local network, ARP uses the physical address of the router, not of the destination machine. After IP receives the physical address of the router from ARP, it formulates the datagram, placing the destination IP address directly above the router's physical address, and sends the data on.

To put it into perspective:

1. Names get converted to IP addresses through one of four methods (HOSTS, DNS, LMHOSTS, or WINS).

2. IP addresses get converted to physical (MAC) addresses through ARP.

3. The data is sent.

Practice Questions

Question 1

> The layer of the OSI model at which name resolution occurs is:
>
> ○ a. Network
>
> ○ b. Physical
>
> ○ c. Application
>
> ○ d. Data Link

The correct answer is c. Name resolution always occurs at the Application layer of the OSI model and is often carried out silently by the applications in use (known as resolvers).

Question 2

> If the following HOSTS file is in use, why can a user reach a host by entering the address 192.168.98.34, but not by the name Ridgeville?
>
> ```
> 192.168.98.1 Portland
> #192.168.98.34 Ridgeville
> 192.168.98.2 Sarasota
> 192.168.98.3 #Angola
> 192.168.98.4 Tipton #Arcadia
> 192.168.98.55 Summitville
> 192.168.98.16 Richmond
> ```
>
> ○ a. The entries are not in numerical order.
>
> ○ b. The comment character prevents the line from being read.
>
> ○ c. The entries are not in alphabetical order.
>
> ○ d. The subnet is incorrect.

The correct answer is b. The pound sign serves as a comment character, and because it is the first item in the line, it causes the whole line to be ignored. The user can reach the site by using the IP address because there is no need to then read this file. When the file is read, however—for name resolution—the needed line is skipped.

Question 3

> What is the maximum number of entries that a HOSTS file can contain?
>
> ○ a. 255
>
> ○ b. 8
>
> ○ c. 2
>
> ○ d. Unlimited

The correct answer is d. There can be an unlimited number of lines within the file, but each line is limited to 255 characters.

Question 4

> The domain that should be used for an institution of higher learning in Oklahoma would be:
>
> ○ a. edu
>
> ○ b. ins
>
> ○ c. gov
>
> ○ d. sch

The correct answer is a. The edu domain is used to signify educational institutions and universities within the United States. Outside the United States, the domain of the country is used. Answer c is incorrect because the domain gov is used for United States government sites. Answers b and d are incorrect because there are no such domains as ins or sch.

Question 5

> Within a DNS record, the entry type used to hold an alias would be:
>
> ○ a. SOA
>
> ○ b. HINFO
>
> ○ c. A
>
> ○ d. CNAME

The correct answer is d. CNAME is the Canonical Name record used to hold aliases for the host. Answer a is incorrect because SOA is the Start Of Authority record, which holds time-to-live and related information. Answers b and c are incorrect because HINFO records hold the TCP/IP address information, as do A records.

Question 6

DNS entries can be set by using which utility?

○ a. Hostname

○ b. ARP

○ c. NSLOOKUP

○ d. SET

The correct answer is c. The NSLOOKUP utility allows you to modify record entries on DNS by using the SET parameter in an interactive session. Answer a is incorrect because the **hostname** command shows the name of the current host only. Answer b is incorrect because ARP is the Address Resolution Protocol used to convert IP addresses to physical addresses. Answer d is incorrect because SET is the command used within the NSLOOKUP utility.

Question 7

Which DNS record type is used for reverse lookup?

○ a. NS

○ b. PTR

○ c. REV

○ d. VER

The correct answer is b. The PTR record holds the pointer information and is used for reverse lookup entries. Answer a is incorrect because NS is the Name Server record, which maps to the primary server for the zone. Answers c and d are incorrect because there are no record types named REV or VER, and they are invalid entries.

Question 8

> Which of the following name resolution methods are dynamic? [Choose all correct answers]
>
> ☐ a. HOSTS
>
> ☐ b. LMHOSTS
>
> ☐ c. DNS
>
> ☐ d. WINS

Trick! question

The correct answer is d. Only the Windows Internet Name Service (WINS) is dynamic and able to add entries on the fly. All other methods require administrative action to add new entries.

Question 9

> What is the syntax of the site **www.ds-technical.com** known as?
>
> ○ a. DNS entry
>
> ○ b. FQDN
>
> ○ c. Zone
>
> ○ d. Alias

The correct answer is b. A Fully Qualified Domain Name (FQDN) includes the service, the host, and the domain. Answer a is incorrect because a DNS entry has record information. Answer c is incorrect because a zone is a database within DNS. Answer d is incorrect because an alias is another name by which a host is known.

Question 10

> A DNS server that has no record file of its own is known as:
>
> ○ a. Primary
>
> ○ b. Secondary
>
> ○ c. Authoritative
>
> ○ d. Caching-only

The correct answer is d. A caching-only server holds the results of queries it has performed, but it does not have a zone file of its own. Primary and Secondary servers hold their own record files, and Authoritative is a bogus distractor that does not apply here.

Need To Know More?

 Dulaney, Emmett. *MCSE Fast Track: TCP/IP*. New Riders Publishing, Indianapolis, IN, 1998. ISBN: 1-56205-937-8. Chapter 2 discusses name resolution technologies.

 Feit, Dr. Sidnie. *TCP/IP Architecture, Protocols, and Implementation with IPv6 and IP Security*. McGraw-Hill, New York, 1999. ISBN: 0-07-022069-7. Chapter 5 covers TCP/IP naming and addressing.

 http://carlton.innotts.co.uk/customer/services/nslookup.html— Offers the ability to enter a Fully Qualified Domain Name and find its corresponding IP address. Appears to work with all domains.

 www.internic.net/whois.html—Allows you to enter an FQDN and see which servers are responsible for the name resolution. Works only for the com, edu, net, and org domains.

 www.osilab.ch/—Offers DNS lookup, allowing you to enter an IP address and see the FQDN associated with it. Works with all domains.

6

Web Service

. . . .

Terms you'll need to understand:

√ Client/server

√ Hypertext Transfer Protocol (HTTP)

√ Web browser

√ Uniform Resource Locator (URL)

√ Cache

√ Proxy server

√ Required and prohibited operators

√ Cookies

Techniques you'll need to master:

√ Understanding the Hypertext Transfer Protocol

√ Identifying the various parts of a URL

√ Using and configuring Web client software

√ Understanding the various types of caching

√ Knowing the functionality of a proxy server

√ Using various methods to search for content on the Web

√ Using advanced search techniques

√ Understanding how cookies are used

The Internet offers a variety of services, such as the World Wide Web (also known as "the Web" and "WWW"), email, FTP, USENET news, Gopher, Telnet, and more. This chapter focuses on the Web—one of the fastest growing and most popular services on the Internet. The Web is composed of a system of servers that support a language called Hypertext Markup Language (HTML), discussed in Chapter 10.

The Client/Server Model

Web services, as well as most other Internet services, use a client/server model. The server provides the services, which are usually requested by the client. A Web client typically uses a Web browser to make requests, and the server responds to those requests by delivering Web pages, for example. While end users (the clients) are generally concerned only with what's going on at their end, you, as an Internet professional, may need to be knowledgeable about both ends. Figure 6.1 shows an example of a Web server responding to client requests.

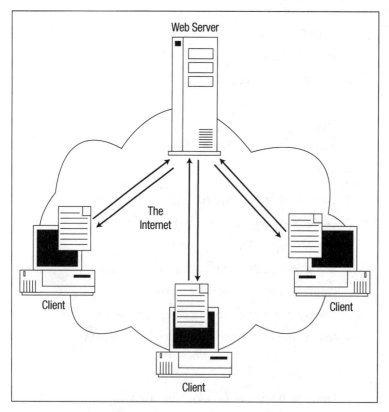

Figure 6.1 The Web uses a client/server architecture.

Hypertext Transfer Protocol (HTTP)

The Hypertext Transfer Protocol (HTTP) is the protocol used over TCP/IP to carry requests and responses between a Web server and a Web client. It can be said that HTTP is to the Web what TCP/IP is to the Internet.

> *Note: HTTP is not a secure protocol. There are, however, a couple of variations of HTTP that provide for encrypted transmission. These variations include the Secure Hypertext Transfer Protocol (SHTTP) and Hypertext Transfer Protocol Secure (HTTPS).*

HTTP is a *stateless* protocol, which means that it cannot remember what occurred previously. (Programs that are *stateful* can remember what happened the last time the program was run and keep track of various configuration settings.)

HTTP uses a series of requests and responses to transfer data. Basically, the client sends a request, and the server responds to the request. This transfer of data on the Web, using HTTP, usually occurs in the following four stages:

1. *Connection*—The client connects to the Web server.

2. *Request*—The client sends a resource request message to the server.

3. *Response*—The server delivers a response to the client.

4. *Close*—The connection is closed between the client and the server.

> *Note: Under the original HTTP specifications, the connection closes after the server response. However, a newer version of HTTP introduces persistent connections; this version maintains the connection and continues to exchange multiple requests until the connection is explicitly closed.*

In addition to HTTP, another Web standard called *Hypertext Markup Language (HTML)* plays a crucial role in the Web's functionality. After the client makes its request and the server responds, the client uses a Web browser to interpret and display the information.

Hypertext Markup Language (HTML)

Hypertext Markup Language (HTML) is the language used for documents on the Web. HTML provides a method for encoding information so that it can be displayed in various types of Web browsers. The i-Net+ exam will expect you to demonstrate the ability to create Web pages using HTML, but not to worry—Chapter 10 deals entirely with HTML.

Web Browsers

The Web browser is the program run by the client that allows the user to view HTML documents sent from Web servers. There are various types of Web browsers, but the two most popular are Netscape Navigator and Microsoft Internet Explorer.

Web browsers provide an easy "point and click" method for navigating the Web. A browser contains several toolbars that provide navigational controls such as moving forward and backwards.

Additionally, most browsers provide controls to adjust their behavior. For example, to help decrease the download time, a client operating over a slow Internet connection can disable pictures to prevent them from being displayed. Instead, a user will see only a "placeholder" where each image should appear. The user then has the option to selectively view pictures by right-clicking on the specific spot and selecting the option to show the picture. Some other methods of customizing the browser include:

➤ Hiding toolbars to create a larger display area

➤ Specifying a "home page" to appear when the browser is first launched

➤ Extending the browser's capabilities with the use of plug-ins (discussed in Chapter 11)

➤ Adjusting the cache settings (discussed in detail later in this chapter)

 You want to be especially aware of the capability to disable the display of pictures. This provides an excellent method of increasing the overall speed, and it is often the problem when users complain that their browsers do not display graphics.

The Uniform Resource Locator (URL)

The ability to easily locate and link to resources on the Web is made possible by the Uniform Resource Locator (URL)—also called an *address*. The general format for a URL is:

protocol://hostname:port/path/filename.ext

The following is an example address that points to the page containing Frequently Asked Questions (FAQs) about the i-Net+ certification. This page is located on CompTIA's Web server:

http://www.comptia.org:80/certification/inetplus/faqs.htm

Next, we will use this example to examine each part of a URL.

The Protocol

The protocol portion of the URL specifies the Internet protocol used to access network resources. Most common is the HTTP protocol, which is used to access Web pages, but other Internet protocols are also supported. Table 6.1 lists many of these protocols. This chapter focuses on the HTTP protocol because it is the most common, but you do need to know how to specify the use of other Internet services in a URL. The next two chapters offer detailed information on other Internet services.

The protocol portion of our sample URL is shown in boldface type:

http://www.comptia.org:80/certification/inetplus/faqs.htm

> *Note: When you're typing Web addresses, you can usually omit the "http://" because Web browsers accept this as the default.*

The Hostname

The hostname (or server address) specifies the name of the server where the resource is located. In Chapter 5, you learned that it is much easier to remember a name such as CompTIA than it is to remember an IP address such as 209.0.85.150. In the following URL, the hostname is shown in boldface type:

http://**www.comptia.org**:80/certification/inetplus/faqs.htm

Table 6.1 Protocols used within a URL.	
Protocol/Data Source	**Description**
http://	Use the Hypertext Transfer Protocol to access a document on a Web server.
ftp://	Use the File Transfer Protocol to access a file on an FTP server.
gopher://	Use the Gopher protocol to access a Gopher file system index on a Gopher server.
mailto://	Send an email message to a specified address.
news://	Use the Network News Transfer Protocol (NNTP) to access news on a USENET newsgroup.
telnet://	Use the Telnet protocol to access a remote session on another computer.
WAIS://	Access indexed files in a database on a Wide Area Information Server.
file://	Access a file on a local disk.

You do not have to specify the DNS hostname; you can also use the numerical IP address.

The Port

In Chapter 3, you were introduced to the various port assignments that services use to communicate. Because port 80 is the well-known port number for HTTP, it is not necessary to specify this number each time you enter a URL; it will be used by default. In the following example, the port number is shown in boldface type:

http://www.comptia.org:**80**/certification/inetplus/faqs.htm

However, the only time that a port number needs to be specified is when the service has been moved from its default port. For example, if CompTIA had configured the Web server to use port 8080, the previous example would not work. In this case, the correct syntax to get to this page on port 8080 would be **http://www.comptia.org:8080/certification/inetplus/faqs.htm**.

 By default, the URL for a Web address will automatically be set to port 80, but if the port number is changed from this default, the number must be specified. To specify a port within a URL, you type a colon and the port number immediately after the hostname.

The Path And File Name

Every computer has a file system. URLs use a directory path to locate a page within the file system. Thus, the *faqs.htm* page located on CompTIA's Web server can be found in the following boldface directory path:

http://www.comptia.org:80/**certification/inetplus/**faqs.htm

The actual destination page—an HTML Frequently Asked Questions page—is the last item in the URL:

http://www.comptia.org:80/certification/inetplus/**faqs.htm**

The Anchor

Additionally, an *anchor* may follow the file name. Web pages that contain a lot of information on one page may use an anchor, which directs the user's Web browser to a specific point on the page so that the user does not have to scroll down to that spot. When an anchor is used, it immediately follows the file name; the anchor is indicated by a pound sign and the anchor name. For example, to refer to a specific point called *benefits* on the faqs.htm page, the URL may hypothetically appear like this:

http://www.comptia.org:80/certification/inetplus/faqs.htm**#benefits**

Web Caching

Web caching stores files from remote Web sites locally or on another computer acting as a proxy, thus allowing for the quick retrieval of images and other files. Retrieving a file locally is much faster than going back out remotely to get the information. The two primary methods used for Web caching involve storing Web data on a proxy server or storing data within the Web browser's cache.

Proxy Caching

The non-technical meaning of a proxy is defined as a person authorized to act for another: an agent or a substitute. Similarly, a proxy server sits between a client and a Web server and acts as the "middleman" between the two. The proxy server intercepts client requests to see if it can fulfill them; if the proxy server can't fulfill a request, it forwards the request to the Web server. The proxy server then receives the response from the Web server, saves a copy for itself, and forwards the response to the client (see Figure 6.2).

Then, if another client later issues a request for the same object, the proxy server can fulfill the request from its cache without having to ask the remote Web server (see Figure 6.3). The freshness of the document is typically controlled by using HTTP headers in the document, which indicate when the proxy server should stop serving cached pages, and retrieve an updated version from the original resource.

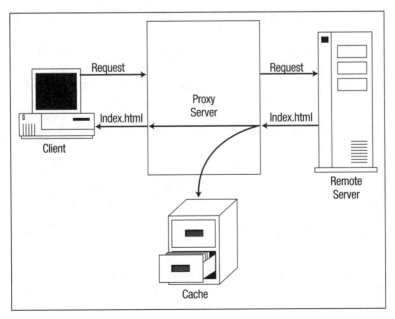

Figure 6.2   A proxy server acts as a go-between for the client and the remote server.

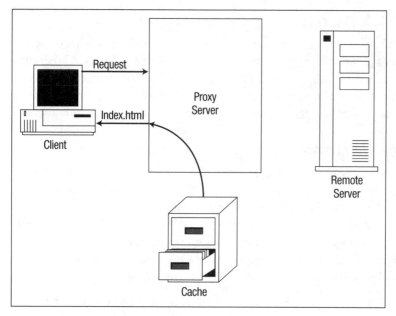

Figure 6.3 A proxy server can deliver subsequent requests for objects from its cache.

The advantages of a proxy server include the following:

➤ *Improved performance*—Proxy servers greatly improve performance by reducing latency and traffic. Web sites appear more responsive because a client receives objects from the proxy server rather than from the original server. Additionally, traffic is reduced because each object is received from the Web server only once while the proxy server then satisfies multiple requests for the objects. By fulfilling these requests, the proxy server prevents clients from consuming excess bandwidth.

➤ *Filtering*—A proxy server acts as a firewall component and can manage traffic to and from the Internet. Filters provide a method of access control, and can prevent employees from accessing certain Web sites.

Proxy servers are usually used in conjunction with a firewall and are typically deployed by various organizations, including most ISPs. A client's browser can then be configured to use a proxy server as a go-between. Most browsers typically require the address and the port number for the proxy server.

Remember that a proxy server acts on behalf of the client, intercepting all incoming and outgoing requests. Be sure you also understand the performance and filtering benefits provided by a proxy server.

Client Caching

In addition to proxy caching, another type of Web caching commonly used is *browser caching*, which is often referred to as client caching. A client's Web browser (such as Internet Explorer) maintains its own cache, which is typically a folder on the hard disk where Web pages and graphics are stored. Consistent navigational images are often used throughout a Web site; in addition to creating a consistent user interface, this practice can speed up the display of pages within the site. With a consistent interface, graphics typically only need to be downloaded once and they can then be retrieved from the cache for display on subsequent pages; thus, a user can browse the site and be issued these images instantly. In addition, this cache enables the user to hit the Back button and instantly see the page without having to request the page from the server again.

Browser Cache Settings

Most Web browsers have adjustable settings that specify how Web pages should be updated. (At any time, however, a user can manually update a Web page, typically by clicking on a button named Refresh or Reload.) For example, Internet Explorer provides several options for specifying when the browser will go back to the originating page to check for a newer version than the one stored in the browser cache. These options, which are shown in Figure 6.4, include:

➤ *Every visit to the page*—Every time you visit a page, the browser checks to see if the page has changed since the last visit. If the page has changed, the browser displays the new page and stores a copy in the cache. This option increases the time it takes for Web pages to appear between pages you have already viewed.

Figure 6.4   Cache settings in Internet Explorer.

➤ *Every time you start Internet Explorer*—The browser checks to see if the page has changed only when the page was viewed in an earlier session. Otherwise, all visits to the same page, in the same work session, pull data from the browser cache. This option increases performance for pages you have already viewed in a single session.

➤ *Automatically*—The browser checks to see if the page has changed only when the page was viewed in an earlier session. The browser also determines if images on the page are changing infrequently over time and check for newer images even less frequently. This option provides the best performance for pages you have already viewed.

➤ *Never*—The browser pulls all previously viewed pages from the cache and never checks to see whether the pages have changed. This option increases performance for pages you have already viewed. To see the most current version of a page when using this option, you will be required to refresh the page.

Note: Microsoft Internet Explorer refers to the browser cache as temporary Internet files.

Most browsers also provide an option to quickly clear the cache. Deleting the cache slows performance upon each initial visit to a Web page but provides the advantage of restoring disk space that was being used to store the cached pages.

Searching For Content

With the mass amount of information available on the Web, the task of trying to find specific information can be overwhelming. Luckily, there are dozens of Web sites that provide *search engines* to assist in locating information. These sites utilize giant databases to record located information provided by special tools called *robots* (robots are also called *spiders* and *crawlers*). Other sites provide directories, which are compiled by people who manually examine information and organize it into categories.

Deciding which type of search tool to use generally depends upon the content you're seeking. A directory might be the best choice when the subject of your search falls under a broad category, whereas a search engine is best used in queries that are more specific. Many search sites provide both options. To initiate a search, a user typically enters keywords into an edit box provided on the Web page. The secret to effectively finding the information you're looking for on the Web is using proper keyword queries with required and prohibited operators.

Required And Prohibited Search Operators

There are several methods for conducting more precise queries using search sites. Many people tend to simply search for the keywords related to their idea. Assume, for example, that you want to find general information about skiing in New England. If you were to type the words **skiing** and **New England** into the edit box of a search engine, this, unfortunately, would produce many results because most search engines will return all pages in which it finds *any* of these words. For example, a page about anything new in the country of England may be returned within the results, although this was not what you wanted.

One solution might be to group New England into a phrase by using quotes; therefore, a search for **skiing** and **"New England"** will return all pages with the word **skiing** or the phrase **New England**. One problem with this, however, is the possibility that one phrase and not the other will be included in the results. For example, the results might include information about skiing in Colorado or beaches in New England.

> *Note: Entering a keyword in all lowercase will find all variants of the word. For example, a search for* england *will find pages that include England, england, ENGLAND, and EngLand. On the other hand, the use of a capital letter will find only that capitalized variant and no others.*

To ensure that you are getting the exact information you are looking for, most search engines support the use of *required* (+) and *prohibited* (-) operators, also called *inclusion* and *exclusion* operators. The use of these operators provides more control over queries. Although not every search site allows the use of these operators, they are supported by most; furthermore, it is important that you understand these because the i-Net+ exam accepts the use of these operators as an important and basic query technique.

The Required Operator

The use of a required operator before a word or phrase indicates that the word or phrase must be included in the search results. To use a required operator, place a plus sign before the term, and allow one space between the previous word and subsequent operators. For example, to find Web pages about skiing in Vermont, you might use the following:

+skiing +Vermont

The required operator may also be used in front of a phrase such as:

+skiing +"New England"

These sample searches will ensure that all of the specified words or phrases appear within the page.

To ensure that a word is included in the results of a search, use a required operator (plus sign). The proper use of a required operator requires the following:

➤ A plus sign typed before the keyword

➤ A space typed after the keyword and before the operator

For example, to find information about hotels in Paris, you would type **+hotels +Paris**.

The Prohibited Operator

Even when you specify what must appear in the page, it is likely that the results will still return many pages with information that you do not want. For example, what if you are not interested in snowboarding? To eliminate any results containing the word "snowboarding," you can use a prohibited operator, thus narrowing the search results down to exactly what you're interested in.

The use of a prohibited operator before a word or phrase indicates that the word or phrase must be excluded from the search results. To use a prohibited operator, place a minus sign before the term, and type one space between each term and subsequent operators. For example, to find Web pages about skiing but not snowboarding, you might use the following:

skiing -snowboarding

As with the required operator, you can also use the prohibited operator before a phrase placed within quotes. Additionally, you can combine the use of required and prohibited operators. For example, if you want information about skiing in Vermont, but you don't want any results that mention snowboarding, you can use the following:

+skiing +Vermont -snowboarding

To ensure that a word is excluded in the results of a search, use a prohibited operator (minus sign). The proper use of a prohibited operator requires the following:

➤ A minus sign typed before the keyword

➤ A space typed after the keyword and before the next operator

For example, to find information about hotels in Paris, but not about Bed-and-Breakfast establishments, you would use **+hotels +Paris -"bed and breakfast"**.

Many search engines also support the use of wildcard characters. A wildcard, typically an asterisk (*), is used as a substitute for one or more letters. Thus, a search for **+skiing +Vermont +child*** will return Web pages about skiing, Vermont, and any variations of the word "child," such as "child," "children," and "childlike." In addition to finding variations of words, wildcards can be helpful when you aren't sure how to spell a specific word. Table 6.2 provides examples of many of the search features discussed thus far.

Advanced Search Techniques

Another popular way to conduct searches is to use Boolean operators. Boolean operators are phrases such as AND, OR, NOT, and NEAR, which are used to create relationships between various words. Table 6.3 lists some of the Boolean operators and their corresponding functions.

Another technique that can be combined with Boolean operators is the use of parentheses. Parentheses can be used to group terms and to specify the order in which the words are searched—much like the use of parentheses in algebraic equations. For example, to find pages with "peanut butter and jelly" or "peanut butter and jam" or even both variations, you might use the following Boolean expression:

(peanut AND butter) AND (jelly OR jam)

Table 6.2 Search examples.	
Search Example	**Description**
peanut butter	Finds all pages that contain "peanut" and/or "butter," as well as any capitalized variations of those words. The found pages can contain one or both words.
Peanut Butter	Finds all pages that contain "Peanut" or "Butter" but does not find any uncapitalized variations.
"peanut butter"	Finds pages that contain the exact phrase "peanut butter," as well as any capitalized variations of the phrase.
+peanut +butter	Finds pages that contain both "peanut" and "butter," but the words don't have to be near each other.
+peanut +butter -jelly	Finds pages that contain both "peanut" and "butter" but not "jelly."
+pea* +butter	Finds pages that contain "butter" and any word starting with "pea."

Table 6.3	Using Boolean expressions with search engines.	
Expression	**Function**	**Example**
AND	Finds pages with all of the specified terms linked by AND.	peanut AND butter
OR	Finds pages containing at least one of the terms linked by OR.	peanut OR butter
NOT	Excludes pages that include a term followed by NOT.	peanut NOT butter
NEAR	Finds pages containing all of the specified terms in close proximity (defined by each search engine) to each other when linked with NEAR.	peanut NEAR butter

Some search engines also permit the use of special keywords to search specific entries within a Web page. Some of the more common special keywords are listed in Table 6.4.

Note: Although most search engines natively support the use of required and prohibited operators, you are usually required to go to the advanced section of a search engine to use other features such as Boolean operators and special keywords.

Table 6.4	Using special keywords with search engines.	
Keyword	**Function**	**Example**
domain:*domain name*	Finds pages with the specified domain name.	Use **domain:ca** to find all pages from Canada.
host:*hostname*	Finds pages with the specified computer name.	Use **host:www.coriolis.com** to find pages on the Coriolis Web server.
link:*URL text*	Finds pages with a link to the specified URL.	Use **link:www.castadream.com** to find pages that link to the castadream.com Web site.
title:*page title*	Finds pages that contain specified words in the page's title, which appears in the title bar of most browsers.	Use **title:certification** to find pages with "certification" in the title.
image:*file name*	Finds pages with the specified image name.	Use **image:logo** to find pages with images named "logo."

Cookies

Web sites often use cookies to identify users and provide customized Web pages. A *cookie* is a small file, no larger than 4K, which contains HTTP header information and which is stored as a plain text file on the client's hard drive.

Cookies are initially sent from a Web server to a client; when the client returns to the site, the cookie can be sent back to the originating Web server. The information stored in the cookie provides enough information for the site to provide a personalized page. For example, an online book retailer that I frequently visit greets me by name and even offers suggested material that it thinks I may be interested in based upon my previous habits.

 Cookies are stored in plain text files on the client computer and are initially provided by the Web server. The primary use of cookies is to provide a personalized experience for the user.

Cookies provide a solution to the otherwise anonymous nature of the Web. As mentioned earlier, HTTP is a stateless protocol that does not monitor all the details of a session. Thus, the use of cookies allows the site to follow the client across various pages within the site and to store information that was volunteered by the user.

Despite much of the hype surrounding the security and privacy implications of cookies, they are relatively harmless. Using cookies is much like walking into a bar and having the bartender greet you by name and remember to put a lime wedge in your drink. Cookies do not have the ability to examine your hard disk and return personal information to a Web server. Furthermore, a Web site cannot access any cookies that it did not issue.

Most Web browsers do, however, provide mechanisms that allow the user to control cookies. For example, cookies can be completely disabled. Unfortunately, doing so would not give the user the benefits provided by cookies. An alternative to completely disabling cookies is an option available in most browsers that will notify the user every time a site wants to deliver a cookie (see Figure 6.5). This option allows the user to decide whether or not a certain site is permitted to place a cookie on the user's hard drive. One obvious disadvantage to this is that the user will most likely be bombarded with sites offering cookies because most sites seek to provide a personalized experience.

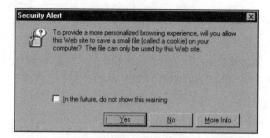

Figure 6.5   Internet Explorer request to store a cookie from a Web site.

Most browsers can be customized to handle cookies in a variety of ways. Generally speaking, cookies can be disabled, automatically accepted, or accepted on a site-by-site basis. That is, a dialog box can alert the user that a particular site wants to deliver a cookie, and the user can either accept or reject the delivery of the cookie.

This discussion primarily focuses on the use of cookies from the end user's point of view. Chapter 12 provides additional information about cookies and discusses how a Web site can use cookies to its advantage.

Practice Questions

Question 1

What does the abbreviation HTTP stand for?

○ a. Hypertext Trivial Transfer Protocol

○ b. Hypertext Trivial Protocol

○ c. Hypertext Transfer Proxy

○ d. Hypertext Transfer Protocol

The correct answer is d. HTTP is the abbreviation for Hypertext Transfer Protocol, which is not to be confused with the Trivial File Transfer Protocol (TFTP—a connectionless protocol used for file transfer). The letter "H" and the letter "T" are taken from the first word, "hypertext." Answers a, b, and c are incorrect because they are not legitimate terms.

Question 2

Which of the following devices sits between a client and a Web server, performs caching functions, and tries to fulfill client requests?

○ a. Router

○ b. Proxy server

○ c. Firewall

○ d. Bridge

The correct answer is b. A proxy server acts as a go-between representing clients to a Web server. Although a proxy server is commonly used in conjunction with a firewall, a firewall is specifically designed to protect a network against external threats; therefore, answer c is incorrect. A router is responsible for message delivery, and a bridge is used to connect two LANs; therefore, answers a and d are incorrect.

Question 3

> Which of the following search criteria would best be used to return the most results for Web sites about Unix but not about Linux?
>
> ○ a. UNIX -LINUX
>
> ○ b. unix+ -linux
>
> ○ c. UNIX+ -LINUX
>
> ○ d. Unix Linux
>
> ○ e. unix -linux

The correct answer is e. To require that a word be included in a search, use a required operator (plus sign) before the word. To exclude a word, use a prohibited operator (minus sign) before the word. In this question, however, because only one word is being searched for, a plus sign is not necessary. Additionally, the use of all lowercase will search for any capitalized variations of the word. Answer a is incorrect because this will not search for capitalized variants, thus it is not the best choice. Answers b and c are incorrect because of the incorrect use of the required and prohibited operators. Answer d will find pages containing Unix or Linux; therefore, it is incorrect.

Question 4

> Configuring a Web browser so that it does not show pictures will result in which of the following?
>
> ○ a. Web pages will not load.
>
> ○ b. Web pages will separately download pictures in a compressed file.
>
> ○ c. Web pages will load faster.
>
> ○ d. Web pages will load more slowly.

The correct answer is c. To provide faster downloads, most browsers can be configured to not display pictures and other multimedia, such as videos. To view a specific picture, right-click on its placeholder and select the option to view the picture. Answers b, c, and d are incorrect.

Question 5

What search criterion is the best choice to find all pages about the phrase *peanut butter*?

○ a. +peanut +butter

○ b. "peanut butter"

○ c. [peanut butter]

○ d. peanut butter

The correct answer is b. To locate a phrase in which the words should appear together, you should surround the phrase with quotes. Answer a is incorrect because this will find pages that contain the words "peanut" and "butter" but not necessarily together. Answer c is incorrect because quotation marks should be used—not brackets. Answer d is incorrect because this will find pages with the word "peanut" or the word "butter" (not necessarily both terms).

Question 6

Which of the following is the correct format for a URL?

○ a. **port://hostname:protocol/path/filename.ext**

○ b. **port://hostname:protocol/filename/path.ext**

○ c. **protocol://hostname:port/path/filename.ext**

○ d. **protocol://hostname:port/path/filename/path.ext**

The correct answer is d. A sample URL is **http://www.domain.com:8080/directory/subdirectory/file.htm**. Answers a, b, and c are incorrect because they do not follow the correct format.

Question 7

Which of the following URLs would you use to access the castadream.com Web site on port 8080?

○ a. **http://8080:www.castadream.com**

○ b. **http://www.castadream.com/8080:**

○ c. **http://www.castadream.com:8080**

○ d. **http:8080//www.castadream.com**

The correct answer is c. When a Web site uses a port other than the default port (80), you must specify a port number by typing a colon and the port number after the hostname. Therefore, answers a, b, and d are incorrect.

Question 8

Which of the following best describes an option that a client can use to control the issuance of cookies?

○ a. Set the Web browser to encrypt the cookie in transit.

○ b. Set the Web server to query the user for acceptance of a cookie.

○ c. Set the Web server to encrypt the cookies in transit.

○ d. Set the Web browser to query the user for acceptance of a cookie.

The correct answer is d. Most Web browsers provide an option to alert you when a Web server wants to send a cookie, and you can accept or decline the cookie. Because this option is set on the browser by the client and not on the Web server, answer b is incorrect. There is not an option to encrypt cookies in transit, and cookies are stored in plain text files; therefore, answers a and c are incorrect.

Question 9

When a client issues a cookie, it stores the cookies as what type of file?

○ a. Executable

○ b. BinHex

○ c. Plain text

○ d. Ciphertext

The correct answer is c. Cookies are stored as plain text files on the client computer. Answer a is incorrect because a cookie is not a program that can be run. Answer b is incorrect because BinHex is a format for converting binary data files into ASCII text. Answer d is incorrect because ciphertext is the encoded text of an encrypted message.

Need To Know More?

 Conner-Sax, Kiersten and Ed Krol. *The Whole Internet: The Next Generation.* O'Reilly & Associates Inc., Sebastopol, CA, 1999. ISBN 1-56592-428-2. Although this book is designed to be an end user's guide, it is actually quite informative because it covers so many aspects of the Internet with several chapters devoted to the Web.

 www.cacheflow.com/friendly/cfengine.py provides a neat utility to check any specified Web page and see how caches will handle them.

 www.ietf.org offers complete information on RFCs and provides several methods for searching the database. Search for "HTTP".

 www.microsoft.com offers plenty of information on HTTP, the Web, and its own Internet browser.

 www.w3.org is the Web site for the World Wide Web Consortium, which was established to promote the evolution and interoperability of the Web. This site is led by Tim Berners-Lee and provides an abundance of resources on HTTP.

Internet Mail And
News Services

Terms you'll need to understand:

√ Mail server

√ List server

√ News server

√ SMTP (Simple Mail Transfer Protocol)

√ POP (Post Office Protocol)

√ IMAP (Internet Message Access Protocol)

√ NNTP (Network News Transport Protocol)

√ MIME (Multipurpose Internet Mail Extensions)

√ S/MIME (Secure Multipurpose Internet Mail Extensions)

√ BinHex

√ UUEncode

Techniques you'll need to master:

√ Understanding the differences between mail, list, and news services

√ Knowing which protocols are used for which services

√ Recognizing which encoding method is best for a given scenario

In this chapter, you'll learn the basics of email and news services. A network without a mail service can be equated to a rowboat without an oar—yes, it can exist, but its functionality and usefulness are greatly enhanced by the addition of this tool.

Differences Between Mail, List, And News Services

Most TCP/IP-based networks provide three services that are closely related to one another—mail, lists, and news. Although similar in that the purpose of each service is to disseminate information, they are drastically different in the way they approach the task.

Mail Servers

With a mail server, one user can send a message to another user or to a selected group of users. For example, if you work in a company of 200 people and you want to know if a certain coworker wants to go to lunch with you, you can send him or her an email asking that question. If you want to know if five others can join you, you can address the message to all five. On occasion, you may need to send a message to all 200 coworkers—telling them, for example, of the new office policy prohibiting the use of email for making lunch dates—but sending a blanket message is an exception to the usual use, rather than the rule. A recipient of your message has the choice of responding to you or replying to all—the recipient cannot pick a subset of the distribution list without manually adding or removing addresses.

List Servers

With a list server, users "subscribe" to a particular list—typically a topic of interest. When any user sends a message (email) to the list server, the message is automatically forwarded to all subscribers. The most popular versions of list servers are Majordomo (freeware for Unix) and LISTSERV (a commercial product available for most platforms). Any user can choose to subscribe or unsubscribe at any given time. Subscribers receive a forwarded copy of *all* messages.

Subscriber lists can be *public* (open to anyone, and also called *open*) or *private* (open only to a select few, and also called *closed*). Although most lists are not moderated, they can be; in moderated lists, an administrator (known as the moderator) prevents messages from being forwarded if they fail to meet certain criteria.

Here's an example of applying a list server: Suppose that 40 of the 200 employees are members of a grievance committee, but they are scattered throughout the workplace (some in sales, some in manufacturing, etc.). A list service can be set up for the members of this grievance committee. When anyone submits a grievance (email) to the list service, it is automatically forwarded to all 40 subscribers to the list. If any member of the committee replies, the reply, as well, is sent to all 40 members. Other reasons for using a list server include the ability to send out electronic newsletters or run email campaigns.

News Servers

A news server is used to publish information of interest to a group; postings are known as *articles* or *threads*. Closely related to a list server, a news server allows users (known as a *newsgroup* and occasionally as a *forum*) to read and post messages for a group. News servers differ from list servers in that the articles are published and must be retrieved, rather than being blindly sent out. With a list server, the messages come in as email and can be deleted locally, never to be seen again. With a news server, the articles are kept on the server and can be organized into topic threads for easy searching. Like lists, newsgroups can be moderated, and one person, a moderator, can prevent the inclusion of messages that can be offensive or irrelevant.

One example of an appropriate use for a newsgroup would be a newsgroup for members of a project team who are working at different locations for the same company. The newsgroup can exist as long as the project is underway and can be disbanded upon completion. All members of the group can view the same articles and post their own. Another example, utilizing an external audience instead of internal, would be for a company's Customer Support department to post fixes to common problems. Customers can read the articles on the Web and solve their own problems.

 There is a distinct difference between these three servers (mail, list, and news), and there is a purpose for each. It is important to be able to differentiate between them on the exam and know which one best fits the needs of a given situation.

Not to be overlooked, ICQ (I seek you) allows for instant messaging. It requires installation of another program (which can be freely downloaded). ICQ essentially turns email into chat, allowing for real-time messaging, file downloading, and such.

Protocols

Several protocols are needed for messaging to take place. This section examines each of them.

SMTP

The Simple Mail Transfer Protocol (SMTP) is used to send email from a client to a server as well as between servers. Working through port 25, the sender and receiver send data back and forth by using commands and responses. The end of the message is identified by a period at the end of a line, followed by a carriage return and a line feed.

Based upon a number of items—such as the operating system and the implementation—the configuration parameters for SMTP can be graphical (as illustrated in Figure 7.1) or command-line based.

Among the options that can be configured are the number of concurrent connections (both incoming and outgoing), the maximum size of messages, and the amount of queuing allowed before messages are sent on.

POP

A counterpart to SMTP, the Post Office Protocol (POP) is used by a client to retrieve email from a server. The first version widely used was POP2, which required and relied upon SMTP to work. The newest version is POP3, which can work without SMTP and which uses port 110 for communications.

Note: POP is also an acronym for Point of Presence—a local access number given by ISPs for use in gaining Internet access.

Figure 7.1   SMTP's operation can be configured and optimized through a plethora of options, as shown by its implementation in Microsoft's Internet Information Server 4.

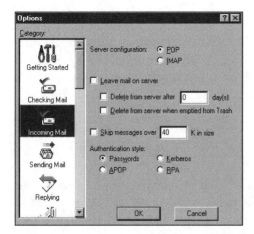

Figure 7.2   When configuring an email application (Eudora Pro is shown here), you must choose between POP or IMAP.

A substitute for POP is IMAP, discussed below, and most email packages allow for the use of either of the two protocols, as shown in Figure 7.2.

In Figure 7.2, notice that you can choose to leave mail on the server, though it is not the default action. If you do choose to leave mail on the server, you must also specify when it can be deleted. Notice, as well, that POP, in this implementation, allows the use of four methods of authentication: Passwords, APOP, Kerberos, and RPA.

➤ Passwords are clear text values that are sent out the same way that they are entered.

➤ APOP is the Authenticated Post Office Protocol; it uses MD5 encryption to send the passwords across the Internet.

> *Note: MD5 (Message Digest version 5) is an algorithm—created by Ronald Rivest (of RSA fame)—which uses one-way hashing and requires a 32-bit operating system.*

➤ Kerberos is another encryption method, considered by many to be the best. Windows 2000 is built around many of its features.

➤ RPA is used for communicating with and retrieving messages from CompuServe.

IMAP

The Internet Message Access Protocol (IMAP) is used instead of POP for retrieving messages from a server by a client. First developed by Stanford University, IMAP is now available in version 4, which allows you to search messages before downloading and to choose which messages to download.

> *Note: The IMAP acronym once stood for Interactive Mail Access Protocol due to the additional interactive features added since its inception.*

IMAP offers more features than POP, but it works through port 143 and is not as popular. One of the reasons for the unpopularity of IMAP is that POP retrieves all messages and places them on the client, while IMAP acts as if they belong on the server. With increased numbers of users and massive quantities of email being generated, it has become less feasible to continually add to and maintain server disk space for users' email messages.

Figure 7.3 shows the configuration options for IMAP and should be contrasted with Figure 7.2 (POP). Notice that the number of authentication styles supported in this implementation has dropped to two: Passwords and CRAM_MD5 (Challenge-Response Authentication Mechanism using MD5).

NNTP

The Network News Transport Protocol (NNTP) uses port 119 and is needed to access newsgroups. It can work with SMTP for moderation and is based on RFC 977.

Figure 7.3   The configuration parameters for IMAP are significantly less than those for POP.

NNTP uses port 119 by default, but this changes to port 563 if SSL (Secure Socket Layer) is used.

When clients (users) pick a newsgroup to view, they request the list of articles. Authentication takes place through the NNTP service, and then the list of articles is sent. The clients then pick articles they want to see, and the NNTP service sends them. During the posting of articles, NNTP verifies that the client is allowed to post to the newsgroup, adds the article to the newsgroup, and updates the index.

Figure 7.4 shows an example of the NNTP configuration options available—in this case using Microsoft's Internet Information Server 4. Notice that the size of postings can be limited, and specifications for moderation can be supplied.

Another option of great importance can be configured either individually for each newsgroup or globally for all newsgroups on a server: expiration. The two most common methods of specifying article expiration are time and size. With time, you specify that articles will be deleted when they are more than x days old. With size, you specify that articles will be deleted, oldest first, when the combined size of the newsgroup exceeds x megabytes. On a few implementations, such as Internet Information Server, you can use both options together: deleting content when it ages *and* when maximum sizes are reached.

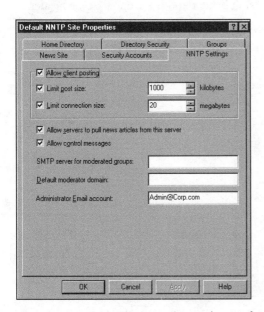

Figure 7.4   NNTP's operation can be configured using a number of options.

Encoding Methods

In addition to the protocols needed for messaging to take place, there is often a need to convert files into a format that can be transmitted and received. The following utilities and standards are commonly referred to as *encoding methods*, and this section examines each of them.

MIME

Multipurpose Internet Mail Extensions (MIME) were first formulated by the IETF (Internet Engineering Task Force) as a means of specifying how non-ASCII (binary) messages (such as graphics and audio) can be sent across the Internet. Almost all email clients and Web browsers currently in use support the usage of MIME and non-ASCII character sets.

 | MIME is used not only by email applications but also by browsers to handle data not written in HTML.

While there are numerous defined MIME types (GIF, for example), users and administrators can define their own types virtually on the fly, making MIME a very flexible specification. Figure 7.5 shows the mapping of known extensions and their associations. To include information about the version and data, MIME uses two headers: the MIME-version header and the Content-type header.

Although MIME is addressed in concept in earlier entries (RFCs 822 and 1341), the heart of MIME's offerings and functionality is covered in RFCs

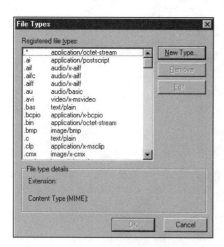

Figure 7.5   MIME maps files to types and applications based upon their extensions.

2045 through 2049. Base64 is the algorithm used for much of the encoding, though variations can also be employed.

S/MIME is touted as the replacement for MIME and is discussed in the next section.

S/MIME

Secure Multipurpose Internet Mail Extensions (S/MIME) enhances MIME by adding message encryption that uses public-key encryption technology from RSA (Rivest, Shamir, and Adelman). RFCs addressing S/MIME are 2311 through 2315, with the framework first begun in RFC 2268. S/MIME also uses the X.509 format for certificates. The current version is S/MIMEv2.

S/MIMEv2 is not a standard because RSA holds the patent on the technology. The IETF has formed an S/MIME working group that is working on a version (S/MIMEv3) that will become a standard, get around the proprietary protocols, and increase security. The RFCs addressing the efforts to derive the new version are 2630 through 2633. Still to be based on X.509, S/MIMEv3 will utilize TripleDES as the encryption algorithm.

BinHex

The purpose of MIME and S/MIME is to allow non-ASCII (binary) data to be sent through email. In contrast to this, BinHex works by converting binary data into ASCII data (with an extension of .hqx), thus allowing it to be sent through email. The binary file in question can be of any type—graphic, executable, etc. BinHex capabilities are included with most email packages, and BinHex is an alternative to MIME, as shown in Figure 7.6.

Figure 7.6   There are three common methods for encoding binary files and sending them through email—MIME, BinHex, and UUEncode.

BinHex is best used for interacting with Macintosh machines. By converting files to ASCII format, BinHex allows binary files to be put into a format understood by all operating systems.

UUEncode

Originally, the acronym represented its purpose: Unix-to-Unix Encoding. Over time, however, UUEncode has come to be available for most operating systems. A substitute for BinHex or MIME, it works by converting files to ASCII (UUEncode), allowing them to be sent as email attachments, and converting them back to binary (UUDecode).

Although most email applications do provide the ability to use this encoding scheme, it is still most prevalently used when one of the parties communicating is running the Unix operating system. Another common use involves older PC operating systems that do not have MIME capabilities.

Comparing The Options

All four of the encoding methods discussed have the same goal of allowing non-ASCII data to be sent as email attachments. Table 7.1 provides situations in which each method is a better choice than the others.

Table 7.1 Encoding Methods and uses.	
Encoding Method	**Ideal For**
BinHex	Communicating with Macintosh operating systems.
MIME	Communicating with any email client that is MIME-capable. This is the best choice, if available, due to its flexibility and ease of configuration.
S/MIME	Communicating with encrypted messages. Unfortunately, it is the newest of the lot and not yet supported by many clients.
UUEncode	Communicating with Unix hosts and with older PCs that do not have MIME capability.

Practice Questions

Question 1

The NNTP protocol is used by which service?

○ a. Mail

○ b. List

○ c. News

○ d. POP

The correct answer is c. NNTP is the Network News Transport Protocol, and it is used for interaction with newsgroups. Mail servers are used to send email to individual users, while List servers are used to send mail to subscribers. POP is the protocol used by a client for retrieving mail. Therefore, answers a, b, and d are incorrect.

Question 2

The Post Office Protocol, by default, utilizes what port for communication?

○ a. 119

○ b. 110

○ c. 80

○ d. 25

The correct answer is b. The Post Office Protocol (POP) uses port 110. Answer a is incorrect because NNTP uses port 119. Answer c is incorrect because the Web service uses port 80. Answer d is incorrect because SMTP uses port 25.

Question 3

> What is the algorithm most commonly used by MIME for encoding files?
>
> ○ a. Base64
>
> ○ b. RSA
>
> ○ c. TripleDES
>
> ○ d. CRAM_MD5

The correct answer is a. MIME uses the Base64 algorithm for encoding files. The other choices do not represent algorithms used by MIME.

Question 4

> You need to communicate with a branch office in Topeka. The branch office has only a few users, and they are running antiquated PCs with the DOS operating system and email applications that were installed several years ago. What encoding method should you use to send attachments to them?
>
> ○ a. MIME
>
> ○ b. S/MIME
>
> ○ c. BinHex
>
> ○ d. UUEncode

The correct answer is d. UUEncode is ideally suited for communication with older PCs and Unix hosts. MIME is used by newer PCs, while S/MIME is a secure version of MIME. BinHex is ideal for communicating with Macintosh clients.

Question 5

> You have sent files to a customer who requested them, and you had to use the BinHex format to send the files as attachments. The customer calls to say that he now cannot find the files on his system. If the files' original extension was .exe, what would their extension be now?
>
> ○ a. ex_
>
> ○ b. _
>
> ○ c. hqx
>
> ○ d. hex

The correct answer is c. BinHex converts files to ASCII format and places an extension of hqx on them to make them readily identifiable. All other choices are invalid.

Question 6

> The protocols that can be used for retrieving messages from a server are: [Choose the two best answers]
>
> ☐ a. NNTP
>
> ☐ b. POP3
>
> ☐ c. IMAP
>
> ☐ d. SMTP

The correct answers are b and c. Messages can be retrieved through the use of either POP3 or IMAP. Answer a is incorrect because NNTP is the Network News Transport Protocol, and it is used for interaction with newsgroups. Answer d is incorrect because SMTP is used for posting messages.

Question 7

> SMTP, by default, utilizes what port for communication?
>
> ○ a. 563
>
> ○ b. 110
>
> ○ c. 80
>
> ○ d. 25

The correct answer is d. SMTP uses port 25. Answer a is incorrect because NNTP uses port 563 if SSL is also used (and port 119 if it is not). Answer b is incorrect because the Post Office Protocol (POP) uses port 110. Answer c is incorrect because the Web service (HTTP) uses port 80.

Question 8

What is the algorithm proposed for use by S/MIMEv3 for encrypting files?

○ a. Base64

○ b. RSA

○ c. TripleDES

○ d. Password

The correct answer is c. S/MIMEv3 will use the TripleDES algorithm for encryption. Answer a is incorrect because MIME uses the Base64 algorithm for encoding files. Answer b is incorrect because S/MIMEv2 uses RSA, which is proprietary, for encrypting files. Answer d is incorrect because passwords are used for authentication and not representative of algorithms.

Question 9

You need to communicate with a branch office in Duluth. The branch office is used for catalog work, and all users are on the Macintosh platform. What encoding method should you use to send attachments to them?

○ a. MIME

○ b. S/MIME

○ c. BinHex

○ d. UUEncode

The correct answer is c. BinHex is ideally suited for communication with Macintosh users. Answer a is incorrect because MIME is used for newer PCs. S/MIME is a secure form of MIME, while UUEncode is used with Unix hosts.

Question 10

> You wish to set up a server to allow for communication between all users
> of your product. One of the advantages of buying your product instead of
> another vendor's is that the users can subscribe to this service and send
> email among themselves. Every email sent to the server will automatically be
> forwarded to all subscribers. What service should you set up to best accom-
> modate this?
>
> ○ a. News
>
> ○ b. Mail
>
> ○ c. List
>
> ○ d. Moderated

The correct answer is c. A list server will forward email sent to it to all users.
The list server can be moderated (have messages scanned by a person before
being posted), but need not be. A News server is used for articles, while a mail
server is used for sending email. Answer d is incorrect as there is no such thing
as a moderated server.

Need To Know More?

 www.academ.com/academ/nntp/index.html—A starting point for information about the Network News Transfer Protocol.

 www.cis.ohio-state.edu/htbin/rfc/rfc1123.html—The RFC covering SMTP and all aspects of it.

 www.cis.ohio-state.edu/htbin/rfc/rfc2060.html—The RFC covering IMAP and all aspects of it.

 www.eudora.com/techsupport/tutorials/glossary.html—If you think your knowledge of email terminology (attachment, alias, etc.) could use some brushing up, peruse the terms defined here.

 www.imc.org/smime-pgpmime.html—An overview of S/MIME and a comparison between it and OpenPGP.

 www.lsoft.com/lists/LIST_Q.html—A listing of known, public lists that can be subscribed to.

 www.lsoft.com/products/email_intro.asp—An excellent article on the differences between email and email lists. Coverage includes how the lists work. Links are provided to the various guides offered.

 www.lsoft.com/products/listserv-history.asp—L-Soft International is the company that markets LISTSERV, the commercial list server. On this page, you can read the history of how the technology came to be.

Other Internet Services

8

Terms you'll need to understand:

√ FTP

√ Gopher

√ LDAP

√ Telnet

√ LPR

Techniques you'll need to master:

√ Understanding the differences between the various services available on the Internet

√ Recognizing which service is best for a given scenario

In this chapter, you'll learn the basics of Internet services other than email and news services (addressed in Chapter 7). You'll see what each service offers and why you would choose to offer it on your site.

The Fine Line Between Services And Protocols

One of the most confusing issues with many services is that the utility that provides the functionality of a service or protocol has the same name as the service or protocol. For example, the FTP (File Transfer Protocol) service allows you to upload and download files to a site. The utility used to perform this operation is also named FTP.

There are dozens of examples like this—for example, ARP is both the Address Resolution Protocol and the utility used to see its cache and to interact with it. There are also examples where this is not the case; for example, HTTP (Hypertext Transfer Protocol) offers Web functionality, but you do not view or post Web pages by using the HTTP command. When you're studying the various technologies, determine whether the discussion pertains to a technology (be it a service or protocol) or a utility. Although the difference, at times, can seem trivial, it can be important in a testing environment.

FTP

FTP (File Transfer Protocol) is the most widely used file-transfer mechanism. First defined in RFC 959, FTP runs on port 21. To use FTP to send or receive files, your systems must meet the following requirements:

➤ The client computer must have FTP client software.

➤ The user must have a user name and password on the remote system. In many cases, a user name of *anonymous* with no password is used.

➤ The remote system must be running an FTP daemon (Unix, VMS, etc.) or service (Windows NT/2000, etc.).

➤ Both systems must be running the TCP/IP protocol.

Figure 8.1 shows an FTP utility (WS_FTP Pro) that can transfer files between remote and local locations.

You can use FTP in either a command-line mode or a command-interpreter mode. The following options are available from the command line:

➤ -a—Use any local interface when binding data connections.

➤ -d—Enables debugging.

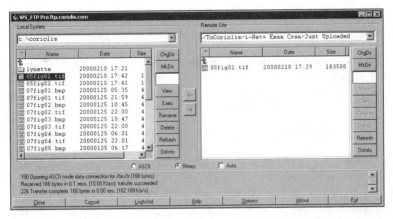

Figure 8.1 WS_FTP Pro adds a graphical interface to the standard FTP utility.

➤ **-g**—Disables file-name globbing (globbing permits the use of wild-card characters such as the asterisk and question mark in local file or path names).

➤ **-i**—Turns off interactive prompting during multiple file transfers.

➤ **-n**—Suppresses auto-login upon initial connection.

➤ **-s:filename**—Specifies a text file containing FTP commands; the commands will automatically run after FTP starts.

➤ **-v**—Suppresses the display of remote server responses.

➤ **-w:buffersize**—Overrides the default transfer buffer size of 4096K.

If you use FTP in a command-interpreter mode, some of the more frequently used options are as follows:

➤ **ascii**—Instructs FTP to treat all transferred files as text.

➤ **binary**—Instructs FTP to treat all transferred files as binary.

➤ **cd**—Changes directories on the remote system. This command functions in much the same way as the DOS **cd** command.

> *Note: If you are using a system that allows spaces in directory names, such as NT, then you must enclose the directory name in quotes.*

➤ **close** or **quit**—Disconnects from a remote system.

➤ **debug**—Turns on debugging commands, which can be useful in diagnosing problems.

➤ **get**—Copies a file from the remote host to your local computer.

➤ lcd—Changes directories on the local system. This command also functions in much the same way as the DOS **cd** command.

➤ ls—Obtains a directory listing on a remote system, much like the **dir** command in DOS.

➤ open—Specifies the remote system to which you connect.

➤ put—Copies a file from your local computer to the remote host.

For the exam, know the basic commands used (e.g., **put** and **get**) with each client (e.g., FTP, Telnet). Know that to place a single file on an FTP site, you use the **put** command. To place multiple files on an FTP site, you can use the **mput** command. To retrieve a single file from an FTP site, use **get**. To retrieve multiple files, use **mget**.

Note: An alternative to FTP—if both the local and remote systems are Unix—is the RCP (Remote Copy) utility.

Configuring The FTP Service

There are as many utilities available for configuring the FTP service on a server as there are FTP flavors. Although they differ slightly in the way they look, most offer the same feature set. For this reason, Internet Information Server (IIS) 4 (shown in Figure 8.2) is used as an example for the following discussion.

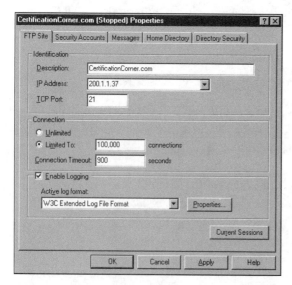

Figure 8.2 Many parameters can be set to customize an FTP site, as shown in Microsoft's Internet Information Server 4.

In this implementation, the parameters are divided into five tabs, each containing specific information about the site. Each tab is discussed in the paragraphs that follow.

FTP Site Tab

The FTP Site tab allows you to change the description (name) of the FTP site, the IP address, and the TCP port. As has been previously mentioned, port 21 is the default TCP port. If you change the port number, it prevents the service from being used by those who do not know and who reference it by the new port number, thus making it hidden. Additional settings on this tab allow you to specify a number of seconds for a connection timeout and limit the number of connections allowed (if bandwidth is an issue; the default is limited to 1,000 connections).

You can also enable logging, and you can choose for the log files to be created in a number of different time period formats. The way in which log files will be created governs the name of the log files created. (The name always consists of some combination of variables.)

Security Accounts Tab

The Security Accounts tab enables you to allow or prohibit anonymous access and to define which NT user accounts have operator privileges. You can also choose to allow only anonymous connections and enable automatic password synchronization.

Implementing security is a two-step process. You cannot configure anonymous access until you have first enabled anonymous access.

Messages Tab

The Messages tab allows you to specify a message to be displayed in each of the following circumstances:

➤ When users enter the site

➤ When users exit the site

➤ When users try to enter the site but can't because there are too many users (the maximum number of connections has been reached)

Home Directory Tab

The Home Directory tab lets you specify a home directory in either of two ways:

➤ On this computer (the default)

➤ As a share on another computer

If you are specifying a directory on this computer, you must give the path. If you are specifying a share on another computer, you must give the UNC path (\\server\share). In either scenario, you then assign permissions of Read and/or Write for that directory, and choose if you want to log access. You also must specify whether directory listings should appear in Unix style or MS-DOS style. Unix is the default and should be used in most implementations for maximum compatibility.

Directory Security Tab

The Directory Security tab allows you to configure IP-address and domain-name restrictions. You would normally do this if you want to restrict access to only a select group of computers (such as one or more subnets) or, conversely, prevent a select group from accessing the site.

TFTP

FTP requires user interaction to work; a user must initiate a download or upload in order for the operation to take place. A derivative of FTP is TFTP—Trivial File Transfer Protocol—that works in the absence of user interaction. Instead of using TCP and port 21, TFTP uses UDP (User Datagram Protocol) and port 69.

The feature sets available in FTP are complex, but those in TFTP are simple. Unlike FTP, TFTP can be used only in a command-line mode; no command-interpreter mode is available. The following options are available:

➤ -i—Specifies binary image transfer mode (also called *octet*). In binary image mode, the file is moved literally byte by byte. Use this mode when you're transferring binary files.

➤ get—Transfers the file destination on the remote host to the file source on the local host.

➤ put—Transfers the file source on the local host to the file destination on the remote host.

TFTP service is not available with all operating systems. For example, Windows NT Server does not include such functionality, but third-party TFTP servers are available.

Note: TFTP can be used to download portions of an operating system from a server to diskless workstations.

Gopher

The Gopher service is an antiquated Internet service defined in RFC 1436 and using port 70. Gopher was used to search for and display documents in a hierarchical structure. As the World Wide Web grew in popularity, the concept of a text-based, document-driven service lost favor. Microsoft's Internet Information Server included Gopher services through IIS 2, but then stopped supporting it.

Gopherspace is the buzzword for the collection of documents and directories on a particular server. One of the good features of Gopher was its ability to organize documents by keywords and allow for Boolean queries to be performed. The Gopher Publishing Service (GPS) relied upon clients such as Archie to display its content. Veronica and Jughead are search engines that work with indexes to find content rapidly.

LDAP

The Lightweight Directory Access Protocol (LDAP) is used by a client to access a directory server, an example of which would be Active Directory in Windows 2000. LDAP was defined as an Internet standard in RFCs 1777, 1778, and 1823. Security principles were introduced with RFC 2253.

 The latest version of LDAP is 3. Its nearest competitor is the Name Service Provider Interface (NSPI), which offers much the same functionality.

LDAP is based upon the X.500 Directory Access Protocol (the directory service of OSI), and uses port 389. The *Lightweight* comes from the fact that it was first envisioned as a simple front end to X.500 that does not have all the features.

LDAP is organized into four models, or major sections: information, functional, security, and naming. The information model consists of attributes and values. The functional model allows for searches and updates. The security model allows for authentication and other features. When LDAP is discussed, however, it is most often in reference to the naming model.

Within the LDAP naming model, every item is defined as an object. Objects can be defined in terms of containers and schemas. *Schemas* are the attributes that can be associated with objects. The objects (and object classes), as defined by the X.500 standard, include the following categories:

➤ Alias

➤ Common Name

➤ Country

➤ Domain

➤ Locality

➤ Organization

➤ Organizational Unit

➤ Organizational Unit Name

➤ Person

The position within a directory hierarchy wherein the entity resides constitutes a *distinguished name (DN)*. A *relative distinguished name (RDN)* does not include the entire distinguished name but is relative to the current position in the hierarchy.

For example, suppose that a user has the LDAP distinguished name of **CN=Karl Buhl,CN=Users,DC=MillerTextiles,DC=COM**—read as "Common Name Karl Buhl, beneath Common Name Users, beneath Domain Miller Textiles, under Domain COM." If the focus is currently at **CN=Users**, the user's LDAP relative distinguished name is **Karl Buhl**. If the search is focused at **DC=MillerTextiles**, the user's LDAP relative distinguished name is **CN=Karl Buhl,CN=Users**.

LDAP is not the only directory protocol in existence, but it has the benefit of being an open protocol supported by almost all vendors.

> *Note: Microsoft's Windows 2000 is dependent upon Active Directory in order to offer all of its features. Active Directory, in turn, needs LDAP in order to work.*

Telnet

Telnet is defined in RFC 854 as a remote-terminal-emulation protocol. It provides terminal emulation for DEC VT100, DEC VT52, and TTY terminals. Telnet uses the connection-oriented services of the TCP/IP protocol for communications at port 23. With Telnet, the command to initiate the session is **Telnet**—either by itself or followed by the location to go to (specified as either an IP address or a hostname). To illustrate, all the following are valid ways to begin a session:

```
Telnet
Telnet CertificationCorner.com
Telnet 209.35.186.218
```

The remote host system must be running a Telnet daemon or service, and after a connection is established, you must log on to the server with a valid username and password (plain text) as if you were sitting at the server. If you use the Connect/Remote system option to connect to a remote host, you may be prompted for the information required for a Telnet session:

➤ *Hostname* —The IP address or hostname of the remote host

➤ *Port* —One of the ports supported by the Telnet application

➤ *Terminal type* —VT100, ANSI (TTY), or VT52 (VTNT is also available in Windows 2000)

Telnet provides some security, insofar as access to the remote system requires a username and password, but there is no encryption of any kind. The password and username are sent as clear text, as is your entire terminal session. If you are using Telnet to perform remote administration, there is a potential for the password and/or session to be intercepted by an unwanted user.

There are a number of Telnet executables. Figure 8.3 shows an example from Windows 2000, and Figure 8.4 shows an example from Windows 98. Both are command-line-based, yet Windows 98 offers menus and a more graphical environment than does Windows 2000.

```
C:\WINNT\System32\telnet.exe                                        _ □ ×

Welcome.

login: ds-technical
Password:
Last login: Wed Feb  9 19:14:00 from iq-ind-as010-17
**********************************************************************
Welcome!

machine:   olive.propagation.net

Please abide by the server policies listed below.

  The following items or activities are not allowed on this server.
    * Pirated software, warez or illegal MP3.
    * Porn or adult material or links to them.
    * IRC and IRC bots (BitchX, eggdrop, etc.).
    * Proxys/Port "Bouncers" etc (BNC, shelld)
    * Unsolicited or bulk email sent from the server or referencing a
      domain on the server.
    * Third party chat scripts (para is OK). We provide 2 chat scripts.
    * Minivend daemons require approval and cost extra to run.
    * Any attempt to exploit, undermine, overload or adversely affect
      the system or it's users.
***Any violation of the above will result in loss of access priviledges.***

                    ****Thank you!****
**********************************************************************
olive:~$
```

Figure 8.3   The implementation of Telnet in Windows 2000 offers execution within a command-prompt environment and no graphical features.

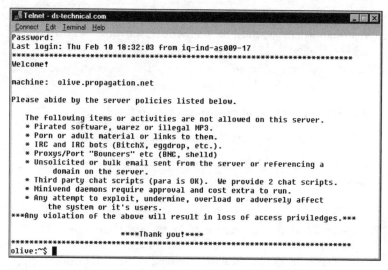

```
Telnet - ds-technical.com                                    _ □ ×
Connect  Edit  Terminal  Help
Password:
Last login: Thu Feb 10 18:32:03 from iq-ind-as009-17
*********************************************************************
Welcome!

machine:  olive.propagation.net

Please abide by the server policies listed below.

   The following items or activities are not allowed on this server.
   * Pirated software, warez or illegal MP3.
   * Porn or adult material or links to them.
   * IRC and IRC bots (BitchX, eggdrop, etc.).
   * Proxys/Port "Bouncers" etc (BNC, shelld)
   * Unsolicited or bulk email sent from the server or referencing a
        domain on the server.
   * Third party chat scripts (para is OK).  We provide 2 chat scripts.
   * Minivend daemons require approval and cost extra to run.
   * Any attempt to exploit, undermine, overload or adversely affect
        the system or it's users.
***Any violation of the above will result in loss of access priviledges.***

                    ****Thank you!****
*********************************************************************
olive:~$ ▮
```

Figure 8.4 The implementation of Telnet in Windows 98 offers a more graphical environment and menu choices.

Within a Telnet session, a limited number of commands are available. The commands include:

➤ **close**—Ends the current connection.

➤ **display**—Shows the values of variables currently in use (TTY, etc.).

➤ **open**—Starts a session.

➤ **quit**—Exits Telnet.

➤ **set**—Changes variable values. Possibilities often include whether both Carriage Returns and Line Feeds will be sent, whether local echo is on or off, etc.

➤ **status**—Shows connection information.

➤ **unset**—Removes variable values.

The ideal use for Telnet is to allow a user to establish a dumb-terminal connection to a server and run processes on the server as if he/she were sitting there instead of at the remote host.

> *Note: Alternatives to Telnet—only if the two machines talking are both Unix—include RSH and REXEC.*

LPR

If you had to pick one item that does not fit with any of the others discussed in this chapter (and on the CompTIA exam), it would be LPR. LPR (Line Printer Request) is the command used to print files to the LPD (Line Printer Daemon) service (in Windows NT/2000) or daemon (in Unix). The remote host system must be running LPD, and you must know the name of the remote host and the printer. This utility has the following command-line options:

➤ **-S server**—Name or IP address of the host providing lpd service

➤ **-P printer**—Name of the print queue

➤ **-C class**—Job classification for use on the burst page

➤ **-J job**—Job name to print on the burst page

➤ **-o option**—Indicates the type of file (by default assumes a text file). Use "-o l" for binary (for example, PostScript) files.

➤ **-x**—Compatibility with SunOS 4.1.x and prior versions

➤ **-d**—Sends data file first

A sample command line would be:

```
lpr -s NTSYSTEM -p NTPRINTER ABC.DAT
```

In this example, ABC.DAT is the file to be printed on the printer named NTPRINTER through the server NTSYSTEM. The system can be specified in a number of ways, including by using a DNS name or IP address.

Several utilities are associated with LPR on most implementations, and the next few sections will look at those utilities.

lpadmin

The lpadmin utility is a standard Unix utility. It's designed to enable an administrator to add and remove printers from the service and to set or change default destinations.

lpusers

The lpusers utility allows you to regulate levels that can be assigned to jobs submitted by users. Levels range from 0 to 39, with 0 having the highest priority and 39 the lowest. In the absence of a priority level, the system default (usually 20) is used.

lpsched

The lpsched utility is *the* daemon managing the print service—the scheduler. It schedules print requests, and it can be started and stopped by the root user only. A number of commands can be used when summoning it, the most important of which are:

➤ **lpmove**—Enables spooled requests to be moved from one destination to another.

➤ **lpshut**—Stops the scheduler. Any printers that are currently printing stop immediately.

lp

An ancestor of LPR, the lp utility exists on most Unix and Linux systems. The lp utility allows you to use a number of parameters when submitting a print job. Among the most important parameters are:

➤ **-c**—Specifies the number of copies of the files to be printed. The default is only the requested copy.

➤ **-d**—Enables you to give a printer destination other than the default printer. If the destination is a class of printers rather than a specific printer, the request is printed on the first available printer in that class.

➤ **-f**—Prints the request on a specified form.

➤ **-H**—Prints the request according to the value of a given variable for special handling.

➤ **-m**—Sends mail to the user after the files have been printed.

➤ **-n**—Prints the given number of copies.

➤ **-o**—Enables you to give options specific for the printer to which the request is going.

➤ **-P**—Prints only the pages specified. You can specify single page numbers or a range of pages. You can use this option only if a filter is available to process it; otherwise, the entire document is printed.

➤ **-q**—Places a priority level in the printing queue, with values ranging from 0 to 39, with 0 being the highest priority.

➤ **-s**—Suppresses return messages to the screen.

➤ **-t**—Prints a given title on the banner page. If this parameter is not used, no title appears.

➤ -w—Writes a message on the terminal after the files have printed. If the requesting user has already logged out, mail is sent to the user's mail file.

lpstat

The lpstat utility prints the status of the line printer operation. If no options are given, the report contains all of a user's requests to lp that are still in the spool.

Comparing The Ports

It is critically important that you know the port numbers for the services discussed in this chapter. Table 8.1 lists the services and protocols covered in this chapter and their associated port numbers.

Table 8.1 The following is a list of common port numbers.	
Port	**Service**
21	FTP
23	Telnet
69	TFTP
70	Gopher
389	LDAP

Practice Questions

Question 1

> The port on which FTP runs by default is:
>
> ○ a. 21
> ○ b. 23
> ○ c. 25
> ○ d. 389

The correct answer is a. FTP runs on port 21 by default. Answer b is incorrect because Telnet runs on port 23. Answer c is incorrect because SMTP runs on port 25. Answer d is incorrect because LDAP runs on port 389.

Question 2

> The command used within FTP to upload multiple files is:
>
> ○ a. **put**
> ○ b. **get**
> ○ c. **mput**
> ○ d. **multi**

Trick! question

The correct answer is c. The **mput** command allows you to post multiple files on a server at one time, while **mget** (not listed here) is used to retrieve multiple files. Answer a is incorrect because **put** is used to upload a single file. Answer b is incorrect because **get** is used to download a single file. Answer d is incorrect because **multi** is an invalid command.

Question 3

> The service that runs, by default, on port 69 is:
>
> ○ a. FTP
> ○ b. TFTP
> ○ c. LDAP
> ○ d. Gopher

The correct answer is b. TFTP runs on port 69. Answer a is incorrect because FTP runs on port 21. Answer c is incorrect because LDAP runs on port 389. Answer d is incorrect because Gopher runs on port 70.

Question 4

Prior to the massive acceptance of the Web, what was a widely used hierarchical method of viewing documents available on the Internet?

○ a. LDAP

○ b. RSH

○ c. RCP

○ d. Gopher

The correct answer is d. Gopher was (and is) used to search for and display documents in a hierarchical structure. Answer a is incorrect because LDAP is a directory service. Answers b and c are incorrect because RSH and RCP are Unix utilities used to start a remote session and transfer files, respectively.

Question 5

LDAP is a lightweight directory service based upon what standard?

○ a. X.25

○ b. X.500

○ c. Telnet

○ d. Gopherspace

The correct answer is b. X.500 is a standard that offers directory services. An-
swer a is incorrect because X.25 is a packet-switching standard. Answer c is incorrect because Telnet is a utility for enabling remote sessions with a host. Answer d is incorrect because gopherspace is the collection of documents and directories on a particular server.

Question 6

> The port on which Telnet runs by default is:
>
> ○ a. 21
>
> ○ b. 23
>
> ○ c. 25
>
> ○ d. 389

The correct answer is b. By default, Telnet runs on port 23. Answer a is incorrect because FTP runs on port 21. Answer c is incorrect because SMTP runs on port 25. Answer d is incorrect because LDAP runs on port 389.

Question 7

> The Telnet command used to start a session is:
>
> ○ a. **start**
>
> ○ b. **begin**
>
> ○ c. **open**
>
> ○ d. **set**

The correct answer is c. The **open** command is used to start a session. Answers a and b are incorrect because Telnet doesn't have **start** or **begin** commands. Answer d is incorrect because the **set** command is used to change the value of variables.

Question 8

> The port on which LDAP runs by default is:
>
> ○ a. 21
>
> ○ b. 23
>
> ○ c. 25
>
> ○ d. 389

The correct answer is d. By default, LDAP runs on port 389. Answer a is incorrect because FTP runs on port 21. Answer b is incorrect because Telnet runs on port 23. Answer c is incorrect because SMTP runs on port 25.

Question 9

The utility used to submit a print job across TCP/IP is:

○ a. LPR

○ b. PRINT

○ c. REXEC

○ d. RSH

The correct answer is a. The LPR utility allows print jobs to be printed on TCP/IP. Answer b is incorrect because **PRINT** is not a valid utility within TCP/IP. Answers c and d are incorrect because REXEC and RSH can be used in place of Telnet on Unix systems.

Question 10

You wish to print a file named velez.txt across TCP/IP. It is to be printed to the printer NICK through the server LODE. The correct command to perform this would be:

○ a. **lpr -s -p VELEZ.TXT NICK LODE**

○ b. **lpr VELEZ.TXT -s NICK -p LODE**

○ c. **lpr -s NICK -p LODE VELEZ.TXT**

○ d. **lpr -s LODE -p NICK VELEZ.TXT**

The correct answer is d. The other choices have incorrect syntax for the LPR utility.

Need To Know More?

 Dulaney, Emmett, Vijay Sankar, and Sharon Sankar. *Integrating Unix and NT Technology: The Definitive Guide.* 29th Street Press, Loveland, CO, 1999. ISBN: 1-882419-84-7. Chapter 12 focuses on TCP/IP printing and the utilities available for it.

 Howes, Tim and Mark Smith. *LDAP: Programming Directory-Enabled Applications with Lightweight Directory Access Protocol.* Macmillan Technical Publishing, Indianapolis, IN, 1997. ISBN: 1-57870-000-0. Although focused on LDAP version 2, this book offers great depth on the LDAP API.

 http://src.doc.ic.ac.uk/computing/internet/rfc/rfc1350.txt— The full RFC for the TFTP protocol.

 www.cis.ohio-state.edu/htbin/rfc/rfc2060.html—The RFC covering IMAP and all aspects of it.

 www.scit.wlv.ac.uk/~jphb/comms/ftp.html—A guide to the File Transfer Protocol (FTP).

 www.uic.edu/depts/accc/inform/docs/vftp.html—An abstract on transferring files between computers with FTP.

 www.webteacher.org/winnet/telnet/telnet.html—An online tutorial on the workings of Telnet.

Programming Languages

Terms you'll need to understand:

√ API (application programming interface)

√ ISAPI (Internet Server API)

√ DLL (Dynamic Link Library)

√ SQL (Structured Query Language)

√ ODBC (Open Database Connectivity)

√ SAPI (Speech API)

√ CGI (Common Gateway Interface)

√ Java

√ Perl (Practical Extraction and Report Language)

√ XML (Extensible Markup Language)

√ VRML (Virtual Reality Modeling Language)

√ ASP (Active Server Page)

√ JavaScript

√ JScript

√ VBScript

Techniques you'll need to master:

√ Understanding the differences between server-side processing and client-side processing

√ Recognizing the basics of several languages

In this chapter, you'll learn the basics of Internet programming and walk through an overview of various options. The main advantages and disadvantages of each programming language will be addressed as well.

Languages And Scripts

In the previous chapter, we mentioned the fine line between services and protocols; a similar situation exists between programming languages and scripts. To use an example, for twenty-some years, Unix was one of the most robust operating systems you could purchase. If it needed to be done, and if it needed to be scalable, Unix could do it. The operating system itself was largely written in the C language, and almost every flavor included at least one C compiler (and often more) for creating your own executables.

Between the operating system and the user lived a command interpreter, known as a *shell*, and every version of Unix included at least one shell (and often more). With Unix, in addition to writing C programs, you could also write *shell scripts*—files containing commands that could be run automatically by the interpreter. Administrators wanting quick-and-dirty automation could whip out shell scripts in no time and edit them on the fly. Administrators wanting robust executables that would not change often could learn the C language and compile such utilities.

The key points here are that there has almost always been more than one way to write something that can give you the results you need—which way is better almost always depends on the setting in question. The C language not only can be used to write executables, but also is robust enough to write the entire operating system in. The shell script has limited functionality and represents a subset of what can be done with the programming language.

Over time, Unix has been joined by other operating systems now able to keep up with its features and functionality. C—still an excellent programming language—has been joined by others that offer similar features but deviate in some way (easier to use, quicker to compile, etc.). Shell scripting has ballooned with Internet technologies, and the interpreter used now is most often not the command interpreter of the operating system, but the browser.

In a nutshell, programming languages:

➤ Require a great deal of training to learn and master

➤ Require the end result to be compiled

➤ Offer a vast array of features

In contrast, scripting languages:

➤ Are usually simple to learn

➤ Are not compiled and require interpretation by a browser or an add-in

➤ Have fewer features than a programming language

Programming Terminology

For the i-Net+ exam, you'll need to be familiar with a number of programming terms and tools. In the next four sections, we will look at several of these: APIs, DLLs, SQL, and SAPI. All differ in their purpose and functionality, and should be well understood for the exam.

API

The *application programming interface (API)* is a feature of most operating systems. APIs are sets of routines, or functions, that programmers can use to interact with the operating system or application. One of the most widely known APIs is the WIN32 API used by most of the current Microsoft operating systems. Programmers who write to it can create programs that run in Windows 95, Windows 98, Windows NT 4, and so on. How the programmer chooses to interact with the API—through Visual Basic, C, C++, or another language—is entirely up to the programmer, and the API makes the same functionality available to all programming languages.

WIN32 API is used for accessing the functionality of the operating system, but within the Internet world, the Microsoft API to use is ISAPI (Internet Server Application Programming Interface). ISAPI is a Microsoft improvement over CGI (Common Gateway Interface) scripting (discussed later in this chapter). ISAPI offers better performance than CGI because applications are loaded into memory at server runtime. This means that they require less overhead and that each request does *not* start a separate process. ISAPI works with OLE (Object Linking and Embedding) connectivity and the Internet Database Connector. ISAPI is implemented as a DLL on the server, and allows:

➤ Pre-processing of requests

➤ Post-processing of responses

➤ Site-specific handling of HTTP requests and responses

DLL

A *dynamic link library (DLL)* file is a library of routines—used in Microsoft operating systems—that can be summoned to perform an operation. DLLs are closely related to APIs, but differ in important ways.

First, there is one WIN32 API for communicating with the operating system, and there is one ISAPI for Internet Server. There are, however, hundreds or thousands of DLLs. Although Microsoft created the APIs in question, any vendor can create (or enhance) a DLL.

Second, APIs do not change with any regularity. DLLs change very regularly. As mentioned earlier, anyone can add functionality to a DLL and enhance what is there. Figure 9.1 shows an example of DLLs running on a Windows 98 machine.

Here's an example of why DLLs exist: A common task on an operating system is to examine how much memory exists on a machine. It would be inefficient to require every programmer to start from scratch every time this task needs to be done and to write all the necessary actions. DLLs allow programmers to incorporate in their programs calls that access the library holding the routines to do this task. Using DLLs makes the results much more uniform and the programmer much more efficient. Drivers and executables depend upon DLLs to provide functionality that can be accessed, making programming much easier.

SQL

The *Structured Query Language (SQL)* is used to interact with relational databases. Databases can be either flat (everything existing within a single file) or

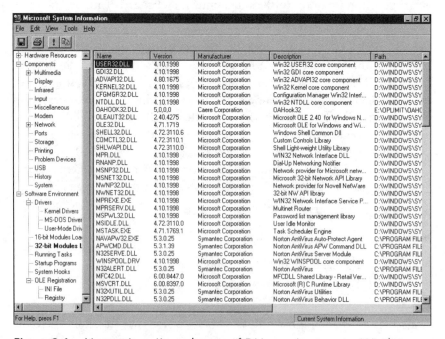

Figure 9.1   At any given time, dozens of DLLs are in use on a Windows-based system.

relational (pointers to data exist within multiple tables). Databases have been around since the early days of computing, and Web servers have been around for a number of years. What is new in the past few years is the integration of the two to create the dynamic Web sites expected today. Databases can supply information to fulfill queries, update information, and add new data through the Web.

For communication to occur between a Web server and a SQL server, something must provide a pathway. Open Database Connectivity (ODBC) is an API that provides a simple way to connect requests to a database (whether that database is Microsoft's SQL or any ODBC-compliant database). ODBC was designed by Microsoft to address the issue of any number of applications needing to interface with SQL server. The greatest advantage of ODBC is that it offers a clear distinction between the application and the database, and thus does not require any specific programming. To use it, you create a query and a template for how the output is to look.

SAPI

The *Speech API (SAPI)* is used to provide telephony and voice functionality to the operating system. Programs are written for SAPI in the same manner as for any other API. SAPI requires the presence of needed peripherals (speakers, microphone, etc.).

Server Languages

Programming can be done so that processing takes place on the server or on the client, and both approaches have benefits. When processing takes place on the server, the client receives only what is to be displayed and can often treat it as it would treat regular HTML—you can't view the source code from the browser. The downside to this, however, is that a server can quickly become overwhelmed on a popular site if it must do extensive processing for every client.

In this section, we will look at a number of languages intended to run on the server—known as *server-side solutions*. A similar look at client languages comes later in the chapter.

CGI

The *Common Gateway Interface (CGI)* is one of the first languages to be closely integrated with HTTP and HTML. CGI runs strictly on the server machine, using only variables that exist there. The calls to CGI can be written in almost anything from shell scripts to C, Perl, or Visual Basic.

While ISAPI works only with Microsoft operating systems, CGI works with all operating systems. CGI runs more slowly than ISAPI, however, because every request creates a new process—making it far more processor-intensive.

The following is an example of a CGI script written to run in Perl and to keep track of the number of users hitting a site:

```
#!/usr/bin/perl
#
#    COUNTER.CGI
#
#    This counter script is meant to be used for a site-wide setup,
# although it can certainly be used by individuals if they want
# counters on their own pages.
#
#    For an explanation of how this script works and how to make
# sure it will work with your server, see:
# http://web.sau.edu/~mkruse/www/info/ssi.html
#
#    To install this script:
# 1. Move it to its own directory, like /cgi-bin/counters/
#    It will create many files in the directory where it is
# located, so put  it somewhere off on its own.
# 2. Make it executable (chmod a+x counter.cgi).
# 3. Make the directory where it is at world-writable (so the
# server can update the counter files).
# That's it!
# Call it as you would any other server-side-include.
#

print "Content-type: text/html\n\n";
($PAGE = $ENV{'DOCUMENT_URI'}) =~ s/\//_/g;
if (!(-e $PAGE)){open(NEW,"> $PAGE");print NEW "0";close(NEW);
_exit(0); }
open(COUNTER,"+< $PAGE");
flock(COUNTER,2);
$_=<COUNTER>;
seek(COUNTER,0,0);
$_++; print; print COUNTER;
flock(COUNTER,8);
close(COUNTER);
```

Java

When Java was created by Sun Microsystems, the original intent was to create a dynamic, object-oriented, multithreading language that programmers could use to develop applications across heterogeneous platforms. Java can be used to create standalone applications and browser applets.

With Java, source code files have the .java extension and are compiled into *bytecode*—files with a .class extension. The compiled programs can be run on almost any platform as long as there is a Java Virtual Machine (interpreter) installed. Common uses for Java include:

➤ Adding controls to a form

➤ Adding animated graphics

➤ Adding non-animated graphics such as charts and diagrams

➤ Creating self-contained applications

The current version of Java is Java 2, version 1.2.2, and the development kit is available for Linux and most other operating systems. Prior to version 1.2, the development environment was known as the Java Development Kit (JDK), while it is now known as the Software Development Kit (SDK).

Perl

The Practical Extraction and Report Language (Perl) was created, as the name implies, to process text. Created by Larry Wall, it is now commonly used to create scripts, most often of the CGI variety.

Perl5 is the latest version, and it is available for almost every operating system. The syntax is a mix between C and shell scripting (with some awk—a Unix utility—tossed in as well). An example, cgi-lib.pl, is shown below:

```
#!/usr/local/bin/perl

# Perl Routines to Manipulate CGI input
# S.E.Brenner@bioc.cam.ac.uk
# $Header: /cys/people/seb1005/http/cgi-bin/RCS/cgi-lib.pl,
# v 1.7 1994/11/04 00:17:17 seb1005 Exp $
#
# Copyright 1994 Steven E. Brenner
# Unpublished work.
# Permission granted to use and modify this library so long as the
# copyright above is maintained, modifications are documented, and
# credit is given for any use of the library.
#
# Thanks are due to many people for reporting bugs and suggestions
# especially Meng Weng Wong, Maki Watanabe, Bo Frese Rasmussen,
# Andrew Dalke, Mark-Jason Dominus and Dave Dittrich.

# see http://www.seas.upenn.edu/~mengwong/forms/  or
#   http://www.bio.cam.ac.uk/web/ for more information
```

```
# Minimalist http form and script
# (http://www.bio.cam.ac.uk/web/minimal.cgi):
# if (&MethGet) {
#   print &PrintHeader,
#     '<form method=POST><input type="submit">Data:
#   <input name="myfield">';
# } else {
#   &ReadParse(*input);
#   print &PrintHeader, &PrintVariables(%input);
# }


# MethGet
# Return true if this cgi call was using the GET request,
# false otherwise. Now that cgi scripts can be put in the normal
# file space, it is useful to combine both the form and the script
# in one place with GET used to retrieve the form, and POST used
# to get the result.

sub MethGet {
  return ($ENV{'REQUEST_METHOD'} eq "GET");
}

# ReadParse
# Reads in GET or POST data, converts it to unescaped text,
# and puts one key=value in each member of the list "@in"
# Also creates key/value pairs in %in, using '\0' to separate
# multiple selections

# If a variable-glob parameter (e.g., *cgi_input) is passed to
# ReadParse,information is stored there, rather than in
# $in, @in, and %in.

sub ReadParse {
  local (*in) = @_ if @_;


  local ($i, $loc, $key, $val);

  # Read in text
  if ($ENV{'REQUEST_METHOD'} eq "GET") {
   $in = $ENV{'QUERY_STRING'};
  } elsif ($ENV{'REQUEST_METHOD'} eq "POST") {
   read(STDIN,$in,$ENV{'CONTENT_LENGTH'});
  }
```

```perl
@in = split(/&/,$in);

foreach $i (0 .. $#in) {
 # Convert plus's to spaces
 $in[$i] =~ s/\+/ /g;

 # Split into key and value.
 ($key, $val) = split(/=/,$in[$i],2); # splits on the first =.

 # Convert %XX from hex numbers to alphanumeric
 $key =~ s/%(..)/pack("c",hex($1))/ge;
 $val =~ s/%(..)/pack("c",hex($1))/ge;

 # Associate key and value
 $in{$key} .= "\0" if (defined($in{$key})); # \0 is the
multiple separator
 $in{$key} .= $val;

}

 return 1; # just for fun
}

# PrintHeader
# Returns the magic line which tells WWW that we're an HTML doc

sub PrintHeader {
 return "Content-type: text/html\n\n";
}

# PrintVariables
# Formats variables in an associative array passed as a parameter
# And returns the HTML string.

sub PrintVariables {
 local (%in) = @_;
 local ($old, $out, $output);
 $old = $*; $* =1;
 $output .= "<DL COMPACT>";
 foreach $key (sort keys(%in)) {
  foreach (split("\0", $in{$key})) {
   ($out = $_) =~ s/\n/<BR>/g;
   $output .= "<DT><B>$key</B><DD><I>$out</I><BR>";
  }
 }
 $output .= "</DL>";
 $* = $old;
```

```
  return $output;
}

# PrintVariablesShort
# Formats variables in an associative array passed as a parameter
# Using one line per pair (unless value is multiline)
# And returns the HTML string.


sub PrintVariablesShort {
  local (%in) = @_;
  local ($old, $out, $output);
  $old = $*; $* =1;
  foreach $key (sort keys(%in)) {
   foreach (split("\0", $in{$key})) {
     ($out = $_) =~ s/\n/<BR>/g;
     $output .= "<B>$key</B> is <I>$out</I><BR>";
   }
  }
  $* = $old;

  return $output;
}

1; #return true
```

C And C++

The C programming language was first developed at Bell Labs by Dennis Ritchie and Brian Kernighan (both of whom were also instrumental in the creation of Unix). C is a high-level programming language that is widely respected for its ability to use less memory than most other languages.

C++ was also developed at Bell Labs, but by Bjarne Stroustrup, with the intent of adding objects and object-orientation to C. C++ is a superset of C in that all programs written for C will run in C++, while not all programs written in C++ will run in C.

Visual Basic

Created by Microsoft, Visual Basic is a derivative of the Basic programming language. Heavy on graphics and objects, Visual Basic allows programs to be quickly developed using controls and event-driven methodology. Visual Basic is not as robust or as object-oriented as other programming languages, but the amount of knowledge needed to create a program is minimal; thus, it is often used when a quick solution or a prototype is needed.

The latest version of Visual Basic is 6, but a newer version should be out in 2001. Visual Basic is now a part of a larger package offered by Microsoft: Visual Studio. Visual Studio contains a number of languages and components to meet as many development needs as possible.

XML

The eXtensible Markup Language (XML) was designed by the World Wide Web Consortium (W3C) to add more functionality to HTML. XML can show data in a browser without the program that originally produced it (think spreadsheets, tables within a word processor, etc.). The files are text-based but not as readable as HTML.

One of the most common uses for XML is to add more than one link to an object—something HTML cannot do. Following is an example of an XML document that adds icons and other items to a table originally created in a word processor:

```
<xml xmlns:o="urn:schemas-microsoft-com:office:office">
 <o:MainFile HRef="../testpro.html"/>
 <o:File HRef="image001.gif"/>
 <o:File HRef="image002.gif"/>
 <o:File HRef="image003.gif"/>
 <o:File HRef="image004.png"/>
 <o:File HRef="image005.jpg"/>
 <o:File HRef="image006.gif"/>
 <o:File HRef="image007.gif"/>
 <o:File HRef="image008.gif"/>
 <o:File HRef="image009.gif"/>
 <o:File HRef="image010.gif"/>
 <o:File HRef="image011.png"/>
 <o:File HRef="image012.jpg"/>
 <o:File HRef="image013.png"/>
 <o:File HRef="image014.jpg"/>
 <o:File HRef="image015.png"/>
 <o:File HRef="image016.jpg"/>
 <o:File HRef="image017.gif"/>
 <o:File HRef="image018.png"/>
 <o:File HRef="image019.jpg"/>
 <o:File HRef="filelist.xml"/>
 </xml>
```

VRML

The Virtual Reality Modeling Language (VRML) is used to create a three-dimensional display within the browser via a VRML plug-in. Files, which have a .wrl extension, define the object as you move throughout the virtual world.

VRML was originally created by Tony Parisi and Mark Pesce; the latest specification is VRML 2.

Within VRML, you start with a world and define your constraints; then you add objects. The objects are defined in terms of geometry (shape) and qualities (such as colors). A coordinate system is used to define height, width, and depth.

ASP

Active Server Pages (ASP), like many things, originated at Microsoft. ASP simplifies server-side programming and offers support for ActiveX objects (a Microsoft phenomenon), for HTML tags, and for all ActiveX scripting commands.

The .asp extension is assigned to all ASP scripts, and the files include text, HTML tags, and ASP script commands. HTML tags begin with "<" and end with ">"; ASP tags begin with "<%" and end with "%>". The tags are also known as *delimiters*, and it is the delimiters that signal the server that processing is required at that point. For example:

```
It is now <%= Time %>
```

will appear as:

```
It is now 14:52:10
```

The easiest way to create ASP files is to start with standard HTML files and add the script commands to them (as well as change the file extensions from .htm to .asp). Active Server Pages can be used with VBScript, JScript, PerlScript, or any other recognized scripting language. Not only can you use a variety of languages, but you can also use multiple languages within the same script. The syntax for doing so is:

```
<SCRIPT LANGUAGE="VBScript" RUNAT=SERVER>
routine
</SCRIPT>
<SCRIPT LANGUAGE="PerlScript" RUNAT=SERVER>
routine
</SCRIPT>
```

In addition to defining variables by an operation (such as DATE or TIME), you can set variables and refer to them within the scripts. Variables are set with the **SET** command, and the variables are referred to in a manner similar to the way the **Time** variable was in the example (It is now <%= Time %>). You can also create an array of data to refer to by using the **Session** variable, which is unique for the life of the session. For example:

```
Session ("City") = "Anderson"
Set Session ("State") = "IN"
How is the weather in <%= Session("City") %>?
```

will appear as:

```
How is the weather in Anderson?
```

As mentioned above, the **Session** variables are kept for the entire duration of the session and are abandoned afterward. To force the purging of the variables, you can use the **Session.Abandon** call. This will remove the variables and end the session.

Client Scripts And Other Solutions

Earlier, we examined programming solutions that run on the server. Their biggest drawback is that they can overwhelm a server if too many requests occur at the same time. An alternative is to use scripting where the processing occurs on the client machine—distribute the load, so to speak. The biggest benefit, of course, is the lessened load on the server. The biggest drawback is that the client sees the code coming down (view, source) and the client must be able to carry out the processing.

Three scripting languages are commonly used for processing on the client: JavaScript, JScript, and VBScript.

JavaScript is a derivative of Java that runs within HTML. The syntax for calling a JavaScript is:

```
<HTML>
<HEAD>
<SCRIPT LANGUAGE="JavaScript">
routine
</SCRIPT>
</HEAD>
</HTML>
```

The **<SCRIPT></SCRIPT>** tags are used to identify the starting and stopping locations of the commands to be processed—represented here by *routine*. Rather than including the commands directly in the HTML file, you can place the commands in another file, and call that file from the HTML file by using the **SRC=** attribute, as shown here:

```
<HTML>
<HEAD>
<SCRIPT LANGUAGE="JavaScript" SRC="MyStuff.js"> </SCRIPT>
</HEAD>
</HTML>
```

Both methods work well; the only advantage of the latter is that you can up-date the code without having to touch the HTML file.

JScript is Microsoft's version of JavaScript. Microsoft began with the original Java specifications and added commands and functionality.

 Although this is always a source for debate, for the exam consider JScript to be not pure Java and thus not capable of running in all browsers.

VBScript is a scripting language based upon Visual Basic. VBScript can be used to summon processing on the server or on the client, and it depends upon Internet Explorer for complete functionality.

Comparing The Options

This chapter examined a great many abbreviations and languages. To review, let's put everything into bite-sized chunks, in alphabetical order. For the exam, you'll need to know the following:

➤ *API*—Application programming interfaces are the building blocks by which software applications are built by programmers.

➤ *ASP*—Active Server Pages run only on the Windows NT platform. They can be processed on the server (which sends back pure HTML) and on the client (which processes them within the browser, but they can be viewed in Source.)

➤ *C*—A programming language that has been around for almost 30 years, C uses a small amount of resources and can run on most operating systems.

➤ *C++*—The object-oriented counterpart to C. C++ is used for graphical environments and runs on most operating systems.

➤ *CGI*—The Common Gateway Interface is a program/language that runs on servers and provides a means to customize output to the user. CGI is server-based and performs all operations there (versus ActiveX and Java applets, which run on the client). Because a process must be initiated each time the program is run, CGI tends to be server-intensive;

in contrast, ISAPI and other server solutions can avoid spawning a new process with each iteration and are therefore not as intensive on the server.

➤ *Client and server-side scripting*—CGI and ISAPI are examples of server-side scripting; Java applets, Active Server Pages, and ActiveX are examples of client-side scripting. Any execution that occurs within the browser is known as client-side programming, and any execution that occurs before data reaches the browser is known as server-side programming.

➤ *DLL*—Dynamic link libraries are the method by which common executable routines are made available in the Windows-based environment. Drivers and executables depend upon DLLs to provide functionality that can be accessed, making programming much easier.

➤ *Java*—An object-oriented programming language created by Sun Microsystems. Java allows programs to be run in almost every operating system (via a Java Virtual Machine).

➤ *JavaScript*—A scripting language created by Netscape to provide active content on Web sites.

➤ *JScript*—A non-compiled scripting language based on Microsoft's implementation of JavaScript.

➤ *ODBC*—Open Database Connectivity allows a Web server to interact with a SQL server.

➤ *Perl*—Practical Extraction and Report Language is an interpretive language (that is, requiring an interpreter) that can be used to write CGI scripts and perform text-processing tasks.

➤ *SAPI*—The Speech API is used for voice and telephony applications.

➤ *SQL*—The Structured Query Language is used to find and to place information in a database. Using ODBC, the Web server can interact with a SQL server, pull up information (from a catalog database, for example), and post the results in HTML to the user.

➤ *VBScript*—A non-compiled scripting language, based on Visual Basic, that allows controls to be added to Web pages.

➤ *Visual Basic*—A graphical programming language that is event-driven. It typically requires an executable to be compiled before it can run on a user's machine.

➤ *VRML*—Virtual Reality Modeling Language is a plug-in that allows the display of 3D objects within Web browsers.

➤ *XML*—Extensible Markup Language allows multiple HTML links (versus the standard one link). XML is a chopped-down version of SGML (Standard Generalized Markup Language). It is useful for shopping sites and other sites that can have multiple results needed for an action. Many people believe that XML will replace HTML eventually for writing Web pages.

Practice Questions

Question 1

> What file extension is used to signify Active Server Pages?
>
> ○ a. ASP
> ○ b. ACT
> ○ c. API
> ○ d. DLL

The correct answer is a. Active Server Pages require an extension of .ASP. Choice b, .ACT, is an invalid extension. APIs are programming interfaces, and DLLs are dynamic libraries of programming functions.

Question 2

> Which of the following commands would make PerlScript active to process the ASP file?
>
> ○ a. **</SCRIPT="PerlScript">**
> ○ b. **</SCRIPT LANGUAGE="PerlScript">**
> ○ c. **<SCRIPT LANGUAGE="PerlScript">**
> ○ d. **<SCRIPT="PerlScript">**

The correct answer is c. The tag used to summon PerlScript is **<SCRIPT LANGUAGE="PerlScript">**, and the tag used to end it is **</SCRIPT>**. The other choices are invalid.

Question 3

> Because a process must be initiated each time the program is run, _____ tends to be server-intensive, whereas ISAPI and other server solutions are not as server-intensive because they can avoid spawning a new process with each iteration.
>
> ○ a. ASP
>
> ○ b. CGI
>
> ○ c. DLL
>
> ○ d. EXE

The correct answer is b. CGI scripts spawn a new process each time they are run, but ISAPI avoids this. Answer a is incorrect because ASPs are Active Server Pages, which are enhanced HTML and not server-solutions. Answer c is incorrect because DLLs are libraries of routines. Answer d is incorrect because EXEs are compiled applications.

Question 4

> What technology is used to allow interaction between a Web server and a SQL server reading from a database?
>
> ○ a. Perl
>
> ○ b. XML
>
> ○ c. SAPI
>
> ○ d. ODBC

The correct answer is d. ODBC—Open Database Connectivity—is used to allow communication with the SQL server. Answer a is incorrect because Perl is a text-processing language. Answer b is incorrect because XML is used to add multiple links and other options to HTML. Answer c is incorrect because SAPI is the Speech API, used for telephony and voice communications.

Question 5

Which of the following is an example of a server-side solution?

○ a. JavaScript

○ b. ISAPI

○ c. ActiveX

○ d. Java applets

The correct answer is b. ISAPI and CGI are *always* server-side solutions. Answers a and d are incorrect because JavaScript *can* run on the client, as *can* Java applets. Answer c is incorrect because ActiveX runs on the client.

Question 6

Which of the following is a plug-in that allows the display of 3D objects within Web browsers?

○ a. XML

○ b. VRML

○ c. SGML

○ d. CGI

The correct answer is b. The Virtual Reality Modeling Language (VRML) allows you to add three dimensions to an object. Answers a and c are incorrect because XML is an enhancement of HTML and a slimmed-down version of SGML. Answer d is incorrect because CGI is a server-side programming language.

Question 7

Which of the following is a library of routines that can be summoned to perform an operation within Microsoft operating systems?

○ a. VBScript

○ b. SQL

○ c. DLL

○ d. Flat database

The correct answer is c. A DLL is a library of routines that can be summoned to perform an operation within Microsoft operating systems. Answer a is incorrect because VBScript is a scripting language. Answer b is incorrect because SQL is a method of communicating with a relational database. Answer d is incorrect because a flat database is a collection of data (stored in a single table), not a library of routines.

Question 8

CGI commands are most commonly written using which of the following?

○ a. SQL

○ b. CGI editor

○ c. ASCII editor

○ d. Perl

The correct answer is d. Perl is commonly used to write CGI commands. Answer a is incorrect because SQL is used for databases. Answer b is incorrect because there is no such beast as a CGI editor. Answer c is incorrect because, although ASCII editors can be used to write CGI commands, most often they are not because of their lack of features.

Question 9

The extension used for VRML files is which of the following?

○ a. .wrl

○ b. .vrml

○ c. .vrl

○ d. .vrm

The correct answer is a. The .wrl extension is used to signify VRML files. The other choices given are invalid extensions.

Question 10

What extension is used for Java source-code files?

○ a. .pl

○ b. .wrl

○ c. .src

○ d. .java

The correct answer is d. The .java extension is used for Java source-code files. Answer a is incorrect because the .pl extension is used for Perl files. Answer b is incorrect because .wrl is used for VRML files. Answer c is incorrect because the .src extension is not used by Java.

Need To Know More?

 Acosta, Nancy, et al. *Webmaster's Professional Reference.* New Riders Publishing, Indianapolis, IN, 1996. ISBN: 1-56205-473-2. Although the book is somewhat dated, Chapter 19 offers good coverage of the basics of CGI, and Chapter 21 does the same for Java.

 Appleman, Dan. *Dan Appleman's Visual Basic 5.0 Programmer's Guide to the WIN32 API.* Ziff-Davis Press, Emeryville, CA, 1997. ISBN: 1-56276-446-2. The best definition and explanation of the API to be found anywhere, regardless of the language you are using.

 http://devcentral.iftech.com/learning/tutorials/c-cpp/cpp/default.asp—A tutorial on *Understanding C++: An Accelerated Introduction,* by Marshall Brain.

 http://java.sun.com/—*The* home page for Java and all aspects of it.

 http://language.perl.com/faq/—The definitive FAQ for Perl, complete with index and recommended links.

 http://msdn.microsoft.com/vbasic—The Microsoft homepage for Visual Basic.

 www.apl.jhu.edu/~hall/java/FAQs-and-Tutorials.html—An online tutorial on Java programming.

 www.w3.org/XML/—The World Wide Web Consortium's Extensible Markup Language home page.

Hypertext Markup Language (HTML)

Terms you'll need to understand:

√ Hypertext Markup Language (HTML)

√ Tags

√ Attributes

√ Hyperlinks

Techniques you'll need to master:

√ Understanding the Hypertext Markup Language

√ Knowing the importance of creating cross-browser coding

√ Understanding the difference between text editors and graphical editors

√ Understanding the basic HTML document structure

√ Demonstrating the ability to use HTML to create Web pages

In Chapter 6, you were introduced to Hypertext Markup Language (HTML). This chapter focuses on HTML because the i-Net+ exam will require you to demonstrate the ability to use HTML to create Web pages. Luckily, you will not be required to construct an entire Web page, but you will be required to identify the proper HTML code for a specific situation.

HTML provides a method for formatting text and other elements to be properly displayed by a Web browser. An HTML document displayed by a Web browser is also simply referred to as a Web page. A Web page, however, can consist not only of an HTML file but also of graphics and other elements, usually located in various directories on a Web server. The Web page is identified by a Uniform Resource Locator (URL) and typically contains links to other Web pages, both internally and externally. That is, Web pages may link internally to other documents located on the same server, or they can link externally to documents located on another server in the same company or anywhere on the Internet.

Tags And Attributes

Before beginning any HTML coding, you need to understand *tags* and *attributes*. An HTML document is coded primarily with tags (words bracketed by "<" and ">"). These tags are the basis for controlling the way a document is displayed in a Web browser.

Most tags come in pairs—they have a beginning tag and an ending tag, as in <**BODY**> and </**BODY**>. (Notice the slash in the ending tag.) In fact, HTML is much like formatting text within an old word-processing program, many of which required the use of "code" to format the document—for example, by placing a <**B**> before and after a word that you wanted to be bold.

Attributes define the tag or modify it to behave in a certain manner (written usually as **name**=*"value"*). For example, if you were to describe an individual, you might say the person is a man. Next, you might describe his attributes, such as his brown eyes or big, furry eyebrows. In HTML, for example, you might define a table and assign various attributes such as a border size or background color to be applied to the table.

Note: The markup for HTML is not case sensitive.

Browser Compatibility

The specifications for HTML are constantly changing. The World Wide Web Consortium (W3C) works to develop new HTML standards. In addition, browser vendors develop their own specifications, which are incorporated into the next version of the vendors' browsers before they (perhaps) become new standards. Because of this, it is imperative that you understand the consequences of *not* coding your Web pages to provide support in various browsers.

Naturally, an analysis of your intended audience is the first step in determining how much you should pay attention to the need to support multiple browsers. If, for example, you're developing a Web site for use on your company's internal network (intranet), you may need to worry about providing support for only one browser. If your site is made public on the Web, however, you should pay careful attention to your HTML to ensure that you do not isolate any one group. Even Netscape Navigator and Microsoft Internet Explorer have major differences, and there are many other browsers being used, including text-based browsers, which don't display pictures or other multimedia. Although it is not mandatory that you ensure cross-browser compatibility, you should at least be aware of these issues. If your site's purpose is to sell digital photographs, for example, you may not be concerned about those people using text-based browsers.

Visit the World Wide Web Consortium (W3C) at **www.w3c.org** to view the latest developments on HTML and other emerging standards, such as Extensible Hypertext Markup Language (XHTML). The W3C is dedicated to the development of open Web standards, such as HTML, to promote interoperability and to help the Web achieve its potential. The organization is led by Tim Berners-Lee, the creator of the Web.

Although not every tag is supported in every browser, it is important to remember that browsers will ignore any unrecognized tags and attributes. Fortunately, visitors can still view your page without errors, but they won't see the page in the way you had originally intended.

While you're constructing a Web page, it may be beneficial to constantly preview your page through as many different browsers as you can, or at least those that you believe your primary audience will be using.

Finally, keep in mind that browsers may have unique names for the various controls. For example, you may be tempted to tell visitors to add your page to their "Favorites folder," but this is a term used by Microsoft Internet Explorer; a browser such as Netscape Navigator uses the term "Bookmark file."

Whenever possible, use generic terms when instructing users to interact with their browsers because not all browsers use the same terminology for their commands and controls.

A new specification called Extensible Markup Language (XML) is being developed by the W3C. XML is an abbreviated version of the Standard Generalized Markup Language (SGML). With HTML (an application of SGML), the W3C and browser vendors are continually extending the definition of HTML in order to provide new tags. In contrast, XML provides a method for developers to define and create customized tags. In essence, XML is not a predefined markup language like HTML—it is actually a metalanguage used to define your own markup language.

Choosing An Editor

Many Web pages are created using a Web-page editor, which is simply a software program used to create and modify HTML documents. There are many types of editors on the market. In fact, Microsoft Internet Explorer and Netscape Navigator both come with their own HTML editors; furthermore, Windows comes with a simple editor, Notepad, which can also be used to create Web pages.

Although Notepad is nothing more than a plain text editor, it works just fine for coding HTML documents. Unfortunately, while you're creating the page, a plain text editor does not allow you to see the page as it will appear in the browser. A GUI (graphical user interface) editor, on the other hand, offers loads of features specifically geared for creating Web pages. These editors save time by providing WYSIWYG (what you see is what you get) capability, which provides immediate visual feedback. Additionally, the Web designer can use the toolbar buttons and menus to easily format the page without having to insert HTML tags.

There are basically two types of editors used to create Web pages. A text editor requires that you code the entire site by hand using HTML, and a Web-page editor uses wizards, toolbars, menus, and other graphical features, which make it easy to develop a Web page using WYSIWYG capabilities.

So, why even learn HTML in the first place? There are several reasons for learning the actual code (the most important being that it's required to pass the i-Net+ exam). In fact, even most WYSIWYG editors also provide the option to view and edit the HTML code directly. Although I would most definitely recommend that one learn the ability to code in pure HTML, I wouldn't recommend a tool like Notepad for constructing an entire site. Unless you're one who takes pride in your ability to create an entire site in a text editor, you may find it more convenient to use a graphical HTML editor. Not only do they simplify routine formatting tasks, but they also provide many site-management tools. Yet your knowledge of HTML will allow you to look underneath the hood of your Web page to make any necessary tweaks and minor adjustments. Figure 10.1 shows an example of a page in development using a GUI Web-page editor; Figure 10.2 shows the same page using a text editor.

Common Tags

At a bare minimum, a Web page should contain the common tags shown in Listing 10.1.

Listing 10.1   The tags needed to create a basic Web page.

```
<HTML>
<HEAD>
<TITLE> Put a title for the Web page here. </TITLE>
</HEAD>
<BODY> Put the contents of the Web page here. </BODY>
</HTML>
```

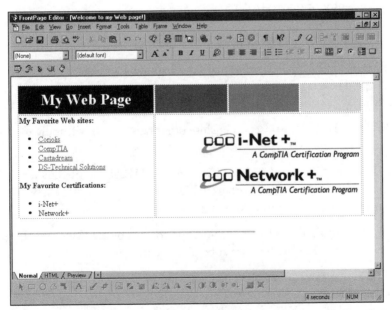

Figure 10.1   Using a GUI Web-page editor to design a Web page lets you avoid using HTML code directly.

```
index - Notepad                                                    _ □ ✕
File  Edit  Search  Help
<HTML>
<HEAD>
<TITLE>Welcome to my Web page!</TITLE>
</HEAD>
<BODY>
<TABLE BORDER="0" WIDTH="1097" HEIGHT="1">
   <TR>
      <TD WIDTH="248" HEIGHT="1" BGCOLOR="#000000" VALIGN="middle" ALIGN="center"><H1><FONT
      COLOR="#FFFFFF">My Web Page</FONT></H1>
      </TD>
      <TD WIDTH="131" HEIGHT="1" BGCOLOR="#535353"></TD>
      <TD WIDTH="127" HEIGHT="1" BGCOLOR="#838383"></TD>
      <TD WIDTH="111" HEIGHT="1" BGCOLOR="#E0E0E0"></TD>
      <TD WIDTH="350" HEIGHT="123" ROWSPAN="2"></TD>
   </TR>
   <TR>
      <TD WIDTH="273" HEIGHT="1"><H4>My Favorite Web sites:</H4>
      <UL>
        <LI><A HREF="http://www.coriolis.com">Coriolis</A>
        <LI><A HREF="http://www.comptia.org">CompTIA</A>
        <LI><A HREF="http://www.castadream.com">Castadream</A>
        <LI><A HREF="http://ds-technical.com">DS-Technical Solutions</A>
      </UL>
      <H4>My Favorite Certifications:</H4>
      <UL>
        <LI>i-Net+
        <LI>Network+
      </UL>
      </TD>
      <TD WIDTH="415" HEIGHT="151" COLSPAN="3" ALIGN="right"><IMG
      SRC="inetlogo.gif" ALT="i-Net+ Logo (2188 bytes)" WIDTH="336"
      HEIGHT="54"><P><IMG SRC="networklogo.gif" alt="Network+ logo (2188 bytes)"
      WIDTH="336" HEIGHT="54"
      <BR>
      </TD>
   </TR>
</TABLE>
<HR WIDTH="67%" ALIGN="left">
</BODY>
</HTML>
```

Figure 10.2 Using a plain text editor to design a Web page requires the entry of only HTML.

To create a simple Web page, you need only these four pairs of tags:

➤ <HTML> </HTML>—Used to mark the beginning and ending of a Web page. These tags identify the document so that it can be interpreted correctly.

➤ <HEAD> </HEAD>—Used to enclose other tags, which will apply to the entire document.

➤ <TITLE> </TITLE>—Contained within the <HEAD> tags. Any text entered between the <TITLE> tags will become the page's title and will appear in the title bar of most browsers.

➤ <BODY> </BODY>—Used to enclose the content of the Web page. In fact, most of the HTML tags must be placed between these two tags.

The <BODY> tag can contain a couple of attributes to specify wallpaper or a background color for your Web page. This is much like displaying wallpaper or a background color on a Windows desktop. To include an image as wallpaper, use the **BACKGROUND** attribute. Use the **BGCOLOR** attribute to define a color either by the standard color name such as "red" or, preferably, by the hexadecimal value for the color. For example, to define a page with a background color of red, use:

```
<BODY BGCOLOR="#FF0000">
```

 Check out **http://hotwired.lycos.com/webmonkey/reference/ color_codes/** for a comprehensive list of colors and their corresponding hexadecimal values.

Adding Comments

To include a comment that will not be displayed by the browser, simply enclose the comment between <!- - and - ->. Use these tags to document your Web page. The following is an example of the use of comment tags:

```
<!--This is a comment. This comment will not appear in the actual
Web page. It will be visible only when you are viewing the source.
-->
```

 The comment tag is used in pairs but is different from most other tags. The beginning tag does not contain a greater-than symbol (>), and the closing tag does not contain a less-than symbol (<) or a slash (/). Remember that the correct format for the comment tag is **<!--** and **-->**.

Formatting Text

Two of the most commonly used tags for formatting text are **<P>**, which is used to begin a paragraph, and **
, which inserts a line break. Neither tag requires an ending tag. Although these tags are similar, using **<P> will leave one blank line, whereas using **
** will insert a line break and start the next line immediately below the previous line.

Other commonly used tags to format text include the **<B>** and **<I>** tags. These tags are used to add emphasis by making text either boldface or italic. For example,

```
<P>This is <B>bold</B> and this is <I>italic</I>
```

would create the following within a Web page:

This is **bold** and this is *italic*

Headings

Just as this book uses varying levels of headings, HTML has several tags that can be used to control the size of headings. The heading tags are used in pairs and include <H1>, <H2>, <H3>, <H4>, <H5>, and <H6>. The largest heading is <H1>, and the smallest is <H6>. Listing 10.2 shows an example of all six headings, and Figure 10.3 shows what the Web page would look like viewed through a browser.

Listing 10.2   Multiple headings in an HTML document.

```
<HTML>
<HEAD><TITLE>Multiple Headings</TITLE></HEAD>
<BODY>
<H1>This is heading level one</H1>
<H2>This is heading level two</H2>
<H3>This is heading level three</H3>
<H4>This is heading level four</H4>
<H5>This is heading level five</H5>
<H6>This is heading level six</H6>
</BODY>
</HTML>
```

Special Characters

To include special (non-alphanumeric) characters within the text of a Web page, you can use the designated character entities. For example, suppose that

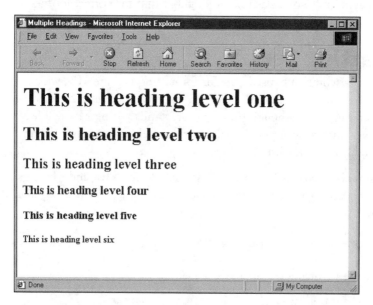

Figure 10.3   <H1> through <H6> heading tags used on a Web page.

you want to include a greater-than symbol (>) within the text of your Web page. As you already know, this symbol is used to code HTML tags; therefore, trying to actually make this symbol appear on your Web page may present a problem. The greater-than symbol and other special characters use a *character entity code* composed of a name or number.

A character entity begins with an ampersand (&) and is followed by the name or number of the character and then by a semicolon (;). Either the character entity name or number can be used, but it is probably much easier to remember the name. When you use a number, you must also include the pound sign (#) before the number. Table 10.1 lists many of the commonly used characters and their associated names and numbers.

Remember that a character entity used in HTML will produce the actual character symbol when viewed through a Web browser. The exam is most likely to test you on the character entity names, but it may be a wise idea to memorize the character entity numbers for these common characters.

Lists

To break up and organize text on a Web page, you may want to consider using one of the following types of lists:

➤ Unordered lists

➤ Ordered lists

➤ Definition lists

Figure 10.4 shows the three types of lists used in Web pages. In the following sections, you will see the HTML that is necessary to create these lists.

Table 10.1 These are some character entities used in HTML.		
Character	**Character Entity (Name)**	**Character Entity (Number)**
Less than (<)	&lt;	&#060;
Greater than (>)	&gt;	&#062;
Copyright (©)	&copy;	&#169;
Registered trademark (®)	&reg;	&#174;
Nonbreaking space		

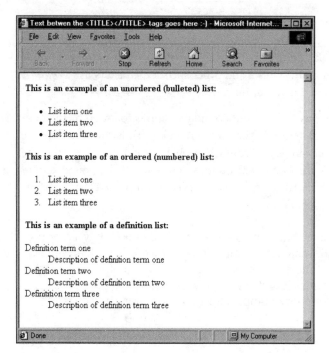

Figure 10.4   Unordered, ordered, and definition lists viewed through a Web browser.

Unordered Lists

Unordered lists, also called *bulleted* lists, are usually used to list items that do not need to be arranged in a particular sequence. In an unordered list, a bullet precedes each item. To create an unordered list, use the <UL> tag to begin the list, use <LI> for each list item, and use </UL> to end the list, as shown in the following example:

```
<UL>
 <LI>Bulleted list item one
 <LI>Bulleted list item two
 <LI>Bulleted list item three
</UL>
```

Note: The <LI> *tag does not require a closing* </LI> *tag.*

Ordered Lists

Ordered lists, also called *numbered* lists, are usually used to arrange items sequentially. In an ordered list, a number precedes each item. The structure for an ordered list is very much like that for an unordered list. The difference between the two is that an ordered list uses the <OL> tag to begin the list and an </OL> tag to end the list. Each list item in an ordered list will also use the <LI> tag. The following example shows the proper use of code for an ordered list:

```
<OL>
 <LI>List item one
 <LI>List item two
 <LI>List item three
</OL>
```

 Make sure you know the difference between an ordered list and an unordered list. Remember that an unordered list presents information in bullets and uses the **<UL>** tag, and an ordered list presents information sequentially, using numerals and the **<OL>** tag.

Definition Lists

Definition lists are usually used to present information in a glossary-like format. A definition list typically lists each definition term followed by an indented description. To create a definition list, use the <DL> tag to begin the list, use <DT> for each definition term, use <DD> for each subsequent definition description, and use </DL> to end the list, as shown in the following example:

```
<DL>
 <DT>Definition term one
 <DD>Definition description one
 <DT>Definition term two
 <DD>Definition description two
 <DT>Definition term three
 <DD>Definition description three
</DL>
```

Note: The <DT> and <DD> tags are not typically required to be used with a closing </DT> or </DD> tag.

Adding Images

Images are used within Web pages for many reasons. You may wish to include an image to grab attention, to establish a theme, or to clarify a concept. Most images in Web pages are either Graphics Interchange Format (GIF) or Joint Photographic Experts Group (JPEG) files. There is, however, another image file format that is gaining popularity and that is designed to take the place of

GIF; this new format is called Portable Network Graphics (PNG). The next chapter discusses multimedia formats in depth.

To insert an image, use the **<IMG>** (image) tag along with the required **SRC** (source) attribute. The **SRC** attribute specifies the picture's name; if the picture is located in a different directory from the HTML document or in another site, the **SRC** attribute also specifies the picture's location. For example, to insert a picture called picture.gif into a Web page, use the following code:

```
<IMG SRC="picture.gif">
```

This code assumes that picture.gif is located in the same directory as the Web page. However, if the image file is stored in a directory called "images", you would use the following:

```
<IMG SRC="images/picture.gif">
```

In the two previous examples, notice that the image file and directory path are enclosed within quotation marks. Additionally, a closing **</IMG>** tag is not required.

Image Attributes

When you are placing an image in the foreground of a Web page, the **SRC** attribute is always required; however, many other attributes can be used with the **<IMG>** tag to control the image.

ALIGN Attributes

The **ALIGN** attribute places an image on the left or right side and also specifies how text should be displayed next to the image. There are five common alignments, which include:

➤ *LEFT*—Places the image on the left side of the page and wraps the text around the right side of the graphic.

➤ *RIGHT*—Places the image on the right side of the page and wraps the text around the left side of the graphic.

➤ *TOP*—Places the image on the left side of the page and places the text even with the top of the graphic.

➤ *MIDDLE*—Places the image on the left side of the page and places the text even with the middle of the graphic.

➤ *BOTTOM*—Places the image on the left side of the page and places the text even with the bottom of the graphic

For example, to insert an image named my_picture.gif with the accompanying text, "This is a picture of me," to the right of the image and aligned with the middle of the picture, use the following code:

```
<IMG SRC="my_picture.gif" ALIGN="middle">This is a picture of me
```

HEIGHT And WIDTH Attributes

The **HEIGHT** and **WIDTH** attributes can be used to define an area in which the image will appear. Although these attributes can be used to stretch and shrink an image, they are best used only to serve as "placeholders" for images. The use of these attributes is not mandatory, but they can improve the overall download speed of your page. To specify the height and width of an image named picture.gif that is 50 pixels high and 30 pixels wide, use the following code:

```
<IMG SRC="picture.gif" HEIGHT="50" WIDTH="30">
```

BORDER Attribute

The **BORDER** attribute is used to put a border, with a specified size in pixels, around images. If you are finding that a border is automatically appearing around your images, and you don't want it to, you may want to ensure that your border size is set to zero. To place a border four pixels wide around an image named picture.gif, use the following code:

```
<IMG SRC="picture.gif" BORDER="4">
```

HSPACE And VSPACE Attributes

The **HSPACE** and **VSPACE** attributes can be used to control the amount of space around an image. Basically, these attributes place a buffer between the graphic and any other elements. The **HSPACE** attribute defines horizontal space to the right or left of the image, and the **VSPACE** attribute defines vertical space above and below the image. To insert an image named picture.gif that has a horizontal 50-pixel buffer and a vertical 25-pixel buffer, use the following code:

```
<IMG SRC="picture.gif" HSPACE="50" VSPACE="25">
```

ALT Attribute

The **ALT** attribute provides an alternate description for an image. Although this attribute is not mandatory, it is highly recommended that you use this attribute with all of your graphics. By using the **ALT** attribute, you can:

➤ Specify text that appears in the place of an image when a browser cannot support images.

➤ Specify text that appears in the place of an image when a user has set the browser for a text-only display.

➤ Specify text that appears while a picture is being downloaded to a user.

➤ Make your site accessible to impaired users who must use special software to read the text from the screen.

For example, assume that you use a graphic file for your company's logo on your Web page. If your company's name is Domain.com and the graphic image is named logo.gif, you might use the following code:

```
<IMG SRC="logo.gif" ALT="Welcome to Domain.com">
```

Although this tag will typically display your company's logo, the text "Welcome to Domain.com" will appear in the logo's place if the user has the graphics display turned off or is viewing your page through a text-only browser.

Adding Hyperlinks

This is the part that actually makes HTML *hyper*. A hyperlink can be text or an image and is also referred to as simply a *link* or *hypertext* (for text). It is these links that have helped launch the popularity of the Web. Several types of links can be created to jump around Web pages. For the i-Net+ exam, in addition to understanding these links, you'll be expected to be able to create a hyperlink to launch a client's mail program to send email.

To create a link, use <**A**> (the anchor tag) to mark text as a hypertext anchor, and use the **HREF** (hypertext reference) attribute to specify the destination. (The anchor is the place you're jumping from [your current position]; the destination is the place you're jumping to.) The basic syntax for a hyperlink is:

```
<A HREF="destination">Text the user will click to go to the
destination</A>
```

The **HREF** attribute indicates the page or the URL that the browser will go to when the user clicks on the anchor. To link to a file in the same directory on the same server, use a *relative* pathname for the **HREF** attribute. For example, to link to an HTML file named page2.htm when a user clicks on "Go to next page," use the following syntax:

```
<A HREF="page2.htm">Go to next page</A>
```

If, however, you want to link to a file on another server, you'll need to enter the *absolute* pathname, which specifies the complete URL. For example, to link to the certification.htm page on the CompTIA Web server when a user clicks "CompTIA certification," use the following syntax:

```
<A HREF="http://www.comptia.org/certification.htm">CompTIA
certification</A>
```

Memorize the proper syntax for creating a hyperlink. Unlike using HTML in the real world, where you can correct your mistakes if you make a slight error, you must be able to recognize the proper syntax the first time for the i-Net+ exam.

Using Graphical Hyperlinks

So far, you have learned how to add images to a Web page and how to create a text hyperlink. Now suppose, for example, that you want to use a graphic as a hyperlink. Many Web sites use graphics to serve as icons, which are hyperlinked to other pages. To do this, simply combine the methods discussed earlier for adding images and creating hyperlinks. Instead of using text in the anchor tag, you use the image code. For example, you may have an image that looks like a house and is called home.gif. The following code will take the user to the home page (index.htm) when the image home.gif is clicked:

```
<A HREF="index.htm"><IMG SRC="home.gif"></A>
```

Instead of specifying text between the <**A**> and </**A**> tags, we have simply substituted an <**IMG**> tag between them. If a user were browsing in text-only mode, this link would not be visible, however, because there is not an **ALT** attribute defined. To provide an alternative for users unable to display graphics, you may consider using the following code:

```
<A HREF="index.htm"><IMG SRC="home.gif" ALT="Return to home"></A>
```

For those browsers not capable of displaying graphics, this code would put the hypertext "Return to home" in place of the graphic.

Linking Within A Page

Thus far you have seen how the anchor tag is used to create links; however, the anchor tag is also used as a reference point within a page. In the previous examples, all of the links direct the user away from the current page onto another page. To create links that jump within the same page (usually used on longer pages), you create one tag to mark the destination and another tag for the user to click to get to the destination. By combining the <A> tag with the **NAME** attribute, you can create the reference point—also called the *named anchor*. For example, the following tag assigns the name "anchor_z" to the text, "Words beginning with Z":

```
<A NAME="anchor_z">Words beginning with Z</A>
```

This tag doesn't change the appearance of the Web page in any way. It is only a reference point for a link that will appear somewhere else on the page, as in the following example:

```
<A HREF="#anchor_z">Z</A>
```

The previous tag is similar to a regular hyperlink except that it contains a pound sign (#) before the hypertext reference. The pound sign indicates that it links to a named anchor. Thus, when a user clicks on "Z", the browser locates the named anchor, "anchor_z", and jumps to that destination.

In addition to using named anchors to jump within the same page, you can also use them to jump to any existing anchor located in any Web page, as in the following example:

```
<A HREF="http://www.castadream.com/glossary.htm#anchor_z">Z Words</A>
```

Linking To An Email Address

In addition to the hyperlinks we have covered so far, you can also create a link that opens the client's email program and automatically puts in a specified destination email address. The syntax for this is similar to that of a regular hyperlink using the <A> tag and the **HREF** attribute, but instead of referring to a URL, you use the **mailto:** protocol designator followed by the destination email address. For example,

```
<A HREF="mailto:info@comptia.org">Email CompTIA</A>
```

will launch the client's email software when "Email CompTIA" is clicked, and it will automatically fill in the "To" field with the specified email address.

Adding Tables

Tables provide a great method for organizing and presenting information on Web pages. Tables consist of columns and rows and are often used simply to chart information as well as to provide the framework for an entire Web page. Tables typically use the following four pairs of tags:

➤ <TABLE> </TABLE>—Used to indicate the beginning and end of a table.

➤ <TR> </TR>—Used to create a row.

➤ <TH> </TH>—Used to create a row or column heading, which typically centers the text and makes it boldface. Used within the <TR> tags.

➤ <TD> </TD>—Used to create a cell. This is similar to <TH>, but it only centers the text. Used within the <TR> tags.

 You must know the difference between the four pairs of tags used to define tables. **<TABLE>** marks the start and end of the table, thus enclosing all other table tags. **<TR>** is used for table rows and encloses the remaining two tags. **<TH>** is used for table headings, and **<TD>** creates a cell that is used for table data.

Listing 10.3 shows an example of a table made of three rows and three columns. Notice that the <TH> tags are used in a manner much like that of the <TD> tags. Additionally, notice that the entire table is between the <TABLE> tags, and both the <TD> and <TH> tags are contained within the <TR> tags.

Listing 10.3   Creating a simple table composed of three rows and three columns.

```
<HTML>
<HEAD>
<TITLE></TITLE>
</HEAD>
<BODY>
<TABLE>
 <TR>
  <TH>Row 1 Heading 1</TH>
  <TH>Row 1 Heading 2</TH>
  <TH>Row 1 Heading 3</TH>
 </TR>
 <TR>
  <TD>Row 2 Column 1 data</TD>
  <TD>Row 2 Column 2 data</TD>
  <TD>Row 2 Column 3 data</TD>
 </TR>
 <TR>
  <TD>Row 3 Column 1 data</TD>
  <TD>Row 3 Column 2 data</TD>
  <TD>Row 3 Column 3 data</TD>
 </TR>
</TABLE>
</BODY>
</HTML>
```

Table Attributes

Just as you can use various attributes with the <IMG> tag to control images, you can use many attributes with the table tags to control the appearance of the table.

 A GUI HTML editor can be extremely helpful when you're designing tables. In addition to letting you "draw" tables without using HTML, these editors typically provide an easy method to define the many available attributes for the table.

BORDER Attribute

The **BORDER** attribute is used to create a border around the table and all of the cells. A value must be given for this attribute, which specifies the border size in pixels. For example, to create a table with a border size of five pixels, use:

```
<TABLE BORDER="5">
```

Figure 10.5 shows how the table listed earlier in Listing 10.3 would appear if we added a **BORDER** attribute specifying five pixels.

ALIGN And VALIGN Attributes

The **ALIGN** attribute specifies the alignment (left, center, or right) of the specific tag for which it's used. For example, to specify that a table is aligned with the right margin, use:

```
<TABLE ALIGN="right">
```

And to specify that the text within a cell is centered, use:

```
<TD ALIGN="center">
```

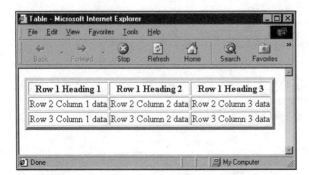

Figure 10.5 A table of three rows and three columns with a border.

The **VALIGN** attribute is similar to the **ALIGN** attribute; however, **VALIGN** defines the vertical alignment (top, middle, or bottom) of the specific tag for which it's used. For example, to specify that data within a <TH> tag is aligned with the top of the cell, use:

```
<TH VALIGN="top">
```

CELLPADDING And CELLSPACING Attributes

The **CELLPADDING** attribute is used with the <TABLE> tag to specify in pixels the amount of space between the cell's borders and its contents. For example, to create a table with five pixels between the borders and each cell's contents, use:

```
<TABLE CELLPADDING="5">
```

The **CELLSPACING** attribute is used with the <TABLE> tag to specify in pixels the amount of space between each cell. For example, to create a table with five pixels between each cell, use:

```
<TABLE CELLSPACING="5">
```

WIDTH And HEIGHT Attributes

The **WIDTH** and **HEIGHT** attributes are used to set the width and height of a table, which can be measured either in pixels or as a percentage of the browser's display area. For example, to create a table 500 pixels wide, use:

```
<TABLE WIDTH="500">
```

Alternatively, to create a table that is 50 percent of the browser's viewable area, use:

```
<TABLE WIDTH="50%">
```

COLSPAN And ROWSPAN Attributes

The **COLSPAN** attribute is used with the <TH> or <TD> tags to define a cell that spans a specific number of columns. For example, to create a cell that spans five columns, use:

```
<TD COLSPAN="5">
```

The **ROWSPAN** attribute is also used with the <TH> or <TD> tags, but defines a cell that spans a specific number of rows. For example, to create a cell that spans five rows, use:

```
<TD ROWSPAN="5">
```

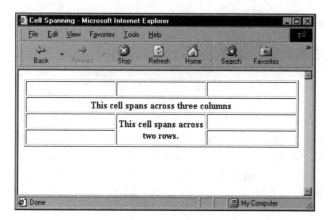

Figure 10.6   Use **COLSPAN** and **ROWSPAN** to span a cell across columns and rows.

Figure 10.6 shows an example of a table using the COLSPAN attribute set to three and the ROWSPAN attribute set to two.

BACKGROUND And BGCOLOR Attributes

The **BACKGROUND** attribute can be used with any of the table tags to display an image in the background of the table, cell, or row. (This attribute is also commonly used with the <**BODY**> tag to create wallpaper for an entire page.) For example, to place an image called logo.gif as the background for a table, use:

```
<TABLE BACKGROUND="logo.gif">
```

The **BGCOLOR** attribute is used to define a color either by the standard color name such as "red" or preferably by the hexadecimal value for the color. For example, to define a table with a background color of red, use:

```
<TABLE BGCOLOR="#FF0000">
```

Adding Forms

Forms are used extensively on the Web for a variety of purposes such as surveys, product and site registrations, and order collections. The form, however, is only the front end of the data collection process. Typically, a form is sent to a Server Side Include (SSI) Web page, which uses SSI commands to save the data from the form to a Web server, to a Common Gateway Interface (CGI) program, or to a server-side JavaScript. A less glamorous, yet still functional, method for sending data from forms is simply to use the **mailto:** protocol designator. For this section, however, we are going to focus primarily on the front end—building the form.

Forms are enclosed between the **<FORM>** and **</FORM>** tags. Forms are composed of one or more elements that provide an input mechanism, such as a text box for entering an email address. Additionally, a form must contain a button to allow the user to submit the information. Thus, the following is the framework for a basic form:

```
<FORM METHOD="value" ACTION="value">
 <!--Form elements are defined here -->
 <INPUT TYPE="submit">
</FORM>
```

First, the **METHOD** and the **ACTION** attributes define how the form will be delivered. The value for the **METHOD** attribute is typically *post*. The value for **ACTION** is typically the location of a CGI script, such as **ACTION= "cgi-bin/sampleform"**, or it can even specify an email address, such as **ACTION="mailto:ihavenocgi@domain.com"**.

Web pages commonly use forms with various elements such as text fields and checkboxes that a user can fill in with data. These forms are created in HTML by using the **<FORM>** tag. Although there are several ways to process form data, CGI scripts and programs are most commonly used.

Form Elements

The form elements are the objects that are placed between the **<FORM>** tags and that the user interacts with to submit information. You need to be familiar with the following form elements:

➤ *Text box*—Provides a box for the user to enter a single line of text.

➤ *Scrolling (large) text box*—Provides a box for users to enter multiple lines of text.

➤ *Radio button*—Used to limit the user to one selection from a list.

➤ *Checkbox*—Used to let the user mark multiple selections from a list.

➤ *Drop-down menu (scrollable menu)*—Used to let users make one or more selections from a drop-down or scrollable list.

➤ *Submit button*—Used to send the form data.

➤ *Reset button*—Used to erase the entered form data (before it's submitted) and start over.

Figure 10.7 shows a sample Web page that utilizes each one of these elements. The basis for most of the elements—with the exception of the scrolling text

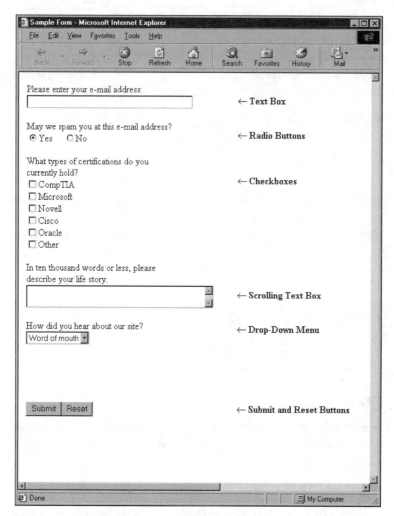

Figure 10.7 A Web page with various form elements.

box and the drop-down menu—involves an **<INPUT>** tag, a **TYPE** attribute, and a **NAME** attribute. The following sections will discuss how these attributes are used with the form elements, as well as some additional attributes that can be defined for each input type.

Text Boxes

A text box provides a single line for the user to enter data such as a name or email address. The **TYPE** attribute is usually set to "text", and the **NAME** attribute can be anything that best describes the specific element. For example, the following tag creates a text box named *email:*

```
<INPUT TYPE="text" NAME="email">
```

To define the appearance and behavior of the input box, you can use a couple more attributes, such as:

➤ SIZE—Specifies the character length of the text box, as it will appear on the Web page.

➤ MAXLENGTH—Defines the maximum number of characters that can be entered.

Scrolling Text Boxes

A *scrolling text box*, also called a *large text box*, allows the user to enter multiple lines of text. This is often used in technical support forms, for example, to provide a description of a problem. Unlike most other elements, a scrolling text box does not use the <INPUT> tag; instead it requires the <TEXTAREA> tag. For example, the following tag creates a scrolling text box named *lifestory*:

```
<TEXTAREA NAME="lifestory">
```

You will typically want to specify additional attributes for a scrolling text box, such as:

➤ COLS—Defines the number of columns for the width of the text box.

➤ ROWS—Defines the number of rows for the height of the text box.

➤ WRAP—Uses various values to specify what happens to typed text that exceeds the borders of the text box, such as a hard or soft wrap.

Radio Buttons

Radio buttons (also called option buttons) are used to present a list of choices to the user, from which he or she may make only one selection. Selecting another choice will automatically unmark the previously selected choice. Radio buttons—like an AM/FM radio—allow you to choose only one "station" at a time. The TYPE attribute should be "radio", and the NAME attribute must be the same within the group of options. Additionally, a VALUE attribute is used—after the form is submitted—to specify the choice that the user selected. Therefore, the following code is used to create the two radio buttons shown earlier in Figure 10.7:

```
<INPUT TYPE="radio" NAME="spam" VALUE="yes">Yes
<INPUT TYPE="radio" NAME="spam" VALUE="no">No
```

Checkboxes

Checkboxes are used to present a list of choices to the user, from which multiple selections may be made. One or more checkboxes may be selected as well as deselected. The format for checkboxes is the same as that for radio buttons except that the **TYPE** attribute should be set to "checkbox". Thus, the following code is used to create the checkboxes shown earlier in Figure 10.7:

```
<INPUT TYPE="checkbox" NAME="certification"
VALUE="comptia">CompTIA<BR>
<INPUT TYPE="checkbox" NAME="certification"
VALUE="microsoft">Microsoft<BR>
<INPUT TYPE="checkbox" NAME="certification"
VALUE="novell">Novell<BR>
<INPUT TYPE="checkbox" NAME="certification" VALUE="cisco">Cisco<BR>
<INPUT TYPE="checkbox" NAME="certification"
VALUE="oracle">Oracle<BR>
<INPUT TYPE="checkbox" NAME="certification" VALUE="other">Other<BR>
```

The <**BR**> tags are used at the end of each line to force the next checkbox to appear on the line beneath it; otherwise, the checkboxes would appear on the same line, as do the radio buttons in the previous example.

Drop-Down Menus

Drop-down menus are often used to present a long list of choices. For example, you may consider using a drop-down menu to have a user select a specific country. Typically these menus allow only one choice to be selected, but they can be made to allow multiple selections if necessary.

This element uses multiple <**OPTION**> tags enclosed between a beginning and ending <**SELECT**> tag. Additionally, a **NAME** attribute is used with <**SELECT**> to specify a name for the set of choices. The following code was used to create the drop-down list shown earlier in Figure 10.7:

```
<SELECT NAME="hear">
 <OPTION>Word of mouth
 <OPTION>Friend
 <OPTION>Banner ad
 <OPTION>Just Surfing
</SELECT>
```

To control the behavior of the menu, you can use a couple more attributes, such as:

➤ **VALUE**—Defines a specific, often short, value to send in place of the text specified by the <**OPTION**> tag.

➤ **SELECTED**—Used to specify a default option; otherwise, the first option will be used by default.

Submit And Reset Buttons

The Submit button must be used on a form. This button, when clicked by the user, will send the data to the intended destination. The format for creating a Submit button is:

```
<INPUT TYPE="submit">
```

Additionally, a **VALUE** attribute can be added to assign a name other than the default "submit", which will appear on the button.

The Reset button, though not required, allows the user to clear any input that has been entered into the form. The format for creating a Reset button is the same as the format for creating a Submit button, but the **TYPE** attribute should be set to "reset".

Including Scripts

The **<SCRIPT>** tag allows you to easily incorporate scripts within a Web page. Although you don't need to know how to write scripts for the i-Net+ exam, you should know how to include them inline with HTML.

Use **<SCRIPT>** to mark the beginning of a script, and use **</SCRIPT>** to mark the ending of the script. First, however, you will need to define the type of scripting language enclosed in the HTML document; you do this by using the **LANGUAGE** attribute with the **<SCRIPT>** tag. The two most common script languages used within HTML documents are JavaScript and VBScript. The value of the **LANGUAGE** attribute will be the corresponding script. Thus, to mark the beginning of a JavaScript within an HTML document, use the following code:

```
<SCRIPT LANGUAGE="JavaScript">
```

 You can include a script within a Web page by beginning the script with **<SCRIPT LANGUAGE=**"*script*"**>**, where the script is typically either JavaScript or VBScript. To end the script, use the closing **</SCRIPT>** tag.

Practice Questions

Question 1

> Which of the following statements is true regarding HTML and browser compatibility?
>
> ○ a. Browser compatibility is a directive issued by the W3C mandating that all Web browsers support only the standard tags.
>
> ○ b. When you're designing a Web page, cross-browser compatibility may be an issue to consider because certain HTML tags may not be supported in all browsers.
>
> ○ c. If an HTML tag is not compatible with a browser, the browser will display a script error.
>
> ○ d. All Web pages should be made so that the HTML is supported in the major Web browsers.

The correct answer is b. Not every Web browser may support every tag; in addition, vendors of Web browsers may implement their own tags, which may not yet be standards. Answer a is incorrect because the W3C does not mandate that vendors support only standard tags. Answer c is incorrect because browsers ignore errors in HTML, and furthermore, HTML is not a scripting language. Answer d is incorrect because not all Web sites necessarily need to be concerned with browser compatibility. An intranet, for example, may only need to support its local clients that may all use only one type of browser.

Question 2

> Which of the following statements is true of editors?
>
> ○ a. A text editor uses wizards to help the Web author insert tags into the document.
>
> ○ b. A GUI editor, also called a do-it-yourself editor, requires the Web author to manually type all the tags.
>
> ○ c. A text editor is a type of editor that is specifically designed for creating HTML documents and that allows a Web author to use menus and toolbars to create the HTML.
>
> ○ d. A GUI editor uses graphical features to assist the author in creating Web pages without manually typing HTML.

The correct answer is d. A GUI editor uses a graphical interface to help the author create Web pages. With a GUI editor, a Web page can typically be created without the author having to insert even a single tag by hand. Text editors, on the other hand, do not provide graphical interfaces, but can be used to manually type HTML and to save a document as an HTML document; therefore, answers a, b, and c are incorrect.

Question 3

What is the correct order for the beginning tags that make up a basic HTML document?

- a. **<BODY><HTML><TITLE><HTML>**
- b. **<HTML><HEAD><TITLE><BODY>**
- c. **<TITLE><HEAD><HTML><BODY>**
- d. **<HEAD><HTML><TITLE><BODY>**

The correct answer is b. The **<HTML>** tag is used to mark the beginning and end of an HTML document. **<HEAD>** is used next and typically contains tags that apply to the entire document. The **<TITLE>** tag is used for the title of the page and is contained within the **<HEAD>** tag. The **<BODY>** tag encloses the contents of the Web page. Answers a, c, and d are incorrect.

Question 4

Which of the following is the correct beginning and ending code for inserting a comment within an HTML document?

- a. **<-- and -->**
- b. **<!-- and /--!>**
- c. **<!-- and -->**
- d. **<--! and !-->**
- e. **<--> and </-->**

The correct answer is c. The comment tag is different from other tags in that the beginning tag does not use a greater-than symbol (>) and the closing tag does not use a slash (/) or a less-than symbol (<). Answers a, b, d, and e are not valid tags within HTML, thus are incorrect answers.

Question 5

> Which of the following is the correct use of the heading tag that uses the smallest heading available?
>
> ○ a.   **<HEAD>Hello World</HEAD>**
>
> ○ b.   **<H6>Hello World</H6>**
>
> ○ c.   **<H1>Hello World</H1>**
>
> ○ d.   **<H5>Hello World</H5>**

The correct answer is b. The <H6> tag creates the smallest heading. <HEAD> is not a valid tag for creating headings; therefore, answer a is incorrect. The <H1> tag creates the largest heading; therefore, answer c is incorrect. The <H5> tag creates neither the smallest nor the largest heading; therefore, answer d is incorrect.

Question 6

> Which of the following is the correct character entity for the copyright symbol (©)?
>
> ○ a.   **<COPY></COPY>**
>
> ○ b.   **©**
>
> ○ c.   **&#copy;**
>
> ○ d.   **<**

The correct answer is b. Answer a is incorrect because <COPY> is not a valid tag for specifying characters. The pound sign (#) is used only with the numbered character entity, such as © used for copyright; therefore, answer c is incorrect. Answer d is incorrect because < is the numbered character entity for the less-than symbol (<).

Question 7

The following code is an example of what type of list?

```
<UL>
  <LI>List item one
  <LI>List item two
  <LI>List item three
</UL>
```

- ○ a. Bulleted, ordered list
- ○ b. Numbered, unordered list
- ○ c. Bulleted, unordered list
- ○ d. Numbered, ordered list

The correct answer is c. The <UL> tag is used to create an unordered list, which uses bullets. Be careful not to let the text within each list item confuse you. A numbered, ordered list is created by using the <OL> tag. Answers a, b, and d are incorrect.

Question 8

Which of the following uses the correct syntax for inserting an image named logo.jpg into a Web page?

- ○ a. **<IMG SRC="logo.jpg">**
- ○ b. **<IMG="logo.jpg">**
- ○ c. **<INS IMG="logo.jpg">**
- ○ d. **<INS="logo.jpg">**

The correct answer is a. To place an image in an HTML document, use the <IMG> tag with the SRC attribute. Answer b is incorrect because the SRC attribute is required. Answers c and d are incorrect because there is no such thing as an INS tag.

Question 9

What is the correct syntax to place a hyperlink to **www.comptia.org** located on port 80 when a user clicks on "CompTIA"?

- ○ a. **<A>http://www.comptia.org HREF="CompTIA"</A>**
- ○ b. **<A>HREF="http://www.comptia.org:80">CompTIA</A>**
- ○ c. **<A HREF="http://www.comptia.org">CompTIA</A>**
- ○ d. **<A HREF="CompTIA">http://www.comptia.org:80</A>**

The correct answer is c. To create a hyperlink, use the **HREF** attribute with the **<A>** tag. Answers a, b, and d are incorrect because they use the incorrect format for a hyperlink. The correct format to use is **<A HREF="*destination*">Text user will click</A>**. The default port for HTTP is port 80, and is used by default. The port assignment only needs to be included if the Web server utilizes a port other than 80.

Question 10

Which of the following is not a valid tag used to create a table?

- ○ a. **<TABLE>**
- ○ b. **<TR>**
- ○ c. **<TC>**
- ○ d. **<TH>**
- ○ e. **<TD>**

The correct answer is c. There is not a specific tag used to create a table column, as **<TC>** may lead you to believe. The tags used to create a table include **<TABLE>**, **<TR>**, **<TH>**, and **<TD>**. The **<TABLE>** tag is used to indicate the beginning and end of the table. The **<TR>** is used to create a table row. The **<TH>** tag is used to create a row or column heading. The **<TD>** tag is used to create a table data cell. Answers a, b, d, and e are valid tags used to create tables, thus are incorrect.

Question 11

Which tag is the best choice for creating a Web page to solicit user feedback, which can then be posted using a CGI script?

- ○ a. <TABLE>
- ○ b. <METHOD>
- ○ c. <FORM>
- ○ d. <ACTION>

The correct answer is c. The <FORM> tag is used to create a form, which can be used for a variety of purposes, including soliciting user feedback. The <TABLE> tag is used to create a table, which is used to organize and display information; therefore, answer a is incorrect. METHOD and ACTION are not tags but are attributes used with the <FORM> tag to define how a form will be delivered; therefore, answers b and d are incorrect.

Question 12

Which of the following is the correct syntax to mark the beginning of a JavaScript within an HTML document?

- ○ a. <SCRIPT="JavaScript">
- ○ b. <LANGUAGE="JavaScript">
- ○ c. <SCRIPT LANGUAGE="JavaScript">
- ○ d. <SCRIPT>"JavaScript"

The correct answer is c. The <SCRIPT> tag used with the LANGUAGE attribute marks the beginning of a script and defines the script to be used in the Web page. Answers a, b, and d use incorrect syntax; therefore, they are incorrect.

Need To Know More?

 Conner-Sax, Kiersten and Ed Krol. *The Whole Internet: The Next Generation.* O'Reilly & Associates Inc., Sebastopol, CA, 1999. ISBN 1-56592-428-2. Although this book is designed to be an end user's guide, it is actually quite informative because it covers so many aspects of the Internet with several chapters devoted to the Web.

 Powell, Thomas A. *HTML: The Complete Reference.* Osborne/McGraw-Hill, Berkeley, CA, 1997. ISBN 0-07882-397-8. An HTML book that not only instructs but also serves as a great reference.

 http://hotwired.lycos.com/webmonkey/ provides great resources for Web design as well as other advanced topics in Web development.

 http://msdn.microsoft.com/ offers advanced information on Web design, and includes an entire site dedicated to XML.

 www.hwg.org/ is home of the HTML Writers Guild, offering resources and support for Web authors.

 www.pageresource.com/ offers a lot of resources for Web development, including great HTML tutorials as well as resources on many other aspects of Web development.

 www.w3.org/ is the organization Web site for the World Wide Web Consortium, established to promote the evolution and interoperability of the Web. This site is led by Tim Berners-Lee and provides an abundance of resources on HTTP.

Multimedia

. . . .

Terms you'll need to understand:

√ Streaming media

√ Vector and bitmap graphics

√ Page Description Language (PDL)

√ PostScript

√ BinHex

√ Plug-in

√ Flash

√ Shockwave

√ QuickTime VR (QTVR)

√ RealPlayer

√ Windows Media Player

√ GIF (Graphics Interchange Format)

√ JPEG (Joint Photographic Experts Group)

√ PNG (Portable Network Graphics)

√ TIFF (Tag Image File Format)

√ BMP (Windows Bitmap)

√ EPS (Encapsulated PostScript)

√ MOV (QuickTime Movie)

√ MPEG (Moving Pictures Experts Group)

√ AVI (Audio Video Interleaved)

√ RTF (Rich Text Format)

√ PDF (Portable Document Format)

Techniques you'll need to master:

√ Understanding the difference between streaming and non-streaming media

√ Understanding the difference between vector and bitmapped graphics

√ Identifying and describing the uses and benefits of popular plug-ins and multimedia file formats

Multimedia refers to the combination of text, sound, graphics, animation, and video. Multimedia on the Internet, however, is still relatively new. It was only in the last decade that multimedia and the Internet became mainstream ideas. Computer hardware performance continues to increase as prices continue to drop, causing multimedia-capable computers to become more commonplace. As a result, the use of multimedia on the Internet—especially on the Web—is everywhere and will continue to grow and become more advanced. Internet professionals will undoubtedly be faced with the need to be familiar with many of the multimedia elements used on the Internet. In fact, understanding the uses and benefits of the various multimedia extensions and file formats is critical for the success of organizations considering making the jump to multimedia or those already using it on the Internet.

Streaming And Non-Streaming Media

Streaming media is commonly used over the Internet as well as on intranets. Streaming media is a method that allows multimedia such as audio and video to be made available in real time. That is, multimedia files can be viewed (and heard) as they are being downloaded. In contrast, non-streaming files typically must first be downloaded entirely before being displayed.

Traditional files such as HTML documents and Web graphics are relatively small and can be downloaded quickly, but files used for streaming media typically take longer to download. Even a short 40-second video clip can take more than a half-hour to download with a traditional modem, but with streaming technologies, videos and other media can begin playback almost immediately. Typically, special software called *controls* or *plug-ins* is used to play the streaming media. These plug-ins first buffer some of the data and then begin to play the streamed data as the rest of the data is sent, arriving in time to be played.

The ability to stream data thus allows media to be viewed either live or on demand. Movie trailer clips and live radio broadcasts are a couple of examples of the content currently being delivered by streaming media. Much of the success, however, for streaming media also depends greatly upon the available bandwidth. As broadband technologies such as DSL and cable modems become more commonplace, the use of streaming media is likely to grow even further. In fact, companies such as MeTV.com are already prepared to provide full-screen and full-length instant movies to users by using streaming media technologies.

Bitmap Vs. Vector Graphics

Vector and bitmap graphics are methods used for representing graphics. *Vector* graphics, also called *object-oriented* graphics, use mathematical formulas to draw images. *Bitmap* graphics, also called *raster graphics*, use a pattern of dots to draw images. Paint programs, such as Microsoft Paint or Adobe Photoshop, are typically used to create and edit bitmapped images, whereas draw programs, such as Adobe Illustrator and Macromedia FreeHand, are typically used to create and edit vector images.

A bitmap image consists of colored dots, or pixels, arranged in rows and columns. Each dot can consist of one bit for simple monochrome graphics, or each dot can consist of several bits, depending upon the number of colors used.

Unlike bitmap images, vector images use mathematical formulas that contain instructions about how to draw the image and where to place each component of the image. An advantage of vector graphics is that they retain their resolution when resized, whereas a bitmap image will appear jagged if enlarged. Figure 11.1 shows an example of a vector graphic and a bitmap graphic, which are enlarged to illustrate the infinitely scalable nature of vector images.

Another advantage of vector graphics is that they are easy to manipulate in a draw program because they are stored as collections of objects that can be ungrouped and edited individually. Unfortunately, most vector images cannot be displayed on the Web and typically need to be converted to bitmap images. Many Web graphics are initially created as vector images and are then converted to bitmap images by using a process called *rasterizing*.

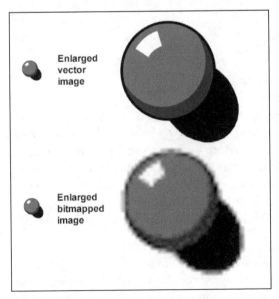

Figure 11.1 The results of enlarging comparable vector and bitmap images.

Page Description Language (PDL)

A *page description language (PDL)* is a language that describes the appearance of a printed page for device independence. A PDL typically resides within the printer as software to provide this functionality. One of the most common PDLs is Adobe PostScript, which is typically used to control laser printers.

PostScript

PostScript has become the standard for desktop publishing. PostScript is a PDL developed by Adobe Systems, and it is a language that describes the appearance of a page, including elements such as text and images, to a printer or other output device. PostScript can take advantage of high-resolution devices such as laser printers and professional presses because it is an object-oriented language. Because PostScript is object-oriented, each object, including text, is treated as a geometrical object instead of bitmaps. This is why PostScript fonts can be easily sized without losing image quality.

BinHex

Chapter 7 introduced BinHex. It is mentioned again here because of its capability to convert binary data, such as multimedia files, into ASCII format with the .hqx extension. A BinHex-encoded file can be passed along to various computers and can be unencoded to be displayed in the original format. BinHex is common to the Macintosh operating system, and its use can prevent files from becoming corrupted in transit.

Plug-Ins

Plug-ins, also called *extensions*, are typically software components that provide feature support for larger programs such as Web browsers. Suppose, for example, that a software company develops a new type of format for displaying streaming video, and this format is not natively supported by a Web browser. The company will also develop a plug-in that is capable of streaming the video and that is seamlessly integrated into the Web browser. For example, Figure 11.2 shows a Web site using a plug-in that allows visitors to view popular television commercials directly within the Web page.

Plug-ins are usually available as a free download from various Web sites; however, the tools needed to create the content cost money, which is typically paid for by the developer. These content creators are allowed to freely distribute the plug-ins, so most Web sites that require the use of plug-ins will typically provide links to retrieve the necessary software.

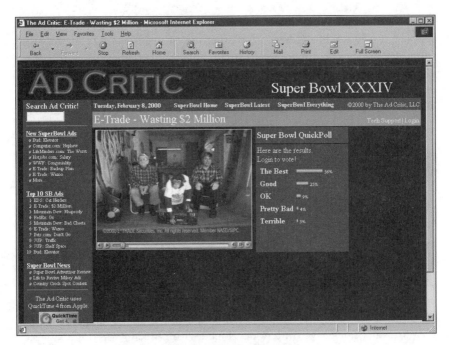

Figure 11.2   The photo in the Web page is actually a video of a TV commercial, which can be played because of the added functionality provided by a plug-in.

Note: Although the term plug-in is used in this text, Microsoft Internet Explorer commonly uses ActiveX controls, which also handle various types of media within the browser.

Although there are many types of plug-ins, most users are not likely to have all of them. Several plug-ins have, however, stood out from the crowd and survived among all the others. Although many of these technologies may seem similar, they also have their differences, and each plug-in needs to be considered depending upon the project being developed.

Flash

The Flash plug-in is used to display Flash content created in the Flash authoring software from Macromedia. Flash, previously known as FutureSplash, was purchased by Macromedia. Flash is designed for producing and delivering stunning Web sites. Flash not only looks good with its smooth graphics, but it is also fast. Because Flash is vector-based, movies created in it have small file sizes and can be streamed quickly, even over slower links. Flash is ideally used to create dazzling Web sites using sound and animation and limited interactivity. In fact, Flash is also being used to create eye-catching advertisements for the Web.

Flash is not without limitations, however. Although it does provide interactive support, it is limited to rollovers and other mouse events, so it is not very well suited for projects that require a great amount of interactivity, such as games. However, another product from Macromedia, called Director, can be used to create highly interactive multimedia. Director can also take advantage of the anti-aliased and fast nature of Flash because of its ability to embed Flash content.

Use Flash to create visually appealing and compact vector graphics, animations, and other effects. Other uses can include creating navigational interfaces, technical illustrations for the Web, and movies.

Shockwave

Director Shockwave Studio is the name of the program used to create Shockwave content, which requires users to have the Shockwave plug-in. Shockwave enables Web pages to display interactive multimedia objects through a combination of graphics, sound, video, text, and animation. Additionally, Shockwave provides support for chat, scripting, HTML manipulation, and file retrieval. Shockwave content developed with Director was originally used to create interactive CD-ROMs and kiosks, but has since been adapted and heavily applied to the Web. Unlike Flash, Shockwave does not typically provide instant playback. Shockwave tends to break things up by displaying a progress bar while the content loads.

Use Director Shockwave Studio to produce a variety of interactive multimedia presentations. Examples can include business presentations, interactive Web content, kiosks, and CD-ROM or DVD titles and games.

Flash Vs. Shockwave

Both Shockwave and Flash are often confused with each other, and you may even see them described together as *Shockwave Flash*. The two are actually developed separately and require two different players. To make matters even more confusing, Shockwave can embed Flash content, thus providing the best of both worlds. In fact, the two are often combined to create compelling Web sites. Although Flash provides fast speeds combined with vector capabilities, it lacks many of the features that Shockwave offers. Deciding which one to use might be tough. Your specific needs should first be examined. You may find that a combination of both is the best solution. As a general rule, however, Flash is best used to provide slick Web interfaces that make a quick impact, and Shockwave is best used for more complex and interactive projects.

QuickTime VR (QTVR)

QuickTime is a video and audio plug-in and standalone player developed by Apple Computer. QuickTime can not only display standalone QuickTime files, but can also be used to play streaming audio and video using industry-standard streaming protocols.

QuickTime VR (QTVR) is an enhanced version of QuickTime that lets the user interact with a spatial environment by rotating the view of a scene 360 degrees (a full circle). A combination of these circles can also be combined to create 3D effects, such as the appearance of actually being at a given location.

RealPlayer

RealPlayer, developed by RealNetworks, plays RealAudio and RealVideo files and is best known as a streaming video and audio plug-in as well as a standalone player. RealPlayer provides features such as picture controls as well as dozens of video channels and hundreds of live radio stations that are preconfigured to retrieve live broadcasts.

Windows Media Player

Developed by Microsoft, Windows Media Player is a plug-in and standalone player that can play streaming and regular video and audio files. Windows Media Player is part of the family of Windows Media Technologies used to create and deliver streaming media. Like RealPlayer, Windows Media Player is ideal for broadcast information such as speeches, radio broadcasts, and movies.

Multimedia File Formats

This section discusses many of the popular file formats, some of which are natively supported in most Web browsers. A file format is identified by a three-letter extension following the file name. Each of the formats generally has specific uses and advantages as well as disadvantages.

GIF (Graphics Interchange Format)

GIF (Graphics Interchange Format) is a bitmap-graphic file format that uses the .gif extension. GIF was developed by CompuServe to provide a highly compressed and compact format that could easily be shared between computers and be uploaded and downloaded from electronic Bulletin Board Systems (BBSs). Unfortunately, GIF uses a patented compression technology called LZW (Lempel-Zif Welsh), which has spawned the need for a new graphics file format.

Nevertheless, GIF has become widespread; it's one of the most-used formats for images and backgrounds on the Web, and it's the one graphic format viewable by all browsers capable of displaying graphics. Because GIF images are 8-bit and limited to 256 colors, GIF is a very compact file format best used for Web images with a limited number of colors. Additionally, GIF is *lossless*, which means that no data is lost during the compression and decompression processes.

GIF images support the following features:

➤ *Interlacing*—Displays a GIF image in two passes of alternating lines rather than displaying the image one line at a time. Interlacing gives the user a quicker view of an image—one that initially appears blurry, but comes into focus.

➤ *Transparency*—Lets the background show through certain parts of an image. Typically a transparent GIF image allows the Web-page background to show through, thus preventing the GIF image from appearing as a square sitting on top of the page.

➤ *Animation*—Stores a series of GIF images in the same file, which will appear animated when viewed through a browser.

> *Note: There are two primary specifications for GIF images—GIF 87a and GIF 89a. The original GIF specification is known as GIF 87a, and the newer specification is known as GIF 89a. Only the GIF 89a specification supports transparency and animation.*

Despite these features, as well as the relatively small GIF file sizes, GIF's primary disadvantage is its ability to display images containing large amounts of color, such as continuous-tone images.

GIF is an 8-bit, 256-color graphic file format commonly used on the Web. GIF is best used for line art and images that are limited in their colors—such as black-and-white images and less complex images that contain large areas of solid color.

LZW Compression

The story of GIF and LZW (Lempel-Zif Welsh) is an interesting controversy. CompuServe originally released GIF as a free and open specification, and its use eventually became widespread. As documented in the original specification, GIF's compression technology is based upon LZW. Later on, it was discovered that Unisys had patented LZW. This took CompuServe, the Web community, and even Unisys by surprise! Unisys later declared that royalties on GIF-based software products would not have to be paid for products developed prior to 1995, as this would be considered inadvertent use; however, programs developed since then would be subject to royalty payments. For more information about LZW, visit **www.unisys.com/unisys/lzw/**.

JPEG (Joint Photographic Experts Group)

Whereas GIF is an 8-bit format limited to 256 colors, JPEG (Joint Photographic Experts Group) is a 24-bit bitmap format that supports up to 16 million colors. JPEG is named after the committee that wrote the original standard, and uses the .jpg extension. Like GIF, JPEG is also in widespread use on the Web.

JPEG images provide a lot more information than do GIF images, so JPEG images are ideal for continuous-tone images such as photographs and detailed 3D renderings. Remember, however, that JPEG does not perform as well as GIF for images that contain lettering, simple cartoons, or line drawings.

 JPEG is a 24-bit, 16-million-color graphic file format commonly used on the Web. JPEG is best used for continuous-tone images such as photographs, 3D rendered artwork, and other realistic images. Generally, use JPEG for more subtly rendered and complex images (e.g., highlights and shading).

A major advantage of JPEG is its ability to compress images while retaining high image quality. JPEG uses a *lossy* compression format, which means that it does lose some quality, but, depending upon the amount of compression applied, this loss of quality can't be perceived by the human eye.

Another advantage of JPEG is that the amount of compression to be applied is adjustable, so you can obtain a balance between image quality and file size. Although the JPEG format can display realistic photographs on the Web, using a relatively small file size, the GIF file format may be a better choice for images that are not continuous-tone. An image that contains large areas of solid colors or text may appear to be noisy (blurred or distorted) when saved in the JPEG format.

If you are creating or scanning images to be used on the Web, you may want to consider experimenting with different formats and levels of compression to find the best image quality with the smallest file size. Some graphics programs—such as Microsoft Image Composer, for example—allow you to preview an image in different formats, and determine the file size and the estimated download time over various modem speeds (see Figure 11.3).

PNG (Portable Network Graphics)

PNG (Portable Network Graphics) is a relatively new bitmap graphic format designed specifically for use on the Internet. PNG uses the .png extension. PNG, which has been approved as a standard, is the result of the need to

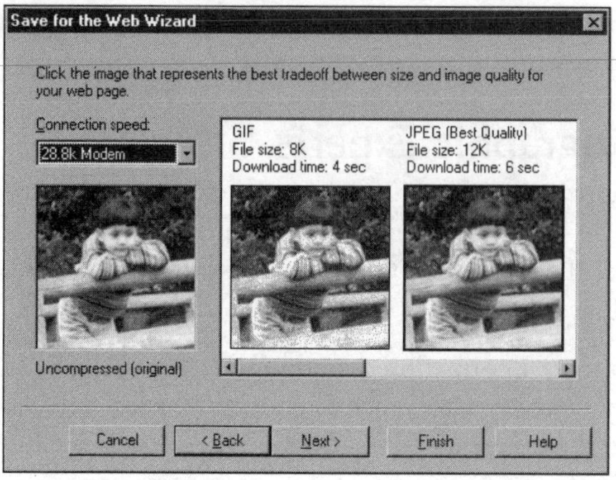

Figure 11.3 Both the file size and the quality of an image need to be considered for images destined for the Web.

replace GIF because of the patented LZW compression algorithm. Not only is PNG patent- and license-free, but it also combines the great features of GIF and JPEG into one file format.

The following are some of the attributes of the PNG file format:

➤ Lossless

➤ Supports 8-bit, 24-bit, 32-bit, and 48-bit color depths

➤ Provides progressive rendering

➤ Provides multiple file-compression options

➤ Provides 254 levels of transparency

➤ Supported in the latest and most popular Web browsers

At the time of this writing (and of the initial development of the i-Net+ exam), PNG is not yet widely deployed on the Web, whereas GIF and JPEG are. Nevertheless, the World Wide Web Consortium (W3C) adopted the PNG recommendation back in 1996, and PNG is expected to become increasingly popular and more widespread on the Web.

TIFF (Tag Image File Format)

TIFF (Tag Image File Format) is a highly flexible bitmap format commonly used in various applications and computer platforms. TIFF, which uses the .tif extension, is a specification originated by Aldus Corporation (now Adobe Systems) and various scanner manufacturers to create an image format for use in desktop publishing.

Note: TIFF may also be referred to as Tagged Image File Format.

TIFF provides a rich and detailed graphics format to take advantage of various imaging devices, including scanners. TIFF has several format variations. TIFF can use various compression schemes and several color modes, including black-and-white, grayscale, and color.

TIFF images are highly portable and are commonly used with scanners, frame grabbers, and paint and photo programs. Additionally, most other applications—such as word processors and desktop publishing programs—understand the TIFF format. TIFF images are typically of higher quality than JPEG or GIF images, and the file size of a TIFF image is much larger. For this reason, TIFF is not a common image file format used on the Web. In fact, most browsers do not support TIFF images without the use of a plug-in.

 TIFF images—which can include grayscale, color, or black-and-white images—are best used in print publishing and when working with scanners. TIFF images are not suited for use on the Web and typically require the support of a plug-in to view them within a Web browser.

BMP (Windows Bitmap)

BMP (Windows Bitmap) is a bitmap image format developed by Microsoft. BMP files use the .bmp file extension and are commonly used in the Windows operating systems. BMP is a device-independent bitmap (DIB), which means that it is designed to retain its original appearance, even in applications other than the one the image was designed in. BMP file sizes tend to be rather large and are not suitable for Web graphics. Additionally, because Windows uses a fixed color palette for BMP files, an image converted to a BMP format may experience a shift in colors.

 The BMP image format is common to the Windows operating system. Images such as the splash screen when Windows starts and the desktop wallpaper are BMP images.

EPS (Encapsulated PostScript)

EPS (Encapsulated PostScript) is a graphics file format used by Adobe's PostScript language. EPS files are commonly used in page layout programs, such as PageMaker and QuarkXPress. Whereas PostScript files contain only PostScript commands for printing graphics, EPS files can also represent graphics as bitmaps onscreen.

MOV (QuickTime Movie)

MOV (QuickTime Movie) is the file format for a movie that uses the QuickTime application. MOV files use the .mov extension; they are often used on the Internet with the QuickTime plug-in discussed earlier in this chapter.

MPEG (Moving Pictures Experts Group)

MPEG (Moving Pictures Experts Group) is a standard for compressing sound and movie files. MPEG files use the .mpg extension. MPEG files may be downloaded or even streamed over the Internet and viewed using an MPEG viewer or plug-in. In fact, newer specifications, such as MPEG-2, are used by digital-video delivery media such as satellite services and digital versatile disks (DVD).

MPEG can achieve high compression rates by storing and encoding only the changes between frames. MPEG files are then decoded using special hardware or software. One of the primary advantages of MPEG is its ability to provide compressed full-motion and full-screen video.

AVI (Audio Video Interleaved)

AVI (Audio Video Interleaved) is the file extension (.avi) used by Video for Windows (VFW). A multimedia technology that is integrated into the Windows operating systems, VFW typically uses the Windows Media Player to play AVI files. Like MOV and MPEG files, AVI is a video format commonly used on personal computers. Unlike MPEG, AVI files are not used for full-screen video, but AVI does not require special hardware.

RTF (Rich Text Format)

RTF (Rich Text Format) is a file format developed by Microsoft; this format uses the .rtf file extension. RTF provides a method for encoding formatted text into ASCII files by using special commands so the document can easily be transferred between applications. For example, a document created in a new version of Microsoft Word using Windows 98 can be converted to RTF and then can be viewed in an old version of WordPerfect using a Macintosh.

RTF provides a convenient way to convert formatted text so that the document can easily be exchanged among various types of word-processing programs and platforms.

PDF (Portable Document Format)

PDF (Portable Document Format) is a file format developed by Adobe Systems; this format uses the .pdf file extension. PDF files provide a method to view documents in their electronic form exactly as they appear in their original form. A PDF document will have the same look as the original document, without the need for the same application and fonts used to create the document. PDF files preserve all of the fonts, formatting, colors, and graphics of the original document.

PDF files are created by using a program named Adobe Acrobat. PDF files can then be read by Adobe Acrobat Reader, which is distributed as both a free standalone application and a plug-in. The use of PDF files is so ubiquitous that Acrobat Reader is often the first plug-in users install.

PDF files have many advantages, including support for file compression, hyperlinks, indexing, and form features. PDF files enable you to create and distribute documents at a cost that is often lower than the paper alternative. As a result, PDF files have many uses, including online manuals, magazine reprints, business reports, archiving, books, and tax forms. Figure 11.4 shows an example of a PDF file as viewed through the Acrobat Reader plug-in.

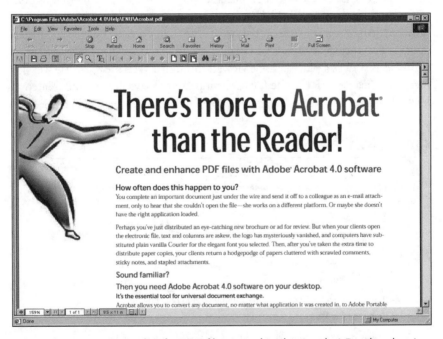

Figure 11.4   An example of a PDF file viewed in the Acrobat Reader plug-in.

Practice Questions

Question 1

All browsers capable of displaying graphics support which of the following image file formats?

○ a. GPG

○ b. GIF

○ c. MPEG

○ d. WRL

The correct answer is b. The GIF and JPEG image formats are ubiquitous on the Web. If JPEG were also a choice and you could choose only one option, you should always go with GIF because it was supported in even the earliest browsers. Answer a is incorrect because GPG is not a valid image file format. Answer c is incorrect because MPEG typically requires special hardware or software as well as a plug-in to be viewed through a Web browser. Answer d is incorrect because WRL is the file extension used to save documents created in Virtual Reality Modeling Language (VRML).

Question 2

Which of the following are true statements regarding MPEG? [Choose the two best answers]

❑ a. It is used to convert binary data, such as multimedia files, to ASCII format.

❑ b. It is a lossless graphic format that supports more than 200 levels of transparency.

❑ c. It maintains a high compression rate by storing only changes between frames.

❑ d. It was developed by Apple Computer and is used for audio and video playback.

❑ e. MPEG is an acronym for Moving Pictures Experts Group.

The correct answers are c and e. Moving Pictures Experts Group (MPEG) is a standard for compressing movie files. It maintains a high compression rate by storing and encoding only the changes between frames. Answer a is incorrect because this describes BinHex. Answer b is incorrect because this describes the PNG image file format. Answer d is incorrect because, although MPEG is associated with audio and video playback, Apple did not develop MPEG. Rather, MPEG standards were defined by a group in the International Standards Organization (ISO) technical committee.

Question 3

You work for a large publishing company, and you deal with screen captures and photographs daily. Which of the following graphic file formats should you use?

○ a. GIF

○ b. JPEG

○ c. PNG

○ d. TIFF

The correct answer is d. TIFF images are most suitable for print publishing and other tasks, such as scanning and storing images and working with photo and paint programs. GIF, JPEG, and PNG are image formats most commonly used to display inline images on Web pages; therefore, answers a, b, and c are incorrect.

Question 4

Which of the following is the best choice for developing a Web-based interactive business presentation?

○ a. Flash

○ b. RealNetworks

○ c. Shockwave

○ d. QuickTime VR

The correct answer is c. Shockwave content is developed with the Director Shockwave Studio program from Macromedia. Shockwave is popular on the Web for interactive games, but it has many uses, including business presentations, interactive Web content, kiosks, and CD-ROM and DVD titles and games. Answer a is incorrect because Flash is best used for designing visually stunning animation and effects. Although Flash can be used to create visually appealing presentations, Shockwave is the better choice because it can embed Flash content as well as provide a level of interactivity that Flash by itself is unable to provide. Answer b is incorrect because RealNetworks is the name of the company that makes the popular RealAudio and RealVideo plug-ins, used primarily for streaming media over the Internet. Answer d is incorrect because QuickTime VR is used primarily for letting users interact in a virtual 3D environment in which objects can be fully rotated and explored.

Question 5

The photography studio you work for wants to get involved in e-commerce. First, you develop a Web site, and next, you need to display various photographs on the site. Which of the following file formats should you select?

O a. JPEG

O b. GIF

O c. TIFF

O d. BMP

The correct answer is a. JPEG images are commonly used on the Web because of the image quality and file size. JPEG files are ideal for photographs or other continuous-tone images. Answer b is incorrect because GIF images support only 256 colors, making GIFs ideal for less complex images that contain solid colors. Both TIFF and BMP are capable of displaying great-looking photographs at the expense of a rather large file size, so neither of these are good choices for use on Web sites. Therefore, answers c and d are incorrect.

Question 6

You need to quickly send an associate a formatted text document you created in your latest and greatest word-processing program, but your associate uses an older version running on a different platform. Which of the following should you use before sending the document to your associate?

O a. Plain text format

O b. Portable Document Format

O c. Rich Text Format

O d. Word Document Format

The correct answer is c. Rich Text Format is used for transferring formatted text between various applications such as Microsoft Word and Corel WordPerfect, as well as those running on different platforms, such as Windows and Macintosh systems. Although a plain text document can be used to transfer files between various applications and platforms, any formatting will be lost; therefore, answer a is incorrect. Portable Document Format (PDF) files maintain the original look and feel of a document. However, to create a PDF file, you will first need to acquire the software to do so, and the recipient will require a reader application, so this would not be the best solution in this case; therefore, answer b is incorrect. Answer d is incorrect because the Word document format describes a document formatted in Microsoft Word, and it does not meet the universal requirement in this scenario.

Question 7

What does the acronym PNG stand for?

○ a. Portable Network Graphics

○ b. Protocol Network Group

○ c. Printable Network Graphics

○ d. Printable Network Group

The correct answer is a. PNG is the acronym for Portable Network Graphics. PNG was developed to replace GIF because of the legal entanglements surrounding the GIF format. Answers b, c, and d are incorrect because these were made up.

Question 8

Which of the following uses vector imaging?

○ a. BMP

○ b. GIF

○ c. JPEG

○ d. Flash

The correct answer is d. Flash uses vector graphics, in which the graphics are defined geometrically. BMP, GIF, and JPEG are all bitmap images, which are made up of a pattern of dots; therefore, answers a, b, and c are incorrect.

Question 9

Which of the following are likely candidates to be viewed as a PDF file? [Choose the two best answers]

❑ a. Tax forms

❑ b. Streaming movies

❑ c. Books

❑ d. Interactive Web pages

The correct answers are a and c. Portable Document Format (PDF) files are ideal for re-creating various types of documents in an electronic form. Typically, PDF files are used for documents that are traditionally printed. Thus, streaming movies and interactive Web pages are not ideal candidates for conversion to PDF; therefore, answers b and d are incorrect.

Need To Know More?

Murray, James D and William VanRyper. *Encyclopedia of Graphics File Formats, 2nd Edition*. O'Reilly & Associates, Inc., Sebastopol, CA, 1996. ISBN 1-56592-161-5. An authoritative and advanced guide to multimedia.

Simpson, Ron Jr. *Cutting Edge Web Audio*. Prentice Hall, Upper Saddle River, NJ, 1998. ISBN 0-13080-075-32. A comprehensive guide to everything about Web audio.

Weinman, Lynda. *Designing Web Graphics 3*. New Riders Publishing, Indianapolis, IN, 1999. ISBN 1-5620-594-91. If you are new to multimedia on the Web, this is a fantastic book that deals with many aspects of the Web and multimedia.

www.adobe.com has complete information about PDF files and PostScript technologies.

www.apple.com contains information about the QuickTime plug-in and QTVR.

www.macromedia.com contains white papers and examples of Flash and Shockwave Web sites.

www.microsoft.com contains information about various multimedia technologies in general and about Microsoft's own products, such as Windows BMP and AVI files.

www.realnetworks.com contains information about streaming media and about RealNetworks' products, including streaming media products such as RealPlayer.

www.w3c.org contains a wealth of information on the various multimedia Web standards.

Site Functionality And Testing

Terms you'll need to understand:

√ Usability testing

√ Functional testing

√ Cookies

√ Full-text index

√ Keyword index

√ Stemming

√ Stop words

√ Reverse proxy

Techniques you'll need to master:

√ Recognizing the importance of usability and functional testing

√ Understanding how cookies can be used to improve your site

√ Recognizing the security and privacy implications of cookies

√ Knowing the concepts related to enabling your site for searching

The process of creating a Web site is evolutionary and cyclical. Creating and maintaining a Web site is much more than just coding HTML. Critical to the success of any site is adequate testing before the site is launched. Additionally, even after the Web site is launched, you need to continually test and evaluate the site as well as constantly consider what can be done to improve its overall functionality.

Web Site Testing And Launching

After developing a Web site, you should plan to perform various tests. These tests should include testing the actual Web pages and possibly the Web server. A company's Web site is a direct reflection upon the company, thus creating the need to ensure that the Web site functions well and that it at least meets customer expectations. In fact, the process of testing a Web site is similar to the process of testing programs and applications.

Before rolling out a completed Web site, you should conduct two types of tests: testing for proper usability and testing for functionality. After the Web site has been thoroughly tested, you can begin preparation for a launch, which might include press releases and registration with search engines. Don't forget, however, that the party is not over—your site will need to undergo continual evaluation, testing, and support.

Although it is critical that you perform these tests before rolling out a Web site, you should also ensure that such tests continue even after a Web site has been made publicly available. Typically, Web sites follow a life cycle, much like that of software and other systems in which the product evolves through a series of steps, which are continuous and ongoing.

Usability Testing

Usability testing typically requires the use of other people not directly involved in the development of the site. These people can be internal to the organization or even select individuals external to the organization. Microsoft, for example, conducts extensive usability tests to determine what the customer expects, as well as to increase the efficiency of delivering the content from its Web site. Microsoft even has a Web site dedicated to usability, which can be found at **www.microsoft.com/usability/default.htm**. If possible, during the design phase of the Web site, you should consider involving users and other people outside the development process.

Functional Testing

Functional testing concentrates on the proper operations of the Web site, ensuring that the site operates as intended. Whereas usability testing is primarily concerned with the user's expectations, functional testing is done to ensure the following:

➤ All links (hot links) work correctly.

➤ The site is accessible through various browsers.

➤ Users are supported at various connection speeds.

➤ The site can support the projected traffic.

➤ Database and e-commerce integration works properly.

Link Checking

Before rolling out a Web site, you should ensure the validity of all your links (hot links). One way to do this is manually—by clicking and following through with all the links. Unfortunately, for larger sites, this method can become quite cumbersome, as well as make it difficult to consistently keep up with any external links that may have been changed. Fortunately, however, many tools and programs can assist in testing links. For example, Figure 12.1 shows how Microsoft FrontPage can be used to monitor the status of all links from your Web site.

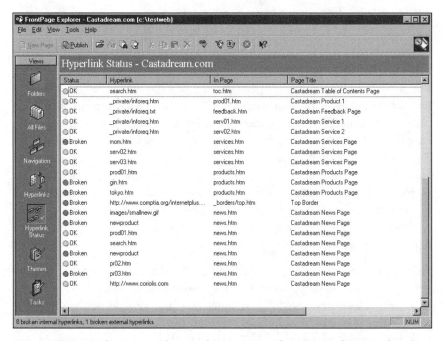

Figure 12.1   Software can be used to monitor the status of internal and external links.

Browser Testing

You will also want to ensure that your pages are displayed properly in the browser that the audience uses. If you are unsure which browser visitors are likely to use, you will, at a minimum, want to ensure that your site appears properly in the most popular browsers. This, unfortunately, means that some visitors—those using lesser-known browsers or using older versions of popular browsers—might experience problems with your Web site.

One way to deal with this is to visually inspect your Web site using different browsers; however, this is not necessarily the most efficient method because there are so many browser types. Additionally, to test different versions of the same browser from one computer can present a problem because it is difficult, if not impossible, to concurrently install two versions of the same browser onto one computer. You may want to consider using one of the many tools available that can check your site's functionality in different browsers.

 If you're serious about your Web site, you may find it important to keep up with current Internet trends. Take a peek at **www. statmarket.com**, which monitors trends such as the percentage of users using various browsers, plug-ins, operating systems, and more.

Speed Connection Testing

You should test your Web site's performance over various connection speeds. If your site is loaded with multimedia extras and large files, you risk alienating many users who use slower modem connections. If your site's primary audience has high bandwidth access, you might consider providing alternatives for those who do not. For example, you could provide an alternate text-only site, and you could specify the size of files so that users could better decide whether to download them. Testing your site at various speeds allows you to get a feel for what the user will experience. If you find that your site does not provide an adequate load time at lower speeds, you may want to consider what can be done to improve the results.

Aside from manually testing your site over various connection speeds, you can also use various tools that can quickly analyze your Web site and provide feedback about your site's load time. Many Web sites—such as **www.netmechanic.com**—provide free and subscription-based services for testing your site. Table 12.1 shows an example of the time it takes to load the home page for **www.useit.com** across various modem speeds.

Table 12.1 Load time by modem speed.	
Modem Speed	**Download Time**
14.4Kbps	8.11 seconds
28.8Kbps	5.05 seconds
56Kbps	3.55 seconds
ISDN (128Kbps)	2.69 seconds
T1 (1.44 Mbps)	2.06 seconds

Load Testing

Adequate load testing helps ensure that your Web site can withstand the computing burden placed on the system by simultaneous user requests. Load testing is critical to ensure that your site can support a specific number of visitors. Load testing allows you to determine your site's response time and provides a means to measure how your site reacts under heavy loads. Load testing can also provide valuable insight in answering the following questions:

➤ Will the site crash if placed under a certain load?

➤ Are the software and hardware optimally tuned?

As your site grows in popularity, proper load testing becomes more critical. Your site should also be prepared as much as possible for the unexpected times as well as for the times you know your site may experience more traffic than usual. A recent high-profile case of a Web site crashing involved Britannica.com, which had to be temporarily shut down because the site was collapsing as a result of the many hits being received. There are also countless other instances in which sites experienced delays and crashes during the holiday season.

Many products are available that can test your systems by simulating thousands of simultaneous requests. Another option might be to use *mirror sites*. A mirror site typically contains copies of files, which can be downloaded from alternate locations spread across the country or even the world. If your site contains large downloadable files, you may want to consider providing these mirrors. In addition to reducing the stress from your primary site by distributing the load, mirror sites also provide an alternative to the consumption of bandwidth across international circuits.

Available from Microsoft is Web Capacity Analysis Tool (WCAT), a free utility for testing client-server network configurations. This free tool and documentation are available for download from **http://msdn.microsoft.com/workshop/server/toolbox/wcat.asp**.

E-Commerce Testing

Extra care should be given to ensuring the functionality of e-commerce sites. Unlike traditional methods of commerce, conducting business on the Web typically requires multitier systems, all of which must properly interact with one another. Many e-commerce sites have millions of visitors who demand that their purchases or other transactions be conducted safely and efficiently.

In addition to ensuring that the e-commerce site can function under heavy loads, you must also be careful with any changes made on the site. If you operate a simple personal Web site, most likely you can easily go in and change the site, but on an e-commerce site, even a simple change—such as adjusting the interface of a form—can corrupt the entire system. Because of the tight integration required among various systems—such as Web servers, application servers, transaction servers, and database servers—it is important that e-commerce sites be looked at as a system rather than as just a Web site.

 A process should be devised for testing each Web site. Remember the considerations listed in this chapter, and understand that such tests are critical both in the pre-launch stage and after the Web site has been publicly released.

Using Cookies

In Chapter 6, you were introduced to cookies and how the client uses them. In this section, we will focus on how the server uses cookies, as well as on the security and privacy implications that need to be considered. Cookies are most commonly used to provide customized Web pages to users.

Cookies serve as a great tool for identifying visitors and providing a more personalized experience. Cookies have, however, received some negative press about the possibility of security and privacy implications. As a result, it is important that you address these concerns for your visitors.

If your site uses cookies, you should also make available a disclosure statement, often included in a site's privacy policy. This statement should make it clear that your site uses cookies, and it should explain why it uses cookies.

 Need assistance in creating a privacy policy? TRUSTe offers a free privacy wizard to assist in creating a privacy statement for your Web site. Visit **www.truste.org/wizard/**.

There are many ways in which cookies can be effectively and responsibly used. Examples include: using cookies to deliver customized sites based upon information collected from your visitors; maintaining online "shopping cart" information; and delivering tailored advertisements.

Another benefit of using cookies, but one that has brought up invasion-of-privacy issues, is the ability to track visitors across your Web site. Monitoring your visitors' tracks across your site can have both positive and negative effects. First, it might give users the impression that they're being watched, and they might feel as though they have no privacy. On the other hand, site tracking can provide an effective tool for monitoring the usability of your site. For example, you may notice a trend that most visitors are leaving the site upon arriving at a certain page. As a result, you may examine the page and discover that this page lacks further links of interest. Again, be sure that you disclose this information and explain how such a policy will ultimately benefit the customer.

There are many positive uses for cookies; however, do not use cookies to store sensitive information! Even if you believe that storing a credit card number in a cookie is safe, the visitors' perception of security is also important; that is, your customers must also believe that their data is secure. Visitors might not be too happy to find that their credit card data or even their passwords are being stored in a cookie. One alternative might be to use cookies to store unique numbers, which can then be referred to a server-side database.

Site Searching

To help users find information, the Web contains many search sites, such as **www.yahoo.com** and **www.altavista.com**. After a site has been found, how-ever, users typically expect to find additional resources for locating information *within* the site. Various methods and technologies can be used to provide users with a better search experience.

One of the simplest methods—and one that most users have come to expect—is the use of a static index or site map. These are roughly the online equivalent of a table of contents or an index that you might find in a book. Figure 12.2 shows an example of the site map from Apple's Web site. Another type of search feature you can provide lets users search for keywords or key phrases via a search form added to your site. This method typically requires that you index your own pages. An index is basically a catalog of keywords.

There are various terms and techniques that relate to indexing your site. These include:

➤ *Full-text index*—An index that contains every word of every document that has been cataloged.

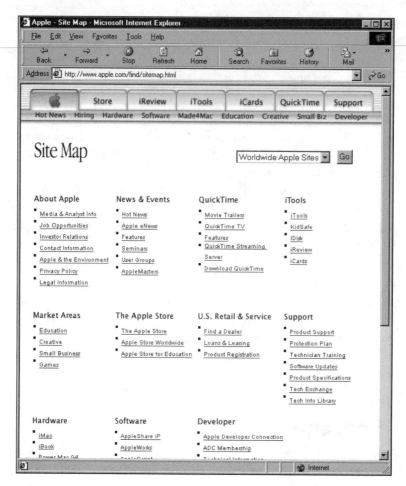

Figure 12.2 An example of a site map from Apple Computer's Web site.

➤ *Keyword search*—A type of search that queries one or more keywords as specified by the user.

➤ *Stemming*—A technique that searches for the base or stem of a word. For example, a search for "chanting" will also return results for the word "chant."

➤ *Stop words*—These include words that are often repeated and by themselves might not mean much. These stop words typically include conjunctions (such as "and"), articles (such as "the"), and prepositions (such as "over" and "through").

Reverse Proxy

In addition to the caching technologies discussed in Chapter 6, another type of caching technology can be deployed on the Web-server side to improve the performance of the site: a reverse proxy. A reverse proxy server can be placed in front of a Web server to make better use of server resources. Although these servers are often called *reverse proxies*, you may also hear the terms *reverse cache*, *inverse cache*, and *accelerator*. A reverse proxy allows the Web server to dedicate its resources to various intensive tasks, while the reverse proxy can concentrate its efforts on delivering responses to the Web clients.

Practice Questions

Question 1

> Which of the following is true of testing Web sites?
>
> ○ a. Only the development staff should do testing.
>
> ○ b. Testing a Web site is similar to program and application testing.
>
> ○ c. Proper pre-launch testing ensures that no testing will be required later.
>
> ○ d. Smarter users are needed to improve a Web site's usability.

The correct answer is b. The development and testing process for a Web site is very similar to that of a traditional program or system—even more so, as more and more Web sites support various tiers and incorporate various programming features. Answer a is incorrect because individuals who have nothing to do with the development or maintenance of the site are often used to test Web sites. The process is much like that of *beta* software, which users test before final software is released. Testing a Web site before launch is critical, but a Web site should also continually undergo testing and evaluation; therefore, answer c is incorrect. Although many developers would like to believe that smarter users are needed, what is really needed is better development; therefore, answer d is incorrect.

Question 2

> Which of the following tasks best describe functional testing? [Choose the three best answers]
>
> ❑ a. Ensuring that all hot links work correctly.
>
> ❑ b. Ensuring that the site can support projected traffic.
>
> ❑ c. Ensuring that the user interface is intuitive.
>
> ❑ d. Ensuring that e-commerce components do not become corrupted.

The correct answers are a, b, and d. Functional testing involves several factors, including ensuring the validity of all hot links, testing the site's performance across various speeds and loads, and ensuring proper integration with database and e-commerce systems. Answer c is incorrect because a Web site's interface, intuitiveness, and ease of use would fall under usability testing.

Question 3

Which of the following sites might you consider if your site offers shareware to be downloaded?

○ a. Stress

○ b. Mirror

○ c. Share

○ d. Load

The correct answer is b. Mirror sites contains duplicate sets of files in order to distribute the load. Web sites that provide large files for download often incorporate the use of mirror sites. Answers a, c, and d are incorrect because these are not valid types of sites.

Question 4

What is *not* a reason for using cookies to improve the user's experience?

○ a. To store the customer's credit card number within the cookie for ease of shopping as well as for security.

○ b. To deliver a Web page with customized content.

○ c. To maintain an online "shopping cart."

○ d. To monitor what users view and do across your site.

The correct answer is a. A cookie should not be used to store sensitive information such as a credit card number. Answers b, c, and d are incorrect because these are valid reasons to use cookies to improve the user's experience. Although following a user's tracks across your Web site may raise privacy concerns, this is still a common action employed by many sites to follow user trends, which are then used to improve the overall site experience. Ensure you implement a privacy statement that clearly describes your site's policies. Make sure you describe not only what you do, but also why you do it.

Question 5

A user searching a Web page for the word "swimming" is returned results for the word "swim." What is this an example of?

○ a. Rooting

○ b. Branching

○ c. Stemming

○ d. Truncating

The correct answer is c. Stemming is the process by which search utilities can look for both the specified word and the base or "stem" of the word. Answers a, b, and d are incorrect and do not relate to any type of search technique.

Need To Know More?

 Lynch, Patrick. *Web Style Guide: Basic Design Principles for Creating Web Sites*. Yale Press, New Haven, CT, 1999. ISBN 0-300-076575-4. A guide that concentrates on the principles of Web site usability.

 Rosenfeld, Louis and Peter Morville. *Information Architecture for the World Wide Web*. O'Reilly & Associates Inc., Sebastopol, CA, 1999. ISBN 1-56592-282-4. This book provides valuable insight and provokes thought on Web usability and functionality.

 www.capacityplanning.com/ provides information and a handful of white papers on capacity planning for Web servers and other types of servers.

 www.cookiecentral.com/ is a Web site dedicated to cookies. Besides in-depth information about cookies, this site also provides various demonstrations.

 www.microsoft.com/usability/ is Microsoft's research site dedicated to usability.

 www.useit.com/ is a Web site from former Sun Microsystem's usability expert, Jakob Nielsen. This site is filled with insightful articles on Web usability.

Security

Terms you'll need to understand:

- √ Intranet
- √ Extranet
- √ Access control
- √ Firewall
- √ Access control list (ACL)
- √ Packet filtering
- √ Authentication
- √ Smart card
- √ Biometrics
- √ Digital certificate
- √ Digital signature
- √ Public Key Infrastructure (PKI)
- √ Encryption
- √ Pretty Good Privacy (PGP)
- √ Secure Multipurpose Internet Mail Extensions (S/MIME)
- √ Secure Sockets Layer (SSL)
- √ Secure Electronic Transaction (SET)
- √ Auditing
- √ Virtual Private Network (VPN)
- √ Anti-virus software
- √ Denial of Service (DoS)
- √ Mail flooding
- √ Ping flood
- √ Smurfing
- √ SYN flood
- √ Spam

Techniques you'll need to master:

- √ Knowing internetworking security concepts and associated technologies
- √ Understanding the purpose of a Virtual Private Network
- √ Recognizing various types of attacks and suspicious activities

The Internet expands our private networks and provides further opportunities to build more powerful and accessible systems, as well as increases the opportunities for e-commerce and corporate globalization. These benefits, however, have increased our susceptibility to intrusion and other security violations. Security is without a doubt a complex and important topic, especially as more businesses rely on networks for their success. Despite security's complexities, there are several underlying principles, such as authentication, access control, integrity, cryptography, and auditing.

Inter-, Intra-, and Extranet Security

Security requirements vary among the different types of networks. Nevertheless, many networks utilize many of the same technologies discussed in this chapter. A Web site, for example, requires that Internet users be able to view the site, but measures must be taken to ensure that the site is not so open that it can be attacked. Even a corporate local area network typically requires that users have easy access to the Internet, yet security must be balanced to ensure that external elements, such as users and services, are unable to access the local area network or resources to which they weren't assigned access.

Intranets and extranets have become increasingly popular and present several new security challenges. An *intranet* is a private network that utilizes Internet technologies, such as TCP/IP. An intranet may be a completely separate entity from the Internet, yet some intranets still require Internet connectivity, in which case a security device such as a firewall is critical. Intranets present many security challenges and become further complicated when organizations extend them to connect with other intranets, thus forming extranets. An extranet, like an intranet, uses Internet technologies, but an extranet extends limited access to various partners such as customers and vendors.

One of the biggest security concerns for intranets and extranets is protecting the networks from inside attacks. The security technologies discussed in this chapter can, however, provide solutions for many of these security concerns. The following are the primary issues of concern for these types of networks:

➤ *Authentication*—Proper identification must be positively established before access privileges can be applied. Access privileges should, of course, be properly defined and enforced.

➤ *Integrity*—The accuracy of data is critical, and it's jeopardized when data is transmitted. Integrity ensures that data is not altered in transit.

➤ *Privacy*—Encryption technologies and Virtual Private Networks (VPNs) provide methods for ensuring that information is viewed by only the intended parties.

➤ *Non-repudiation*—The origin of information (such as messages) needs to be positively established so that it later cannot be said to have been forged.

You need to understand the access requirements of Internet sites, intranets, and extranets. Typically, an Internet site should be accessible to everyone. An intranet is private and should be accessible only to the internal organization. An extranet allows business partners, customers, and vendors to gain limited access to an organization's intranet.

Access Control

There are many methods for controlling access to networks. These mechanisms are typically the first line of defense in internetworking security. The goal of access control is to selectively permit or deny users' access to resources. This, however, is one of the trickier parts of access control—determining who needs what information. Ideally, users are given access to only the information needed and nothing more.

Firewalls

Again, multiple methods of controlling access exist. A dial-up server, for example, might control access by calling back a predefined number to ensure that access is attempted from a specific location. On networks, one of the first and best-known methods for controlling access is a firewall. A *firewall* is a security system that can be used to permit or deny traffic based upon specific criteria. A firewall is like a club bouncer who lets in only people who are 21 or older.

A firewall can be hardware- or software-based, and is typically a combination of both. A dedicated firewall, a proxy server, a standard operating system, and routers can all provide firewall-type features by controlling access from one network to the next.

Access Control Lists (ACLs) And Packet Filtering

Access control lists (ACLs) are used to filter network traffic by either permitting (forwarding) or denying (blocking) packets to and from a network. Depending upon the criteria specified in the ACL, the incoming or outgoing traffic can be filtered. For example, an ACL configured on a router's interface can be set to deny all incoming traffic from network address 209.0.85.1, or it can deny traffic based on protocols, such as the User Datagram Protocol (UDP).

Firewalls and ACLs are usually only the first line of defense. Basic access lists do not authenticate, as do passwords and certificates, discussed later in this chapter. This first security perimeter is an important obstacle to the potentially malicious attacker, but it should never be relied upon as the only defense.

File Access Control

Another important control mechanism is *file access control*. This control is also sometimes referred to as an *access control list*, but in contrast to the lists discussed previously, the file-access-control list pertains primarily to an operating system and to a user's or group's ability to access or modify a file.

Each user is assigned an account on the system, and each user can belong to one or more groups. Depending upon the control given, a user will have certain privileges pertaining to files and folders. For example, one person might have full control over a specific document, whereas others can only view the file and cannot delete or change it. Table 13.1 lists general types of permissions for controlling access to files and folders.

 Permissions on Unix hosts come in three types: Read, Write, and Execute. The Write permission enables you to change a file, but in order to delete the file, you must be assigned the Write permission for the directory in which the file resides. On Windows systems, you should also be aware of the *no access* permission, which overrides any other given permission and, as its name implies, prevents access to files and folders. *No access* on a Unix host is specified by not assigning Read, Write, or Execute permissions.

Authentication

Authentication is a verification process that ensures the identity of a user. For example, suppose that someone is knocking at your door, and after asking, "who is it?" you hear the person identify himself as the mail courier. To ascertain the identity of the individual, you might then look through the peephole to verify that the individual is who he says he is. In a computing environment and especially on the Internet, it is often difficult, if not impossible, to visually verify the identity of a user—thus, the importance of verification methods such as passwords, smart cards, digital certificates, and digital signatures.

Table 13.1 File and folder access control types.	
Control	**Description**
Read (R)	View attributes, permissions, and the contents of folders and files.
Write (W)	Change attributes and file and folder content; search directories.
Execute (X)	Run files, such as executable programs.
Delete (D)	Delete files and folders.

Passwords

A password is generally the simplest and most used form of authentication. A password is composed of a string of characters, which are used to identify a user before permitting access to system resources. Ideally, a password should be committed to memory and never divulged to anyone else. Following are additional guidelines for creating passwords:

➤ Do *not* use any word that can be associated with you, such as your child's name or your vehicle type.

➤ Do *not* use any word that is found in a dictionary.

➤ Do *not* use your user ID.

➤ Do *not* use patterns such as QWERTY or AABBCC.

➤ Do use a minimum of six to eight characters.

➤ Do use mixed case, but do not mix only the case of the first or last character.

➤ Do include numerals or punctuation characters, but do not simply replace an "O" with "0" or an "I" for a "1."

➤ Do change your password often, and ensure password uniqueness—that is, do *not* reuse old passwords.

Passwords provide a secure means of authentication—but only if passwords are properly chosen and guarded. Cracking passwords does not necessarily take a supercomputer or an experienced hacker; in fact, many tools can take advantage of the fact that often users choose words that they can easily remember. Even a password policy that requires passwords to be eight characters, mixed case, and containing at least one number will still allow users to choose an easy-to-guess password such as "Passw0rd." Figure 13.1 shows an example of a password-cracking program from L0pht Heavy Industries in action, cracking the accounts on a Windows NT machine. Such a tool can be a valuable asset for administrators to ensure the integrity of passwords on the network.

 Perhaps, educating users about the importance of a strong password is the most important first step. I know one administrator who—to ensure that everyone on the network had a strong password—made it known that he would occasionally run a password-cracking utility; anyone whose password he discovered would face serious consequences.

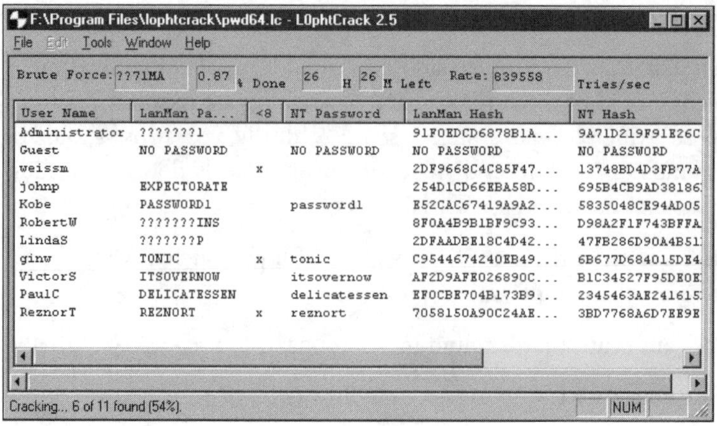

Figure 13.1 A password cracker in action.

Smart Cards

Password authentication relies upon what a person knows, but the level of authentication can be further layered by combining a password with something a person physically has possession of, such as a key or a smart card. This is similar to using your bank's automatic teller machine—you must not only know your personal identification number or password, but you must also have physical custody of a card. A *smart card* is typically a credit-card-size device that contains an integrated circuit and that's used with a smart card reader.

Biometrics

Biometrics is traditionally defined as the statistical analysis of biological observations and phenomena, yet it is also the term given to a more recent technique for computer authentication. In addition to authenticating with something you know and something you have, biometrics presents a third layer, which relies upon something that is part of a person's biological makeup, such as speech, retinas, or fingerprints. Biometrics is successful because everyone has different biological characteristics, and certainly the use of biometrics authentication will continue to rise as the cost of associated hardware and software continue to fall.

Digital Certificates

Digital certificates provide a means of ensuring an individual's or organization's identity. These can be thought of as the online equivalent of a driver's license or passport. Digital certificates are used to ensure the validity of information transferred over the Internet and across intranets by positively identifying the involved parties. Figure 13.2 shows an example of my digital certificate.

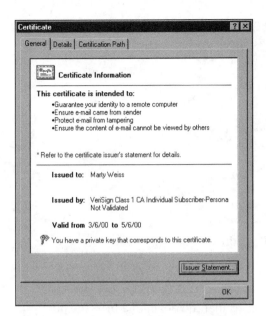

Figure 13.2   A personal digital certificate.

*Note: You may also hear digital certificates referred to as Digital IDs.
Keep in mind, however, that digital certificate is the generic term, and
Digital ID is a servicemark of VeriSign, Inc.*

Digital certificates are used to validate the identity of an organization and its
servers. Digital certificates are also used by individuals for exchanging messages with others. In addition, developers use digital certificates in their software
to authenticate the software and its authors for clients who might download
the software. In the latter case, the certificate ensures that the software being
downloaded is genuine (see Figure 13.3).

Digital certificates are issued and signed by a Certification Authority (CA)—
typically a trusted third party such as VeriSign. Alternatively, a CA may also
exist internally to an organization by establishing an internal authority responsible for certificate management using a certificate server product such as
Netscape Certificate Server or Microsoft Certificate Server. A CA must perform many important duties, such as validating the identity of an individual or
organization, maintaining the life-cycle services of certificates, and maintaining very high standards of security. Digital certificates use public key encryption,
which is an encryption process discussed shortly. Ultimately, a CA provides
the "keys" used in digital certificates for authentication and encryption.

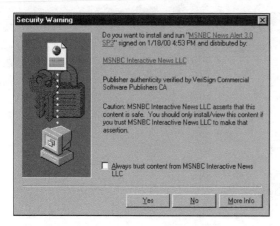

Figure 13.3 Installing software, verified to be authentic.

 Digital certificates provide a non-repudiated means of authentication and are defined under the X.509 standards. *Non-repudiation* implies that the origin of a message, for example, is in fact true and cannot later be claimed to have been forged.

Digital Signatures

Digital signatures are similar to their handwritten counterparts—only more secure. A digital signature relies on public key encryption. Widely used in electronic correspondence, a digital signature assures the recipient of the message's integrity. A digital signature is used with a digital certificate, thus providing the means to validate the identity of the sender. It can be said that a digital certificate authenticates a digital message.

Do not confuse a digital signature with the block of identification information—such as the sender's name and telephone number or a digitally created image of a signature—usually appended to the end of an email. A digital signature is really nothing more than a one-way hashing algorithm and key encryption used to ensure that information was not altered.

Cryptography

When cryptography is discussed, the term "key" is often used, but it doesn't describe the traditional metal object used with a physical locking device; rather, the term is analogous. *Cryptography keys* describe a string of bits, which are used for encrypting and decrypting information.

The two types of cryptographic systems in use are secret key and public key. *Secret key cryptography* is a symmetric process in which the same key is used for both the encryption and decryption processes. *Public key cryptography* is an asymmetric process that relies upon two keys—a public key and a private key.

Secret key cryptography is not well suited for the needs of the Internet. Secret key cryptography requires that each person trust the other to guard the secret key; in addition, the exchange of secret keys is not feasible considering the distributed nature of the Internet. Finally, the nature of the Internet and the success of e-commerce and communications over the Internet rely upon fundamental issues such as authentication and non-repudiation, which secret-key cryptography does not address.

> *Note: Data Encryption Standard (DES) is the most popular secret-key system in use. DES was developed by IBM and later adopted by the U.S. government as a standard. The most popular public-key system is the RSA Public Key Cryptosystem. RSA stands for the developers of this system: Rivest, Shamir, and Adleman.*

Public Key Infrastructure (PKI)

Public Key Infrastructure (PKI) provides the infrastructure for TCP/IP networks to apply the security mechanisms available in the "real" world to the Internet, as well as to intranets and extranets. Relying upon public key cryptography, this infrastructure is the system of digital certificates, digital signatures, and Certificate Authorities that provide the means to match or exceed the level of security provided by mechanisms such as physical signatures, envelopes, seals, and identification cards.

Digital Certificates

Digital certificates are based upon public key cryptography and use two keys: a private key and a public key. The private key is kept a secret, and only the owner should have access to this key, whereas the public key is distributed within the certificate and made available to others. The authenticity of this public key is verifiable via the Certificate Authority of the issued certificate.

The private and public keys are inversely related—that is, what one does, only the other can undo. Therefore, the public key can decrypt only data that is encrypted with the private key, and data encrypted with the public key can be decrypted only with the private key.

Digital Signatures

A digital signature by itself does not encrypt the actual contents of a message, so the recipient does not require a digital certificate to view the signed message.

In order to encrypt a message, the sender must encrypt the contents by using the receiver's public key. A digital signature does ensure, however, that the message was not modified in transit.

Encryption is used with digital signatures to encrypt the message digest. To create a message digest, a hash function (complex mathematical algorithm) is performed on the message before it is sent, and this same function is in turn performed on the receiving end. Even if the message was modified only slightly, the hash function will return hash results much different from the original. The signature or message digest is encrypted, and it is decrypted on the recipient's end by using the sender's public key.

Pretty Good Privacy (PGP)

Pretty Good Privacy (PGP) is a technique used for encrypting and digitally signing messages. PGP software, which is available for free on the Internet, uses public key cryptography. By using the PGP encryption package, you can encrypt messages and allow others to decrypt your messages by using a public and private key pair.

Philip Zimmerman developed PGP. He became the subject of a criminal investigation when PGP was published as freeware in the early 1990s and found its way overseas, violating United States export restrictions on cryptographic software. Further information on government encryption concerns is detailed here shortly.

Secure/Multipurpose Internet Mail Extensions (S/MIME)

Secure/Multipurpose Internet Mail Extensions (S/MIME) adds secure support to the widely used MIME email protocol. S/MIME supports message encryption and digital signatures, and it has been endorsed by many companies, including Microsoft, Lotus Development Corporation, Novell, Netscape Communications, and VeriSign.

By using a combination of digital signatures and encryption, S/MIME provides additional security support, such as authentication, integrity, and non-repudiation. The S/MIME process using encryption and digital signatures also uses the public and private key pair.

PGP and S/MIME both support email encryption and digital signatures.

Web Security

Earlier in the book, you learned that the Hypertext Transfer Protocol (HTTP) is the communications protocol for the Web. HTTP by itself, however, does not provide the security needed for e-commerce. To address the issue of security, the following protocols have been developed:

➤ Secure Sockets Layer (SSL)

➤ Secure Electronic Transaction (SET)

> *Note: A third method developed, called Secure Hypertext Transfer Protocol (S-HTTP), also enhances the security of HTTP. S-HTTP is a symmetric key technology that does not secure the communications channel but secures individual messages.*

Secure Sockets Layer (SSL) is a protocol developed by Netscape Communications to provide secure and private client and server authentication over the Internet. Although SSL is most used for Web transactions, the SSL protocol can be layered with other connection-oriented protocols, such as FTP and SMTP. A secure connection between a client and a server using SSL requires the server to send its digital certificate to ensure that the client it's communicating with is a trustworthy source. The two will continue a handshaking procedure to negotiate a method for key exchange, the encryption algorithm, and the hash function to be used.

 Secure Sockets Layer (SSL) connections are identifiable and initiated with a Uniform Resource Locator (URL) that begins with *https:* in the client's Web browser.

Secure Electronic Transaction (SET) is a protocol developed by several organizations, including Visa and MasterCard, to provide a secure method for credit card transactions over the Internet. SET uses public key encryption to ensure that the involved parties are the only ones that can view the account information. Additionally, SET uses digital certificates to verify the legitimacy of a merchant. SET can even be used to validate the cardholder's authorization to use the card, provided that the cardholder has obtained a certificate from the credit card provider.

 The Secure Electronic Transaction protocol provides the following three benefits:

➤ Ensures the safe transfer of credit card or other payment information.

➤ Assures consumers that a merchant is authorized to accept credit cards.

➤ Assures merchants that a consumer is authorized to use a particular credit card.

Encryption Concerns

Strong cryptography is on the United States Munitions List and is an export-controlled commodity along the same lines as bombs, missiles, and other technologies that present a potential use for criminals or as weapons of war. Many Internet users first become familiar with these political issues when attempting to download a Web browser. Typically, Web browsers are offered in a 40-bit version and a 128-bit version. In the past, downloading a browser with 128-bit encryption required you to agree to various statements about such things as your citizenship. Furthermore, the server from whom you received your browser most likely checked your Internet Protocol (IP) address to ensure that you were not located in a foreign country. The government takes the export of such munitions very seriously, and even posting strong encryption technologies on your private Web site might constitute exporting, which may land you in serious trouble.

Just recently, however, the U.S. government has relaxed its encryption export policy. Despite the relaxed regulations, strict rules still exist concerning exports to many countries, such as Cuba, Iran, Iraq, North Korea, and other U.S.-embargoed destinations. For more information on encryption concerns and the latest export laws, visit the Web site of the Department of Commerce's Bureau of Export and Administration at **www.bxa.doc.gov/**.

Auditing

Auditing is an important part of security, which unfortunately is often overlooked. *Auditing* is the process of recording and identifying events related to security. This process typically provides feedback via a log in which security-related events are documented. Some implementations of auditing provide mechanisms to push the alert to an administrator or other person in charge of security.

A well-defined and well-implemented auditing policy plays an important role in security. The practice of maintaining and verifying security logs provides several benefits, including:

➤ Tracking potential and existing security problems

➤ Helping to ensure accountability

➤ Providing evidence in the event of a security breach

Figure 13.4 shows an example of the security log generated by Windows 2000 Server. In this example, a log is kept that quickly identifies the security events set to be logged. Additionally, each item can be further analyzed as shown with the active dialog box in Figure 13.4, which provides details about an attempt to log on with an incorrect password.

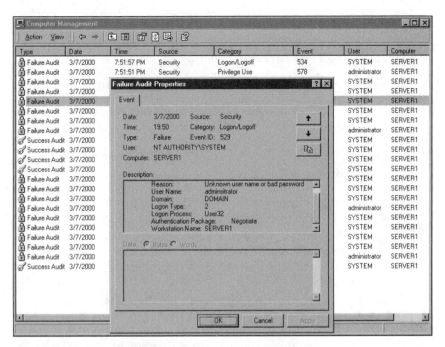

Figure 13.4   The Windows 2000 Server security log.

Virtual Private Networks

A Virtual Private Network (VPN) is a secure method for connecting two or more nodes using a non-secure public network such as the Internet. For example, rather than have a remote office or user connected directly to the corporate office via an expensive private leased line, the remote sites can connect to their local Internet Service Provider (ISP) to gain Internet access, and then use the Internet as the medium for communications. By implementing VPN technologies such as encryption and encapsulation, you create a private "tunnel" through the Internet for the two offices to communicate.

The packets of data that use a VPN to traverse the Internet are encrypted and then encapsulated. Several protocols are involved in creating a VPN. These protocols (discussed in Chapter 4) include:

➤ *Point-to-Point Tunneling Protocol (PPTP)*—Encapsulates secure packets inside an IP packet.

➤ *Layer 2 Forwarding (L2F)*—Encapsulates secure packets and is protocol-independent.

➤ *Layer 2 Tunneling Protocol (L2TP)*—Combines the features of PPTP and L2F and relies upon IPSec for encryption.

➤ *IP Security (IPSec)*—Provides authentication, integrity, and encryption.

VPNs can be used in a variety of scenarios. VPNs provide the framework for intranets and extranets, as well as for connecting individual remote users to a site. Three types of VPNs have been defined:

➤ *Access VPN*—A link between a corporate network and mobile users.

➤ *Intranet VPN*—A link between a corporate network and remote offices and branch offices.

➤ *Extranet VPN*—A link between a corporate network and its strategic partners, customers, and suppliers.

 A Virtual Private Network (VPN) creates a virtually private passageway through the Internet by using encapsulation and encryption technologies. Access, intranet, and extranet VPNs give remote users, remote offices, and business partners a secure and cost-efficient means of connecting to corporate networks.

Anti-Virus Software

Anti-virus software (also called *virus protection software*) is designed with the specific purpose of protecting your systems from viruses. Anti-virus software, however, is only as good as its database of known viruses. Because new viruses are introduced every day, anti-virus programs need to be constantly updated. Most programs provide a feature to accomplish this task by automatically updating the program from the Internet.

Systems can be vulnerable to viruses in a variety of ways. Originally, viruses were usually transferred from computer to computer via a floppy disk, but with the widespread use of networks and the Internet, viruses can now be transmitted and received in a number of ways. Because of this, computers in client/server environments are far more vulnerable to infection, even more so than are standalone systems. Symantec Corporation is one example of a company that makes anti-virus software for client operating systems, network operating systems, email servers, gateways, and firewalls.

Viruses can be introduced not only at the desktop but also at various types of servers, gateways, and firewalls. As a result of these increasing possibilities, anti-virus software companies have introduced a variety of products designed specifically for the various types of systems.

Anti-virus software runs in the background of computer systems. The software should typically be set to run automatically when the system turns on, and it should stay on as long as the computer is on to continually monitor the system for virus activity. It may be necessary, however, to temporarily disable anti-virus software under certain circumstances, such as when you're installing software. Most software manufacturers will even notify you that any anti-virus utility should be temporarily suspended during the installation process. Installing software while running anti-virus software may result in the unexpected halting of the installation process. Whenever you disable your anti-virus software to install a program, you should always first scan the program to be installed for any viruses.

 Generally, viruses can be introduced to a system regardless of whether the computer is a standalone system, is connected to the Internet, or is secured behind an intranet. Because of this consistent threat, anti-virus software should be installed on all systems and should constantly monitor the systems for viruses. Temporarily disabling anti-virus software, however, is acceptable when you're installing software. Just ensure that you first scan any programs before installing them, and be sure to re-enable the anti-virus software after you have finished performing any installations.

Suspicious Activity

To provide internetworking security, you must understand and recognize the many types of attacks and suspicious activities that can occur. Before you can prevent and defend against such activity, you must first know what to look for. Although many types of attacks can occur on networks, many of these are beyond the scope of this book and of the i-Net+ exam. Generally, security attacks can be classified into the two following broad categories:

➤ *Theft, destruction, and alteration of data*—There are countless ways that someone can illegally penetrate your systems to destroy or steal data. The simplest method of obtaining access is with a password. Therefore, you should vigilantly be on the lookout for multiple failed attempts to gain access to a system. Log files, discussed earlier, provide the best method for noticing multiple logon failures or individuals who have failed to properly log on to a system. Multiple logon failures do not necessarily mean that an individual is trying to gain illegal access, but such failures should be taken seriously because they might indicate an attempt to gain access into a system to steal, alter, or destroy information.

➤ *Denial of Service (DoS) attack*—This is typically a planned assault that results in system resources being depleted, thus preventing legitimate use of the system. A DoS attack performed over a computer network is analogous to continually and repeatedly calling a pizza delivery establishment, preventing legitimate customers' phone calls from getting through.

Spam And Mail Flooding

Spam, or *unsolicited commercial email (UCE),* is the electronic equivalent of junk mail. It is typically email sent to multiple recipients at one time, as well as simultaneous postings to news groups. Spam in general is annoying to most people, yet for the person sending the spam, it is a cost-efficient way to reach many people quickly. Instead of the spammer paying for the costs, as one would pay to the U.S. Postal Service in the "real" world, it is the Internet Service Providers, network administrators, and users who endure the cost of spam inflicted upon their resources—both hardware and software. Tracing the origin of spam is often difficult because the originator will typically forge the email header information or use a "disposable" email account.

Mail flooding, or *mail bombing,* is similar to spam in that large amounts of email are sent, but mail flooding typically involves sending these messages (or even one very large message) to only one account in an attempt to crash the system or create delays. Because of this, mail flooding is considered a type of Denial of Service and thus a criminal offense.

Ping Floods

PING (packet Internet groper) is a protocol and utility commonly used by administrators to check for the presence of another host on the network by sending Internet Control Message Protocol (ICMP) echo requests. Although PING is a useful and often-used utility, a ping flood is a type of Denial of Service attack aimed at preventing a remote host from responding to legitimate requests.

A ping flood is basically an assault of many pings in a short period of time. Because a PING asks a host if it's "alive," the remote host, if it is present, will return a response; thus, the assault of pings in a ping flood consumes the remote system's resources as it attempts to respond to the flood.

A variation on this attack, called *smurfing,* sends simultaneous ping requests to a broadcast IP address, which then broadcasts the pings to up to 255 computers on the target network. In turn, all these machines will respond, but to a spoofed (forged) address—in this case, the victim's computer.

SYN Floods

TCP/IP uses a three-way handshake in which a synchronous idle character (SYN), used to establish timing, is sent from the client and acknowledged (ACK) by the service with a SYN-ACK, and the client completes the handshake with a SYN-ACK. A SYN flood, a Denial of Service attack, ties up a system's network services. This attack is performed when the attacker spoofs the source IP address and sends multiple SYN packets to various resources on the target computer. Upon receiving these packets, the target computer begins allocating resources to handle them and starts responding. Because the source IP address was spoofed, the target computer can't get a final response, so it retransmits the SYN-ACK a number of times. As a result, the victim's computer is robbed of its resources if the SYN packets from the attacker are sent faster than the timeout rate of the victim's system.

Practice Questions

Question 1

> Your organization needs to filter incoming traffic based upon IP address. Which of the following should you implement?
>
> ○ a. Denial of Service
>
> ○ b. Firewall
>
> ○ c. Strainer server
>
> ○ d. Intranet

The correct answer is b. A firewall is a system designed for protecting a network against threats, and it can be used to permit or deny traffic based upon an IP address or protocol. Answer a is incorrect because Denial of Service is a type of attack intended to disrupt services. Answer c is incorrect because a strainer server does not exist. Answer d is incorrect because an intranet is a private network that will often implement a firewall solution if the intranet is connected to external networks.

Question 2

> What access permission should you assign to anonymous users on the *up-load* directory located on a Unix FTP server in order to allow them only to upload files?
>
> ○ a. Read
>
> ○ b. Write
>
> ○ c. Execute
>
> ○ d. Read and Execute

The correct answer is b. *Write* permissions on the directory will allow users to create and delete files in the directory. Answer a is incorrect because the Read permission allows the user to only list the contents of the directory. Answer c is incorrect because the Execute permission allows the user to search the directory. (Execute permissions on a file enable you to run a program.) Answer d is incorrect because the users will still need the Write permission on the directory.

Question 3

TiMe2g0 is an example of a good password for which of the following reasons?

○ a. Is not found in a dictionary

○ b. Contains more than one type of character

○ c. Uses a keyboard pattern

○ d. Both a and b

○ e. All of the above

The correct answer is d. The given password is not a word that can be found in a dictionary, and it contains numbers as well as letters. The fact that this password also uses mixed case makes it even better. Because you should not choose a password that uses patterns, answers c and e are incorrect.

Question 4

Which of the following is the online equivalent of an ID card or passport and is issued by a CA?

○ a. Digital identification

○ b. Microsoft Passport

○ c. Digital certificate

○ d. Digital signature

The correct answer is c. A digital certificate, issued by a Certificate Authority (CA), is the online equivalent of an identification card or passport. A digital certificate is also called a Digital ID, which is a servicemark of VeriSign. Answer a is incorrect because, although digital identification may initially appear to be correct, it is not the best choice. Answer b is incorrect because Microsoft Passport is a feature offered by Microsoft and its partners to provide a "single sign-in" and "wallet" service for the Web. Answer d is incorrect because a digital signature is only part of a digital certificate—just because you sign your driver's license, that does not make your signature a license.

Question 5

> What is the most widely used standard for defining digital certificates?
>
> O a. X.400
>
> O b. X.25
>
> O c. X.200
>
> O d. X.509

The correct answer is d. The X series is a set of recommendations from a division within the International Telecommunications Union (ITU). X.509 is the defining standard for digital certificates. Answer a is incorrect because X.400 is a standard for transmitting email at the Application layer of the OSI model. Answer b is incorrect because X.25 is the standard interface for connecting packet-switched networks. Answer c is incorrect because X.200 covers the seven-layer OSI reference model.

Question 6

> What does the abbreviation PKI stand for?
>
> O a. Pass Key Infrastructure
>
> O b. Protocol Key Instructions
>
> O c. Public Key Infrastructure
>
> O d. Public Key Intranet
>
> O e. Protocol Key Infrastructure

The correct answer is c. PKI is the abbreviation for Public Key Infrastructure, which is the foundation for public key cryptography over TCP/IP networks. Answers a, b, d, and e are all incorrect because these are made-up terms.

Question 7

> Public key encryption uses which of the following?
>
> O a. Public and private keys
>
> O b. Public key only
>
> O c. Private key only
>
> O d. A pair of public keys

The correct answer is a. Public key encryption uses a pair of keys—one private and one public. Because they are inversely related, what one does the other will undo. Because a private key and a public key are used, answers b, c, and d are incorrect.

Question 8

What is the protocol jointly developed by Visa and MasterCard that enables secure credit card transactions to take place over the Internet?

○ a. SCCT.X

○ b. SSL

○ c. SET

○ d. X.509

The correct answer is c. Secure Electronic Transaction (SET) is a standard vital to e-commerce support. SET enables various types of payment card transactions to take place securely over the Internet. Answer a is incorrect because this answer is made up. Answer b is incorrect because SSL is a handshake protocol developed by Netscape Communications to provide secure and private transmissions over the Internet. Answer d is incorrect because X.509 is an International Telecommunications Union (ITU) specification for digital certificates.

Question 9

Which of the following make it possible to send secure email messages? [Choose the two best answers]

❏ a. MIME

❏ b. PGP

❏ c. S/MIME

❏ d. S/PGP

The correct answers are b and c. Pretty Good Privacy (PGP) and Secure/Multipurpose Internet Mail Extensions (S/MIME) use encryption to secure messages. S/MIME adds encryption support to MIME, which is a specification for formatting messages to be sent over the Internet. Because MIME does not support encryption, answer a is incorrect. Answer d is incorrect because S/PGP does not exist.

Question 10

> What does the abbreviation PGP stand for?
>
> ○ a. Preferred Gopher Protocol
>
> ○ b. Pretty Good Privacy
>
> ○ c. Packet Gateway Privacy
>
> ○ d. Private Gateway Protocol

The correct answer is b. PGP is the abbreviation for Pretty Good Privacy, a method for encrypting email messages. Answers a, c, and d are incorrect because these options do not exist.

Question 11

> Which of the following are examples of a DoS attack? [Choose the three best answers]
>
> ❑ a. Spam
>
> ❑ b. Mail bomb
>
> ❑ c. Smurf attack
>
> ❑ d. SYN flood
>
> ❑ e. Gargomel attack

The correct answers are b, c, and d. Mail bombing, smurfing, and SYN flooding are all Denial of Service (DoS) attacks in that they deplete a system's resources, preventing legitimate use. Answer a is incorrect because spam is generally more of an annoyance and is not intended to prevent legitimate use of systems. Answer e is incorrect because a Gargomel attack does not exist.

Question 12

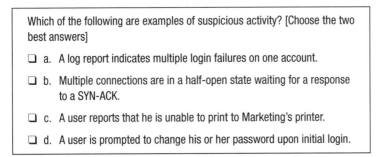

Which of the following are examples of suspicious activity? [Choose the two best answers]

- ❏ a. A log report indicates multiple login failures on one account.
- ❏ b. Multiple connections are in a half-open state waiting for a response to a SYN-ACK.
- ❏ c. A user reports that he is unable to print to Marketing's printer.
- ❏ d. A user is prompted to change his or her password upon initial login.

The correct answers are a and b. Multiple login failures should raise suspicion because they might be an attempt to gain unauthorized access to a resource. Multiple connections in a half-open state indicate a possible SYN flood and might indicate a Denial of Service attack. Answers c and d are incorrect because these more closely resemble typical network problems or controls set by the administrator.

Need To Know More?

 Feghhi, Jalal, Peter William, and Jalil Feghhi. *Digital Certificates: Applied Internet Security*. Addison-Wesley Professional, Boston, MA, 1998. ISBN: 0-201-30980-7. Jalal Feghhi, one of the book's authors, is a senior software engineer at VeriSign, Inc, which is a leading provider of Internet trust and security services. This book details many technologies, including digital certificates, authentication, and S/MIME.

 Garfinkel, Simson and Gene Spafford. *Web Security & Commerce (O'Reilly Nutshell)*. O'Reilly & Associates Inc., Sebastopol, CA, 1999. ISBN 1-56592-269-7. Great technical book explaining security risks and methods of protecting systems from them.

 www.antionline.com/—This site provides the latest security news as well as a bunch of resources on everything hacker- and cracker-related.

 www.cert.org/—Home page of the CERT Coordination Center. The site also contains a wealth of security tips, tools, and security advisories.

 www.microsoft.com/security/default.asp—Microsoft's security Web site contains security bulletins, white papers, and other useful security tidbits.

 www.w3.org/Security/Faq/—A security FAQ maintained by Lincoln D. Stein. This is one of the best general security resources available for Webmasters.

Business Concepts

Terms you'll need to understand:

√ Copyright

√ Trademark

√ Patent

√ Fair use

√ Unicode

√ Intranet

√ Extranet

√ Virtual Private Network

√ Push technology

√ Pull technology

√ EDI (Electronic Data Interchange)

Techniques you'll need to master:

√ Understanding the basic concepts of Internet-based business

√ Recognizing the legalities of copyrights and the terms of their use

In this chapter, you'll learn the basics of Internet business and walk through an overview of legal and cultural issues. The main concepts to know for the real world, as well as for exam preparation, are addressed in detail.

Copyrights Vs. Trademarks And Patents

A *copyright* is a legal protection placed upon a written work by Section 17 of the United States Code, known as the Copyright Act of 1976. It applies to original works of "authorship" and protects them for the entire life of the author plus 50 years.

A *trademark* is an original and unique name or symbol used for identification purposes. Trademarks can be phrases, numbers, notes, or other entities that uniquely identify an entity. Trademarks are not covered by the Copyright Act but are governed by the United States Patent and Trademark Office and are provided legal protection indefinitely.

A *patent* is a protection offered for 17 years to inventions (or for fewer years for designs only). Given to the first person to file them for a given invention, patents prevent anyone else from using the same invention for their duration. Like trademarks, patents are governed by the United States Patent and Trademark Office.

Of these three ways to protect one's work, the only one that applies to Web content is the copyright. Copyrights are obtained by submitting the appropriate forms, available at any library, to the Library of Congress in Washington, DC. When submitting the forms, you should submit two hard copies of the works. If the work is not completed when the application forms are submitted, you can submit copies of the work within three months of publication.

After the copyright has been granted, it covers the work—whether or not the copyright notice appears on the work. The copyright notice is *required* on all works published before 1989, and it *should* appear on all works copyrighted after that, although the absence of the notice does not waive the protection. The notice can begin with the character ©, the three characters **(c)**, or the word **copyright**. Following that, the year of the notice should appear, followed by the name of the copyright owner. Examples include:

➤ © 2000 Emmett Dulaney

➤ Copyright 2000 Emmett Dulaney

➤ (c) 2000 Emmett Dulaney

Certain kinds of written works cannot be copyrighted. These include:

➤ Names, including titles, subtitles, and so on

➤ Unembellished facts and numbers, such as Pi or the date of a war

➤ Advertising expressions, such as slogans, phrases, and other entities qualifying for trademark protection

➤ Ideas, inventions, and entities qualifying for patent protection

➤ Ingredient lists

➤ Blank forms

The possession of a copyright offers you exclusive use of the work. If anyone else uses that work without your permission, you are free to use the courts to seek legal recourse. You can also transfer the copyright or grant licenses (exclusive or non-exclusive) to it.

There are, however, several ways your material can be used without your permission and for which there is no recourse. These fall into a category collectively known as *fair use*. Examples of fair use include:

➤ Parody

➤ Limited use (500 words of an entire book, for example)

➤ Educational use, particularly among schools and not-for-profits

➤ Archiving

Four factors are often used to determine if the use of copyrighted material—without permission—is worth awarding damages:

➤ How much material was used in relation to the whole work

➤ The effect of the use on the original

➤ Whether the use was for commerce or education

➤ Whether the material is factual or original (as in literature)

Working In A Global Environment

As the Internet brings the world together and removes geographic boundaries, it opens a number of problems related to localization and understanding. An example of this would be a company that sells lawn ornaments. In over half the world, Web-site visitors would have no idea what a lawn is, and in much of the other half, they would wonder why you would want to put ornaments in it.

Contrast this with the state of Indiana, where the cement goose seems to be the state bird.

For the exam, you should be aware of four main areas of diversity:

➤ Language

➤ Legal issues

➤ Cultural issues

➤ Regulatory issues

Legal, cultural, and regulatory issues can be resolved by carefully researching those areas within the regions you intend to do business in. Great care should be taken to verify that nothing posted on a site could be misinterpreted in such a way as to damage your business or appear in any way inappropriate.

Language issues can be greatly lessened by embracing Unicode. With the Unicode Character Set (UCS), each character is composed of a 16-bit value. This allows the same character to be interpreted by 65,536 different entities.

 Whereas Unicode uses 16 bits for each character, ASCII uses only 8. The additional possibilities allow Unicode to represent alphabets such as Japanese.

Note: Windows 2000 embraces Unicode and puts it to good use. You can change languages on the fly, and the change is carried throughout WordPad, Notepad, and other editors.

Intranets, Extranets, And The Internet

The Web site you establish can fall into one of three categories, based upon area of coverage:

➤ Internet

➤ Intranet

➤ Extranet

With an Internet site, you are open to the public and wanting everyone to come. Security is not a high priority, and more often than not, anonymous users are allowed to come to the site. Internet sites can be used for marketing, promotion, and education, and the sites can be listed with search engines to increase traffic. The Internet site must operate at port 80.

The exact opposite of an Internet site is an intranet site. An intranet is a private site set up only for internal business use. (For example, a Human Resources department could post HR documents and forms for use by company employees only.) Intranets can be set up in a number of ways—including not connecting the server to the Internet at all, separating it with a firewall, or changing to a port number other than 80 (opting to use a higher number, non-common port).

Between the Internet and an intranet is an extranet. An extranet is not open to the public and is almost an intranet. It differs from an intranet in that those accessing it are not all internal users—they can be customers, vendors, or others that you grant access to. For example, an extranet could contain a just-in-time inventory database used by a manufacturing company. The company could give database access to a steel vendor who monitors the database and automatically ships steel to the company when the inventory gets low. A *Virtual Private Network (VPN)* is an extranet built by using tunneling technologies.

Push And Pull Technology

Two types of technology are used to send information from one machine to another: push and pull. In *push technology*, the browser gets information pushed to it without requesting it. In *pull technology*—on which most of the Web is based—a user requests data before it is sent.

To use an analogy, Windows 2000 allows an administrator to move software applications from a server to a client in two ways: assigning or publishing. If the software application is *assigned,* then it is automatically sent to the client machine the next time it is booted, regardless of who uses the machine. If the software application is *published,* then its existence becomes known to a user, who must choose to download and install it. Assigning is the same as push technology, and publishing is the same as pull technology.

Business Terms And Concepts

For the exam, you'll need to know several business terms, including:

➤ Means of distribution

➤ Commerce and merchant systems

➤ EDI

➤ Marketing

➤ Relationships

We will look at each of these categories in the following sections.

Means Of Distribution

The two major methods of distribution are *business-to-business* and *business-to-consumer*. Each model utilizes a different mindset, and it is important to use the right one for your distribution priorities.

With the business-to-business model, your company is selling directly to other businesses. The businesses you deal with need the products or services you provide and want to be able to find information about them quickly and easily at your site.

With the business-to-consumer model, your company is selling directly to the consumer. The customers you deal with have lots of options, and you want them to find your site quickly, be impressed enough by it to come back often, and have ease of ordering.

Commerce And Merchant Systems

Internet commerce is transacted through Web packages that offer online store-fronts. Such storefronts can offer such services as inventory management, online ordering, and product display. Products can be purchased using digital cash, smart cards, or traditional payments (charge cards or checks). Most sites accepting payment use SSL (Secure Sockets Layer) and other technologies to encrypt the transactions.

Electronic commerce servers are also referred to as *merchant systems* or *online catalogs*. Many, such as WebClerk, combine e-commerce features with a database and an application server. There are a vast number of products available in these areas, many specializing in a particular area. Examples of payment solutions include:

➤ ProCart

➤ Signio

➤ PrivacyBank.com

Examples of storefront software include:

➤ CustomCart

➤ Freemerchant.com

➤ Merchant Builder

Electronic Data Interchange (EDI)

Electronic Data Interchange (EDI) is used for transferring files from one data format to another. The ANSI (American National Standards Institute) standards upon which EDI is based are known as X12. EDI is intended to reduce the need to rekey data (thus reducing errors), reduce the cost of paper trails, and eliminate the dependence on paper documents and records.

Three issues related to EDI include data security, confidentiality, and storage.

The Importance Of Marketing

Marketing and promotion help businesses become known in the Internet world as well as in the traditional world. One of the adages for business goes something like this: When times are good, you should advertise; When times are bad, you have to advertise.

Advertising can come in many forms, from swapping links with another site to running commercials during the Super Bowl. For the exam, know the difference between promotion and publicity: promotion is advertising or other forms of marketing that you pay for; publicity is attention drawn to your company in other ways (such as through press releases) that you don't pay for directly.

> *Note: An alternative method of generating publicity, but requiring you to pay for it indirectly, is to hire a publicity agency.*

The Value Of Relationships

After you spend the time and effort to get customers, it is important that you keep them. One of the best ways to keep customers is to let them know that you value their relationship and are willing to work with them. One of the most difficult aspects of the relationship occurs when the customers become dissatisfied with your product.

The best solution is to have a detailed policy on how to handle returns. A detailed written policy ensures that all customers receive the same treatment and are treated fairly. Make certain that all employees who will interact with customers know the company's policy and are empowered to carry it out.

Practice Questions

Question 1

> What is the length of life for a copyright given to an author who obtained it
> and then died two years later?
>
> ○ a. 2 years
>
> ○ b. 50 years
>
> ○ c. 52 years
>
> ○ d. infinite

The correct answer is c. A copyright is good for the life of the author plus 50
years. The only infinite protection is for trademarks, not copyrights.

Question 2

> How many years does a copyright offer protection for an invention?
>
> ○ a. 0 years
>
> ○ b. 17 years
>
> ○ c. 50 years
>
> ○ d. The life of the author plus 50 years

The correct answer is a. Copyrights do not apply to inventions, which are
governed by patents.

Question 3

> Which of the following represents the correct format for a copyright no-
> tice for a document copyrighted in the year 2000 by the company D S
> Technical Solutions?
>
> ○ a. 2000 © D S Technical Solutions
>
> ○ b. © 2000 D S Technical Solutions
>
> ○ c. D S Technical Solutions © 2000
>
> ○ d. © D S Technical Solutions 2000

The correct answer is b. The other entries are not valid formats for the copyright notice.

Question 4

A Webmaster for one site "borrows" content from another site and places it on his own. The content was protected by copyright, and the Webmaster did not obtain permission to use it. Under what circumstance can the Webmaster do so without legal ramifications?

- a. He did not know the material was protected.
- b. He posts a notice that the material is borrowed.
- c. He is sampling.
- d. He is doing a parody.

The correct answer is d. Parody is one possible "fair use" right under which the material can be borrowed without permission.

Question 5

Which of the following would not be eligible for copyright protection?
- a. A dissertation on why taxes are unjust
- b. An ingredient list
- c. A classified ad
- d. An employment application

The correct answer is b. An ingredient list cannot be protected by copyright. All other examples given can be protected.

Question 6

The Unicode character set uses how many bits to represent each character?
- a. 4
- b. 8
- c. 16
- d. 65,536

The correct answer is c. Unicode uses 16 bits to represent each character, allowing for 65,536 possibilities. The ASCII character set uses 8 bits.

Question 7

A Virtual Private Network is an example of which type of site?

○ a. Extranet

○ b. Internet

○ c. Intranet

○ d. Open

The correct answer is a. A Virtual Private Network (VPN) is an example of an extranet. Answer b is incorrect because the Internet is generally open to the public. Answer c is incorrect because an intranet is closed to the public. Answer d is incorrect because there is no such site category known as "open."

Question 8

The type of technology wherein a browser must go to a site and bring information down is known as which of the following?

○ a. Known

○ b. Assign

○ c. Push

○ d. Pull

The correct answer is d. With pull technology, the browser goes to a site and brings the needed information down. Answer a is incorrect because "known" is not a type of push or pull technology. Answers b and c are incorrect because, with push technology (of which assigning is one method), the information is automatically sent to the browser.

Question 9

The ANSI standard upon which EDI is based is which of the following?

○ a. X.400

○ b. X12

○ c. X.25

○ d. VRM

The correct answer is b. The X12 standard is what Electronic Data Interchange (EDI) is based upon.

Question 10

Using a portion of a document protected by copyright—as long as it does not take away from the original document or is used for an educational purpose—falls under the realm of which of the following?

○ a. Pull

○ b. Unicode

○ c. Exception

○ d. Fair use

The correct answer is d. Fair use governs the right to use a document that has been protected as long as the use is for a specific purpose, such as parody or education, and does not take away from the original.

Need To Know More?

 Warda, Mark. *How to Register Your Own Copyright, 2nd Edition*. Sphinx Publishing, Naperville, IL, 1998. ISBN: 1-57071-225-5. An easy-to-understand overview of the copyright laws, complete with forms needed for registering.

 http://ecommerce.internet.com—The electronic commerce guide from IBM.

 www.loc.gov/copyright/forms/—The Library of Congress and the copyright forms page.

 www.asca.com/unicode.html—The Unicode Character Encoding Standard as posted by the Arabic Scientific Alliance.

 www2.echo.lu/oii/en/edi.html—The Electronic Data Interchange Standards and relevant links.

 www4.law.cornell.edu/uscode/17/—The Legal Information Institute's complete listing of the United States Code, Title 17, on copyrights.

Troubleshooting

Terms you'll need to understand:

√ File corruption

√ PING

√ TRACERT

√ Ipconfig

√ Winipcfg

√ Ifconfig

√ NETSTAT

√ ARP

Techniques you'll need to master:

√ Understanding how problems can occur and how to deal with them

√ Recognizing the tools to use for troubleshooting problems

In this chapter, you'll learn the basics of troubleshooting problems with TCP/IP and Internet sites. The main troubleshooting tools you should know for the real world, as well as for exam preparation, are addressed in detail.

Content Problems

When a user attempts to download a file from your Internet site and has difficulty doing so, this can reflect badly on your site in a number of ways. Not only do you have a frustrated user, but you also have the potential of losing a large number of customers. For example, assume that you are in the shareware business and distribute your wares through Web and FTP sites. The primary way that you get more business is by word of mouth. If a user downloads a file and likes it well enough to purchase it, then not only are you making money from the purchase, but you stand to make exponentially more money as that user recommends your product to other users.

If the same user spends thirty minutes downloading a file that turns out to be corrupt, then not only are you losing the money from that user's registration, but you are also losing all the potential customers he or she could have directed your way. It is extremely important that you take every conceivable precaution to ensure that your files are error-free and that the risk of problems is minimal.

Problems themselves fall into one of two categories in relation to this discussion: correctable by administrators or caused by users. Administrators need to think through and correct every error they can come up with to prevent the errors from happening. Some tips for so doing include:

➤ Keep file sizes as small as possible. The smaller the file, the less prone it is to be affected by download times, modem speeds, and disconnects.

➤ Check the posted files regularly. Make certain that checksums have not changed and that corruption has not occurred without your knowledge.

 A checksum is a mathematical number generated by adding the values of all characters within the file. Monitoring checksums is an easy way to make certain that the file content has not changed drastically.

➤ Avoid resolution problems whenever possible. When creating files or programs, always do so for the lowest common denominator and not for the smallest market. For example, the desktop on Windows 2000 Professional, Windows 98, and a number of other operating systems can be set to True Color (32-bit). With graphic resolution, the greater the number of bits, the better the graphic's appearance. Although 32-bit graphics are perfect for an ideal world, if you want to serve all users, you should use 8-bit graphics because that resolution is as high as you can go if you want to support the 256-color monitors still used by many.

Some problems you cannot prevent, no matter how hard you try, and these fall into the category of user error. It should never be assumed that the user has intentionally caused problems, however; sometimes problems occur because of the user's environment. Examples of this would include:

➤ *Using antiquated browsers*—Naturally, they do not contain all the capabilities provided by newer, more popular browsers. Although you should be careful when including Web-site items that work only with the newest browser, there is nothing wrong with including functionality understood by most browsers.

➤ *Connecting at the speed of which moss grows*—Yes, at one point in time, 300-baud modems were all the rage, and there are plenty around that still work. Trying to download a 5MB file with one, however, is certain to cause a timeout or corruption. Although you should not create a site for the public that works with only DSL connections, there is nothing wrong with expecting customers to be able to connect at a minimum of 28Kbps (which is about as low as most 56K modems with a bad connection will drop to before giving up).

➤ *Using antiquated monitors*—Problems can occur if you are mixing color palettes and the user is using a monochrome monitor. Know your audience and whether you are creating content for third-world countries (where equipment can be dated) or select customers. If it is the latter, it should be safe to assume that most users won't be using antiquated monitors, and you can encourage those who are to upgrade.

If files become corrupt on the server, the best recourse you have is to replace them. If files become corrupt during a download by the user, their best recourse is to replace them. If a user repeatedly tries to download a file from your site and has difficulty (and you have ascertained that the problem is isolated to the user), then you can always send the file as an email attachment. Take care when doing this if your files are large, however, because many SMTP servers restrict the size of the attachments they will allow.

If your files are large and download time is lengthy, consider dividing the file into multiple sections or compressing it. Dividing a file into an EXE and the needed support files (DLL, OCX, etc.), for example, creates two smaller files, decreases the download file (though not the overall time), and reduces the possibility of errors during the download. Compressing downloads can be done with packages such as PKZIP and related products.

Site Problems

Internet sites are prone to problems in the same way network servers and other computers are. Some of the problems encountered can be the result of administrator error, and others can be caused by load, bottlenecks, and media constraints. Table 15.1 lists some common problems and possible solutions.

In all cases, troubleshooting must be approached methodically. A suggested order of action would be:

1. Investigate and document the symptoms. Look for records on past similar occurrences and the resolutions.

2. Isolate the problem as much as possible: is it only this server, only these clients, or only this application?

3. Hypothesize a solution or multiple solutions. Try each solution one at a time and document the results of each one until the problem is fixed.

Table 15.1 Common site problems.

Problem	Solution
Cannot find site	Verify that the site is up. Try accessing the site by both the URL and the IP address. If the site is down, bring it back up. If the site can be accessed by the IP address but not by the URL, then there is a problem with the DNS resolution that must be corrected.
400-level errors	Caused by the client. Try to isolate the reason: is it just this client, just this application, etc.
404 errors in FTP	Some browsers cannot accept more than one line of a Welcome message.
500-level errors	Caused by the server, and the user is usually given an instruction to notify the administrator if the problem persists. Verify that the site is up and the Web pages have not become corrupted. Replace the HTML files as needed, and double-check permissions.
Applications will not run	Check MIME mapping and add needed entries.
Cannot see all files	Use Unix listing styles rather than DOS for compatibility with all browsers.
File contains no data	Typically bad header information or formatting.
General network failure	Has the server been renamed? If so, change all references.

(continued)

Table 15.1 Common site problems (continued).	
Problem	**Solution**
Inadequate permissions	Within FTP, a user must have Write permission to upload files and Read permissions to download files. On a Web site, a user must have Script permission to run ISAPI and similar scripts and Execute permissions for compiled entities and other type scripts. Check also that the authentication in place can be used by the browsers visiting the site.
Performance	Find the bottleneck and replace it. This can be the network card, the disk drive, the processor, the amount of RAM, or a plethora of other possibilities. Monitor the site over time and find out what one entity is holding up all other resources; then, replace it.
Security	Use SSL, require authentication, and change the port used by the service.
Unable to locate host	Correct an incorrect URL.

Tools To Use

A number of tools can be useful in solving site-related or protocol-related problems. In the next few sections, we will examine each of them.

PING

The **PING** command (short for Packet Internet Groper) is one of the most useful commands in the TCP/IP protocol. It sends a series of packets to another system, which in turn sends back a response. This utility can be extremely useful in troubleshooting problems with remote hosts.

In all operating systems, the PING utility is used as a command-line program that indicates whether the host can be reached and how long it took for the host to send a return packet. On a local area network, the time is indicated as less than 10 milliseconds, but across wide area network links, this value can be much greater.

TRACERT

Not available with all implementations of TCP/IP, TRACERT is a command-line utility that enables you to verify the route to a remote host. Execute the command **TRACERT** *hostname*, where *hostname* is the computer name or IP address of the computer whose route you want to trace. TRACERT will return the different IP addresses that the packet was routed through to reach the final destination. The results also include the number of hops needed to reach the destination. Execute the **TRACERT** command without any options to see a help file that describes all the command switches.

As with the **PING** command, **TRACERT** returns the amount of time required for each routing hop. The TRACERT utility determines the intermediary steps involved in communicating with another IP host. It provides a road map of all the routes an IP packet takes to get from host A to host B.

Ipconfig, Winipcfg, And Ifconfig

The purpose of the Ipconfig, Winipcfg, and Ifconfig utilities is to show the IP configuration parameters on the current host. They all do roughly the same job, but they each reside in different operating systems. Ipconfig is the most generic, residing in a number of operating systems, including Windows NT and Windows 2000. Winipcfg resides only in Windows 95 and Windows 98, and Ifconfig is generally found in Unix and Linux installations.

Ipconfig

Figure 15.1 shows an example of the output generated by Ipconfig. When called on a command line by itself, it reports the IP address, subnet mask, and default gateway values. When used with the /**ALL** parameter, it adds the hostname, DNS suffix, node type, information on routing and proxy, and as much information as possible about the network interface card. Two other parameters that can be used with Ipconfig are /**RELEASE** and /**RENEW**: the former is used to release an IP address if DHCP (Dynamic Host Configuration Protocol) leases are employed, and the latter renews the address from the DHCP server.

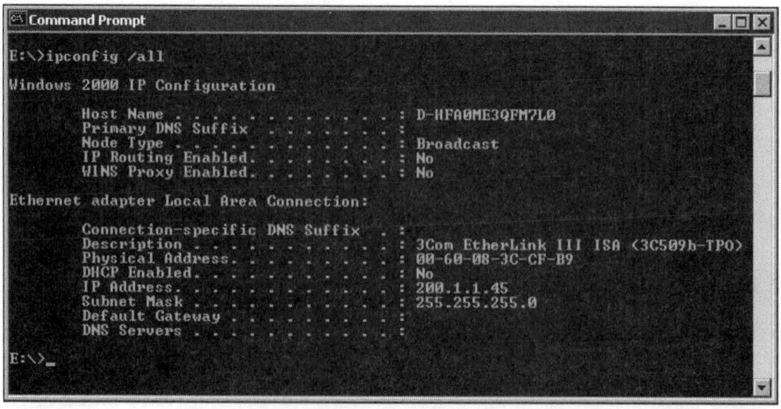

Figure 15.1   The command **IPCONFIG /ALL** shows all available parameters.

Winipcfg

The Winipcfg utility can be thought of as a graphical version of Ipconfig. As shown in Figure 15.2, it offers the same basic information when first summoned. The More Info >> button will add the additional information about node type, hostname, and so on. The Release button returns the IP address to a DHCP server. The Release All button returns all IP addresses to the DHCP server (if more than one card is installed in the machine). The Renew button renews the lease for the IP address with the DHCP server; the Renew All button assumes that there is more than one networking card installed in the machine.

Ifconfig

The Ifconfig utility (usually located in the /sbin directory) works by showing the status of active interfaces. Using the -a parameter, it shows the status of all interfaces. Interfaces traditionally are denoted by a name representing their type and unit number; for example, **eth0** means that it is Ethernet and the first interface. An example of the output generated by Ifconfig follows:

```
Eth0    Link encap:Ethernet    Hwaddr 00:60:97:DD:E8:36
        inet addr: 200.1.1.0 Bcast:200.1.1.255 Mask: 255.255.255.0
        UP BROADCAST RUNNING MULTICAST MTU:1500 Metric: 1
        RX packets: 41025 errors: 3 dropped: 0 overruns: 0 frame:3
        TX packets: 12 errors: 0 dropped: 0 overruns: 0 carrier: 0
        Collisions: 0 txqueuelen: 100
        Interrupt:10 Base address: 0x300
```

Whether you use Ipconfig, Winipcfg, or Ifconfig is almost always a decision based solely upon which operating system you are using.

NETSTAT

NETSTAT is a command-line utility that enables you to check the status of current IP connections. Executing the **NETSTAT** command without switches displays protocol statistics and current TCP/IP connections.

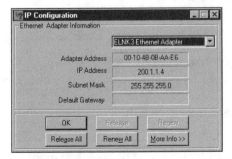

Figure 15.2 Winipcfg, where available, is a graphical version of Ipconfig.

When you have determined that your base-level communications are working, you will need to verify the services on your system. This involves looking at the services that are listening for incoming traffic and/or verifying that you are creating a session with a remote station. The **NETSTAT** command allows you to do this.

ARP

Mentioned briefly in an earlier chapter as the Address Resolution Protocol, ARP as a utility can be used to see the entries in the Address Resolution table. It is the Address Resolution table that maps network card addresses (MAC addresses) to IP addresses. You can check to see if the IP addresses you believe should be in the table are there and if they are mapped to the computers they should be. Usually, you do not know the MAC addresses of the hosts on your network. However, if you cannot contact a host, or if a connection is made to an unexpected host, you can use the **ARP** command to check this table and begin isolating which host is actually assigned an IP address.

Network Analyzers

A network analyzer can go by many names, including *sniffer*, *probe*, and *packet tool*. Whatever the name, the purpose is to examine traffic on the network and help you find bottlenecks. One example of this, from the Microsoft world, is Network Monitor. This tool comes in two flavors (both going by the same name); one version comes with Windows NT Server and is a subset of the full-blown tool included with SMS (Systems Management Server). The differences are significant because the lesser tool captures incoming and outgoing traffic for only the local machines and not for the full network.

To get true traffic statistics, in almost all cases, the network card that the tool is running on must support *promiscuous* mode—meaning that it can hear all the traffic on the network and not just the traffic intended for that card.

Other Troubleshooting Tools

A number of other tools that have been mentioned in other chapters of this book provide some level of troubleshooting in specific situations. These include:

➤ *NSLOOKUP*—Used for verifying entries on a DNS server.

➤ *ROUTE*—Used to see the local routing table and add entries to it.

➤ *NBTSTAT*—Used to check the resolution of NetBIOS names to TCP/IP addresses.

➤ *DHCP*—Used to get around manual configuration (misconfiguration) issues.

➤ *Event Viewer (NT/2000 only)*—Used to look at the system logs for instances of errors during loading and configuration.

➤ *FINGER*—Returns information about a remote host and the services and/or users on it.

➤ *HOSTNAME*—Returns the name by which the current host is known.

For pure TCP/IP troubleshooting, one of the best things you can do is install SNMP (Simple Network Management Protocol). The SNMP protocol enables TCP/IP to export information to troubleshooting tools such as NT's Performance Monitor or other third-party tools. By itself, SNMP does not report any troubleshooting information, but the reports and information it does generate can be invaluable for troubleshooting.

Here are some general rules for TCP/IP-specific troubleshooting:

➤ If TCP/IP cannot communicate from a local host to a remote host system, the utilities discussed in this chapter will not work correctly.

➤ If the systems are on different subnets and cannot communicate, remember that TCP/IP requires routing to communicate between subnets.

➤ If the systems previously were able to communicate but can no longer communicate, suspect either your router(s) or changes in software configuration.

Earlier in this chapter, we spoke of approaching a problem systematically. Microsoft recommends that you approach a possible connectivity problem by following these steps:

1. Run **IPCONFIG** to verify that there is a valid IP address (whether it's manually configured or supplied by DHCP).

2. **PING** the loopback address (127.0.0.1). This will verify that the TCP/IP stack is properly functioning but will not go out across the wire.

3. **PING** your own IP address. A success should show that address resolution is not a problem.

4. **PING** the default gateway.

5. **PING** a remote host.

If all the steps are completed successfully, the problem lies in something other than the TCP/IP protocol and connectivity.

Practice Questions

Question 1

> What is a mathematical number generated by adding the values of all the characters within the file?
>
> ○ a. Algorithm
>
> ○ b. Bit
>
> ○ c. Checksum
>
> ○ d. Baud

The correct answer is c. A checksum is a mathematical number generated by adding the values of all the characters within the file. Answer a is incorrect because an algorithm is any formula. Answer b is incorrect because a bit is a component of a file. Answer d is incorrect because baud represents transmission speed.

Question 2

> For maximum compatibility with 256-color monitors, resolution on graphics should be:
>
> ○ a. 8-bit
>
> ○ b. 16-bit
>
> ○ c. 24-bit
>
> ○ d. 32-bit

The correct answer is a; 256-color monitors can handle only 8-bit graphics. The trick is to remember that there are only 256 possibilities with 8-bits. When moving to a higher number of bits, such as 32, the number of possibilities enters the millions.

Question 3

> How many bits can Windows 2000 and Windows 98 handle for graphic files?
>
> ○ a. 8 bits
> ○ b. 16 bits
> ○ c. 24 bits
> ○ d. 32 bits

The correct answer is d. Windows 2000, Windows 98, and many other operating systems can handle True Color, 32-bit graphics.

Question 4

> Which of the following error messages was likely caused by the user?
>
> ○ a. 400
> ○ b. 503
> ○ c. 502
> ○ d. 501

The correct answer is a, 400, which represents a bad file request. All 400-level error messages point to the client, while 500-level error messages point to server problems. Error 503 comes when the server is busy, 502 comes when the server is temporarily overloaded, and 501 comes when the server fails to support a requested item.

Question 5

> Which troubleshooting tool can be used to see the IP configuration data given by a DHCP server to a Windows 98 client?
>
> ○ a. PING
> ○ b. Ipconfig
> ○ c. Winipcfg
> ○ d. Ifconfig

The correct answer is c. Winipcfg shows the IP configuration parameters on Windows 9x. Ipconfig does a similar job on Windows NT and Windows 2000, and Ifconfig does a similar job on Unix and Linux. PING is used to check host availability.

Question 6

Which troubleshooting tool can be used to check the availability of a host and see the path taken to get there?

○ a. TRACERT

○ b. PING

○ c. DHCP

○ d. NETSTAT

The correct answer is a. TRACERT will show the availability of a host and trace the route used to reach it. Answer b is incorrect because PING will show only the availability of a host. Answer c is incorrect because DHCP is used to automatically issue IP configuration from a server to clients. Answer d is incorrect because NETSTAT shows network statistic information.

Question 7

Of the following, which step should you take first to troubleshoot a suspected connectivity problem?

○ a. **PING** the default gateway.

○ b. Run **IPCONFIG** to verify that there is a valid IP address.

○ c. **PING** the loopback address.

○ d. **PING** a remote host.

The correct answer is b. You should first run **IPCONFIG** to verify that there is a valid IP address. Then you should **PING** the loopback address, followed by the default gateway, and then a remote host.

Question 8

> Which of the following error messages was likely caused by the server?
>
> ○ a. 404
>
> ○ b. 503
>
> ○ c. 400
>
> ○ d. 401

The correct answer is b, 503, which represents an unavailable service. All 400-level error messages point to the client, while 500-level error messages point to server problems. Error 404 usually comes when the requested file name is misspelled, 400 comes when the URL is incorrect, and 401 comes when a given password is incorrect.

Question 9

> What is the troubleshooting tool that can be used to check the status of current IP connections?
>
> ○ a. TRACERT
>
> ○ b. PING
>
> ○ c. DHCP
>
> ○ d. NETSTAT

The correct answer is d. NETSTAT shows network statistic information and current IP connections. Answer a is incorrect because TRACERT will show the availability of a host and trace the route used to reach it. Answer b is incorrect because PING will show only the availability of a host. Answer c is incorrect because DHCP is used to automatically issue IP configuration from a server to clients.

Question 10

Which troubleshooting tool can be used to see the IP configuration data given by a DHCP server to a Windows NT Workstation client?

○ a. PING

○ b. Ipconfig

○ c. Winipcfg

○ d. Ifconfig

The correct answer is b. Ipconfig shows the IP configuration parameters on Windows NT and Windows 2000. Winipcfg does a similar job on Windows 95 and Windows 98, and Ifconfig does a similar job on Unix and Linux. PING is used to check host availability.

Need To Know More?

 Feit, Dr. Sidnie. *TCP/IP Architecture, Protocols, and Implementation with IPv6 and IP Security.* McGraw-Hill, New York, 1999. ISBN: 0-07-022069-7. Good coverage of the TCP/IP utilities.

 http://coverage.cnet.com/Resources/Tech/Advisers/Error/— Internet errors explained by Shirley Malcolm.

 http://ftp.arl.mil/~mike/ping.html—The story of the PING program, by Mike Muuss (its creator).

 www.ea.com/techsupp/network/network.htm—Setting up and troubleshooting a network.

 www.webopedia.com/quick_ref/error.html—Internet error messages.

 www.webopedia.com/quick_ref/fileextensions.html—Data (MIME) formats and their file extensions.

 www.zdnet.com/anchordesk/story/story_1495.html—A comparison of PING implementations.

Sample Test

In this chapter, we provide pointers to help you develop a successful test-taking strategy. We'll discuss how to choose proper answers, how to decode ambiguity, how to work within the CompTIA testing framework, how to decide what you need to memorize, and how to prepare for the test. At the end of the chapter, we include 72 questions on subject matter pertinent to the CompTIA i-Net+ Certification Exam. Good luck!

Questions, Questions, Questions

There should be no doubt in your mind that you are facing a test full of specific and pointed questions. The i-Net+ exam that you take will include 72 questions, and you will be allotted 90 minutes to complete the exam.

The i-Net+ test uses five types of questions:

➤ Multiple choice with a single answer

➤ Multiple choice with multiple answers

➤ Multipart with a single answer

➤ Multipart with multiple answers

➤ Simulations whereby you click on a GUI screen capture to pick graphics

Always take the time to read a question at least twice before selecting an answer, and always look for an Exhibit button as you examine each question. Exhibits include graphics information related to a question. An *exhibit* is usually a screen capture of program output or GUI information that you must examine to analyze the question's contents and formulate an answer. The Exhibit button displays graphics and charts used to help explain a question, provide additional data, or illustrate page layout or program behavior.

Not every question has only one answer; many questions require multiple answers. Therefore, you should read each question carefully, determine how many answers are necessary or possible, and look for additional hints or instructions when selecting answers. Such instructions occur in brackets immediately following the question.

Picking Proper Answers

Obviously, the only way to pass any exam is to select enough of the right answers to obtain a passing score. However, CompTIA's exams are not standardized, as the SAT and GRE exams are; they are far more diabolical and convoluted. In some cases, questions are strangely worded, and deciphering them can be a real challenge. In such cases, you might need to rely on answer-elimination skills. Almost always, at least one answer for a question can be eliminated immediately because it matches one of these conditions:

➤ The answer does not apply to the situation.

➤ The answer describes a nonexistent issue, an invalid option, or an imaginary state.

➤ The answer can be eliminated because of information in the question itself.

After you eliminate all answers that are obviously wrong, you can apply your retained knowledge to eliminate further answers. Look for items that sound correct but that refer to actions, commands, or features that are not present or not available in the situation that the question describes.

If you're still faced with a blind guess among two or more potentially correct answers, reread the question. Try to picture how each of the remaining answers would alter the situation. Be especially sensitive to terminology; sometimes, the choice of words ("remove" instead of "disable") can make the difference between a right answer and a wrong one.

Guess at an answer only when you've exhausted your ability to eliminate answers but you remain unclear about which of the remaining possibilities is correct. An unanswered question offers you no points, but guessing gives you at least some chance of getting a question right; just don't be too hasty when making a blind guess.

You can wait until the last round of reviewing marked questions (just as you're about to run out of time or out of unanswered questions) before you start making guesses. However, guessing should be a last resort.

Decoding Ambiguity

CompTIA's exams have a reputation for including questions that can be difficult to interpret, confusing, or ambiguous. The only way to beat CompTIA at its own game is to be prepared. You'll discover that many exam questions test your knowledge of things that are not directly related to the issue raised by a question. This means that the answers you must choose from, even incorrect ones, are just as much a part of the skill assessment as the question itself.

Questions often give away their answers, but you have to be Sherlock Holmes to see the clues. Often, subtle hints appear in the question text in such a way that they seem almost irrelevant to the situation. You must realize that each question is a test unto itself and that you need to inspect and successfully navigate each question to pass the exam. Look for small clues, such as one question toward the end of the exam that states the answer to a question that appeared earlier in the exam. Little things such as these can point to the right answer if properly understood; if missed, they can leave you facing a blind guess.

Another common difficulty with certification exams is vocabulary. Be sure to brush up on the key terms presented at the beginning of each chapter. You might also want to review the glossary at the end of this book the day before you take the test.

Working Within The Framework

The test questions appear in random order, and many elements or issues that are mentioned in one question might also crop up in other questions. It's not uncommon to find that an incorrect answer to one question is the correct answer to another question and vice versa. Take the time to read every answer to each question, even if you recognize the answer to a question immediately. That extra reading might spark a memory or remind you about a networking feature or function that helps you on another question elsewhere in the exam.

Remember, you can revisit any question as many times as you like. If you're uncertain of the answer to a question, check the box that's provided so that you can return to it later. You should also mark questions that you think might offer information that you can use to answer other questions. On the fixed-length tests we've taken, we have usually marked somewhere between 25 and 50 percent of the questions. The testing software is designed to let you mark every question if you choose; use this framework to your advantage. Everything you'll want to see again should be marked; the testing software can then help you return to marked questions quickly and easily.

For fixed-length tests, we strongly recommend that you first read the entire test quickly before getting caught up in answering individual questions. This will help jog your memory as you review the potential answers, and it can help identify questions that you want to mark for easy access to their contents. The key is to make a quick pass over the territory to begin with—so that you know what you're up against—and then to survey that territory more thoroughly on a second pass, when you can begin to answer all questions systematically and consistently.

If you see something in a question or in one of the answers that jogs your memory on a topic or that you feel you should record if the topic appears in another question, write it down on your piece of paper.

Don't be afraid to take notes on what you see in various questions. Sometimes what you record from one question—especially if it's not as familiar as it should be or if it reminds you of the name or use of some network device, utility, or network interface details—can help you on other questions later on.

Deciding What To Memorize

The amount of memorization you must undertake for an exam depends on how well you remember what you've read and how well you know the material by heart. If you're a visual thinker and you can picture a network design and how all the components interact with each other, you won't need to memorize as much as someone who's less visually oriented. However, the exam will stretch your abilities to memorize internetwork features and functions, development technologies, and security and business concepts.

At a minimum, you'll want to memorize the following kinds of information:

➤ Basic information about networks including the Internet

➤ Types of servers and their functions

➤ Internet clients and their configuration and use

➤ The fundamentals of the TCP/IP protocol

➤ The different types of remote connectivity

➤ Internet design, development, and troubleshooting

➤ Internetworking security and business issues

Don't forget that The Cram Sheet at the front of the book is designed to capture the material that's most important to memorize; use this to guide your studies as well.

Preparing For The Test

The best way to prepare for the test—after you've studied—is to take at least one practice exam. We've included one here in this chapter for that reason. The test questions are located in the pages that follow, and, unlike the preceding chapters in this book, the answers don't follow the questions immediately; you'll have to flip to Chapter 17 to review the answers separately.

Give yourself 90 minutes to take the exam, and keep yourself on the honor system—don't look back at the text in the book or jump ahead to the answer key. When your time is up or you've finished the questions, you can use Chapter 17 to check your work. Pay special attention to the explanations for the incorrect answers; these can also help reinforce your knowledge of the material. Knowing how to recognize correct answers is good, but understanding why incorrect answers are wrong can be equally valuable.

Taking The Test

Relax. Once you're sitting in front of the testing computer, there's nothing more you can do to increase your knowledge or preparation. Take a deep breath, stretch, and start reading that first question.

You don't need to rush, either. You have plenty of time to complete each question and to return to those questions that you skip or mark for return. If you read a question twice and remain clueless, you can mark it if you're taking a fixed-length test. Don't spend more than five minutes on any single question—if it takes you that long to get nowhere, it's time to guess and move on.

You can read through the entire test, and before returning to marked questions for a second visit, you can figure out how much time you've got per question. As you answer each question, remove its mark. Continue to review the remaining marked questions until you run out of time or complete the test.

Set a maximum time limit for questions, and watch your time on long or complex questions. If you hit your limit, it's time to guess and move on. Don't deprive yourself of the opportunity to see more questions by taking too long to puzzle over questions, unless you think you can figure out the answer. Otherwise, you're limiting your opportunity to pass.

That's it for pointers. Here are some questions to help you practice for the actual test.

Sample Test

Question 1

Which of the following is a benefit of public key encryption?

○ a. It's the most secure encryption method.

○ b. It is not necessary to exchange private keys.

○ c. It increases the amount of bandwidth available.

○ d. All of the above

Question 2

Which of the following was designed to replace the GIF image format?

○ a. Tag Image File Format (TIFF)

○ b. Encapsulated PostScript (EPS)

○ c. Joint Photographic Experts Group (JPEG)

○ d. Portable Network Graphics (PNG)

Question 3

What is wrong with the following HTML markup?

```
<TITLE>Welcome to my Home page<title>
```

○ a. The closing tag is in lowercase.

○ b. The closing tag is missing a slash before the less-than symbol.

○ c. The opening tag is in uppercase.

○ d. The closing tag is missing a slash following the less-than symbol.

Question 4

Which of the following statements is true of a digital signature?

- ○ a. It verifies the identity of a person.
- ○ b. It encrypts the contents of a message.
- ○ c. It's typically created in a paint program to provide a graphical representation of one's signature in an email.
- ○ d. It does not provide non-repudiation of origin.

Question 5

What does the abbreviation AVI stand for?

- ○ a. Audio Visual Integration
- ○ b. Apple Video Internet
- ○ c. Audio Visual Information
- ○ d. Apple Video Interchange
- ○ e. Audio Video Interleaved

Question 6

Which of the following is a line protocol that supports only TCP/IP?

- ○ a. PPP
- ○ b. LSLIP
- ○ c. LPPP
- ○ d. SLIP

Question 7

ADSL and SDSL are:

- ○ a. Also known as advanced and simple digital support lines
- ○ b. The two main categories of DSL
- ○ c. Digital subscriber lines used over fiber optics
- ○ d. Specifications for HDTV

Question 8

Which one of the following is not a tunneling protocol?

○ a. PPP

○ b. L2TP

○ c. PPTP

○ d. L2F

○ e. IPSec

Question 9

Which part of the URL **http://www.comptia.org/index.htm** is the protocol used to access resources on the Web server?

○ a. **http://**

○ b. **www**

○ c. **comptia.org**

○ d. **index.htm**

Question 10

To create a link in a Web page, so that you can view a file on the local hard drive, which protocol designator should you use?

○ a. **c://**

○ b. **drive://**

○ c. **disk://**

○ d. **http://**

○ e. **file://**

Question 11

A client using Microsoft Internet Explorer to browse the Web must use which of the following protocols?

○ a. NetBEUI

○ b. IPX/SPX

○ c. TCP/IP

○ d. TCP and SPX

Question 12

What is the name for a text file that is given by the Web server, stored on the client, and then—on subsequent visits to the same site from the same client machine—sent back to the Web server?

○ a. BinHex

○ b. Cookie

○ c. PING

○ d. Comma-delimited

Question 13

What search criteria would best be used to find information about animals in Africa but not about elephants?

○ a. **+animals +africa -elephants**

○ b. **africa+ animals+ elephants-**

○ c. **"africa animals" elephants-**

○ d. **africa animals**

○ e. **+africa +animals ONLY**

Question 14

All of the following attributes are common to both images and tables except:

○ a. **WIDTH**

○ b. **BORDER**

○ c. **ALT**

○ d. **ALIGN**

Question 15

Which of the following is the correct syntax to mark the ending of a Visual Basic script within an HTML document?

- ○ a. **<SCRIPT="vbscript">**
- ○ b. **</LANGUAGE="vbscript">**
- ○ c. **</SCRIPT LANGUAGE="vbscript">**
- ○ d. **</SCRIPT>**

Question 16

The following code is an example of what type of list?

```
<OL>
  <LI>Frosting filled yellow sponge cakes
  <LI>Highly caffeinated yellow soft drink
</OL>
```

- ○ a. Bulleted, ordered list
- ○ b. Numbered, unordered list
- ○ c. Bulleted, unordered list
- ○ d. Numbered, ordered list
- ○ e. None of the above. **<OL>** is not a valid tag; instead **<UL>** should be used in its place.

Question 17

Which of the following uses the correct syntax to create a hyperlink named **email** to send an email message addressed to Aaron Gazer?

- ○ a. **If you have a question,**
  <A HREF="http:\\aarongazer@domain.com">
  email</A> me immediately.
- ○ b. **If you have a concern,**
  <A HREF="mailto:aarongazer@domain.com">
  email</A> me immediately.
- ○ c. **If you have a problem,**
  <mailto:aarongazer@domain.com:email> me immediately.
- ○ d. **If you have gripe, please email (aarongazer@domain.com)**
  me immediately.

Question 18

Your company wants to implement a fun and interactive online site for children. Your boss asks you to recommend a technology to create games that can be played from the Web. What should you recommend?

○ a. Flash

○ b. QuickTime VR

○ c. Shockwave

○ d. RealPlayer

Question 19

What type of file uses a .pdf extension?

○ a. PostDefinitions

○ b. Adobe Acrobat

○ c. Portable Web graphic files

○ d. Macromedia Flash

Question 20

Which of the following are benefits provided by SET? [Choose the three best answers]

❏ a. Ensures the safe transfer of credit card information

❏ b. Enables merchants to ensure that the consumer is authorized to use the credit card

❏ c. Enables the consumer to ensure the validity of the merchant

❏ d. Provides safe mechanisms for the transfer of payment card information via secret key encryption

Question 21

What is the default subnet mask for a Class A network?

○ a. 255.255.255.255

○ b. 255.255.255.0

○ c. 255.255.0.0

○ d. 255.0.0.0

Question 22

Which of the following are Application-layer protocols? [Choose the four best answers]

❏ a. HTTP

❏ b. FTP

❏ c. TCP

❏ d. SMTP

❏ e. Telnet

❏ f. UDP

Question 23

Which of the following Class B subnet masks will provide for 12 subnets with at least 4,000 hosts per subnet?

○ a. 255.255.0.0

○ b. 255.255.192.0

○ c. 255.255.240.0

○ d. 255.255.255.0

Question 24

What is the well-known port for FTP?

○ a. 21

○ b. 25

○ c. 80

○ d. 119

Question 25

You need to ensure that TCP/IP is properly installed on a client computer. Before you do anything else, you want to ping the loopback address. What address will you ping?

○ a. You must first type **IPCONFIG** to determine the client IP address

○ b. 127.0.0.1

○ c. 255.255.255.255

○ d. 207.55.86.2

Question 26

Which of the following is an extension to the Point-to-Point protocol developed by Microsoft and is commonly used for creating Virtual Private Networks?

○ a. PSTN

○ b. MS-DOS

○ c. L2F

○ d. PPTP

Question 27

Microsoft Internet Explorer and Netscape Navigator are two popular examples of what type of Internet client?

○ a. FTP software

○ b. Email

○ c. News

○ d. Web browser

Question 28

Which of the following protects a network from unauthorized access via the Internet?

○ a. Firewall

○ b. Certificate Authority

○ c. Denial of Service system

○ d. Anti-virus software

Question 29

When would it be appropriate to disable anti-virus software?

○ a. Never

○ b. When you suspect an email may have a virus-infected attachment

○ c. When installing software

○ d. When downloading software

Question 30

Which of the following protocols is a connectionless protocol?

○ a. TCP

○ b. UDP

○ c. UPS

○ d. TAPI

Question 31

The TCP/IP stack consists of ___ layers, and the OSI reference model consists of ___ layers.

○ a. 5 and 8

○ b. 4 and 7

○ c. 8 and 5

○ d. 7 and 4

Question 32

What is the correct syntax for placing an image named picture.jpg on a Web page?

○ a. **<IMG SRC="picture.gif">**

○ b. **<IMG HREF="picture.jpg">**

○ c. **<IMG SRC="picture.jpg">**

○ d. **<IMG PIC="picture.gif">**

Question 33

What is the term given to authentication methods that use fingerprints, hand-prints, voice recognition, and retina scans?

○ a. Bionics

○ b. Cybernetics

○ c. Authametics

○ d. Biometrics

Question 34

Which of the following is not needed to use a Web browser to browse the Internet?

○ a. TCP/IP configuration

○ b. FTP client

○ c. Internet connection

○ d. Computer or other Internet-accessible hardware device

Question 35

Which of the following by nature is most secure from outsiders?

○ a. Internet Web site

○ b. Intranet

○ c. Extranet

○ d. Internet FTP site

Question 36

Which of the following are two of the most popular file formats for displaying graphics in Web pages?

○ a. GIF and TIFF

○ b. JPEG and WAV

○ c. BMP and GIF

○ d. JPEG and GIF

Question 37

Which port, by default, is used by the SMTP service?

○ a. 21

○ b. 23

○ c. 25

○ d. 389

Question 38

Which of the following is an example of a server-side processing implementation?

○ a. Java applets

○ b. Java scripts

○ c. CGI

○ d. ActiveX controls

Question 39

Which of the following commands is used within FTP to upload multiple files to a remote site?

○ a. **put**

○ b. **get**

○ c. **mget**

○ d. **mput**

Question 40

What tool can be used to query a DNS server and find the name/IP-address translation?

○ a. NSLOOKUP

○ b. TRACERT

○ c. PING

○ d. NETSTAT

Question 41

Which of the following organizations is responsible for approving all standards for the Internet?

- O a. ISO
- O b. OSI
- O c. IETF
- O d. IEF

Question 42

Which of the following programming languages is used to create compiled executables?

- O a. Perl
- O b. JavaScript
- O c. JScript
- O d. C

Question 43

Which of the following tools is used to check the resolution of MAC addresses to IP addresses?

- O a. Ifconfig
- O b. ARP
- O c. Ipconfig
- O d. Winipcfg

Question 44

Print jobs are typically submitted across TCP/IP by using which of the following?

- O a. HTTP
- O b. NNTP
- O c. SMTP
- O d. LPR

Question 45

Which of the following are two methods of resolving names to IP addresses on Unix hosts?

- ❏ a. DNS
- ❏ b. LMHOSTS
- ❏ c. HOSTS
- ❏ d. DHCP
- ❏ e. WINS

Question 46

Which of the following protocols, by default, would run on port 110?

- ○ a. HTTP
- ○ b. NNTP
- ○ c. SMTP
- ○ d. POP3

Question 47

Data can be transferred between a SQL server and a Web server through the use of which of the following?

- ○ a. ODBC
- ○ b. OSI
- ○ c. API
- ○ d. ISAPI

Question 48

A vendor of a popular Web-based add-on routinely sends unsolicited ads from its server to clients running their browsers. Which technology would this be an example of?

- ○ a. Pull
- ○ b. Push
- ○ c. Thrust
- ○ d. XML

Question 49

A Web site that can be accessed only by internal employees and outside vendors, but not by the rest of the world, is an example of which of the following?

○ a. Regional

○ b. Intranet

○ c. Extranet

○ d. NAP

Question 50

Which of the following is an interconnectivity device that can be used to join two, and only two, subnets?

○ a. Hub

○ b. Bridge

○ c. Router

○ d. Brouter

Question 51

Links on a Web page can refer to more than one location if which of the following technologies is employed?

○ a. SET

○ b. XML

○ c. Java

○ d. VRML

Question 52

Which of the following characters signifies the beginning of comments within a HOSTS file?

○ a. @

○ b. $

○ c. !

○ d. #

Question 53

The Webmaster for CertificationCorner.com wants to apply for a copyright on the content displayed within the company's Web pages. To what agency must he/she apply?

○ a. IETF

○ b. Library of Congress

○ c. IAB

○ d. U.S. Office of Patents and Copyrights

Question 54

The Webmaster for CertificationCorner.com has been granted a copyright on the content displayed within the company's Web pages. What is the extent of the rights provided to the copyright holder?

○ a. Exclusive

○ b. Fair Use

○ c. Limited

○ d. Common

Question 55

LDAP, by default, runs at what port?

○ a. 110

○ b. 80

○ c. 119

○ d. 389

Question 56

What is the extension used to signify files encoded with BinHex?

○ a. .bnx

○ b. .hqx

○ c. .bin

○ d. .hex

Question 57

Which of the following protocols is commonly used to send email between servers?

○ a. POP3

○ b. IMAP

○ c. SMTP

○ d. MAPI

Question 58

Which two of the following protocols are commonly used by clients to retrieve and view email from servers?

❏ a. POP3

❏ b. IMAP

❏ c. SMTP

❏ d. MAPI

Question 59

Which of the following is the speed at which a T3 connection can transfer data?

○ a. 43Mbps

○ b. 1.544Mbps

○ c. 64Kbps

○ d. 56Kbps

Question 60

Which of the following is an interconnectivity device that can be used to transfer email between two networks?

○ a. Bridge

○ b. Gateway

○ c. Router

○ d. Hub

Question 61

A company that exists to provide Internet access to small companies and individuals is which of the following?

○ a. URL

○ b. NAP

○ c. ISP

○ d. ASP

Question 62

A Web site used to announce and market your products to the world is an example of a service over which of the following networks?

○ a. Internet

○ b. Intranet

○ c. Extranet

○ d. VPN

Question 63

Which of the following data technologies is the European equivalent of a T1 connection?

○ a. T3

○ b. E1

○ c. E3

○ d. NAP

Question 64

Which of the following technologies allows a hub to receive a signal and direct it to the port for which the data is intended?

○ a. Passive

○ b. Managing

○ c. Switching

○ d. Cascading

Question 65

> Which of the following is a high-bandwidth switching technology that uses only 53-byte cells?
>
> ○ a. Frame Relay
>
> ○ b. X.25
>
> ○ c. X.500
>
> ○ d. ATM

Question 66

> On Unix hosts, the DNS server can be specified within which of the following files in the /etc directory?
>
> ○ a. HOSTS
>
> ○ b. resolv.conf
>
> ○ c. network
>
> ○ d. services

Question 67

> Which of the following DNS record types is used for reverse lookups?
>
> ○ a. REV
>
> ○ b. NS
>
> ○ c. PTR
>
> ○ d. SOA

Question 68

> Which of the following services would be best for sending individual messages between individual users?
>
> ○ a. News
>
> ○ b. List
>
> ○ c. Terminal
>
> ○ d. Mail

Question 69

Which of the following is a command that can be used to transfer files from a local Unix machine to a remote Unix host?

- ○ a. Telnet
- ○ b. RCP
- ○ c. SMTP
- ○ d. BinHex

Question 70

Which of the following standards allows characters to be easily translated from one language set to another?

- ○ a. Unicode
- ○ b. EDI
- ○ c. XML
- ○ d. MAPI

Question 71

For which of the following purposes would SAPI be used when you're adding functionality to a system?

- ○ a. Monitoring
- ○ b. Mail
- ○ c. Voice
- ○ d. Troubleshooting

Question 72

Which of the following protocols, by default, runs at port 21?

- ○ a. FTP
- ○ b. Telnet
- ○ c. SMTP
- ○ d. HTTP

Answer Key

1. b	19. b	37. c	55. d
2. d	20. a, b, c	38. c	56. b
3. d	21. d	39. d	57. c
4. a	22. a, b, d, e	40. a	58. a, b
5. e	23. c	41. c	59. a
6. d	24. a	42. d	60. b
7. b	25. b	43. b	61. c
8. a	26. d	44. d	62. a
9. a	27. d	45. a, c	63. b
10. e	28. a	46. d	64. c
11. c	29. c	47. a	65. d
12. b	30. b	48. b	66. b
13. a	31. b	49. c	67. c
14. c	32. c	50. b	68. d
15. d	33. d	51. b	69. b
16. d	34. b	52. d	70. a
17. b	35. b	53. b	71. c
18. c	36. d	54. a	72. a

Question 1

The correct answer is b. Public key encryption is a method of asymmetric encryption that uses a public key and a private key. Unlike secret key encryption, public key encryption does not require the exchange of private keys. Although public key encryption is very secure, it is not necessarily the most secure means of encryption; therefore, answer a is incorrect. Answer c is incorrect because key encryption is not designed to increase bandwidth. Because answers a and c are incorrect, answer d is also incorrect.

Question 2

The correct answer is d. PNG was designed as a replacement for GIF, primarily due to the legal restrictions on the compression algorithms used with the GIF file format. Answers a, b, and c are incorrect because these describe file formats that were not meant to replace GIF images.

Question 3

The correct answer is d. The closing tag should have a slash immediately following the less-than symbol and not before, such as </TITLE>; therefore, answer b is incorrect. Because HTML is not case-sensitive, answers a and c are incorrect.

Question 4

The correct answer is a. In addition to ensuring that a message was not altered, a digital signature is also used with a digital certificate to verify the identity of the sender. Answer b is incorrect because a digitally signed message does not necessarily encrypt the contents of a message—it is the message digest that is actually encrypted. Answer c is incorrect because, in terms of security, this does not describe a digital signature. Answer d is incorrect because a digital signature does provide non-repudiation of origin and therefore could hold up in court.

Question 5

The correct answer is e. AVI is the abbreviation for Audio Video Interleaved. This is a format developed by Microsoft that supports full-motion video and sound; therefore, answers a, b, c, and d are incorrect.

Question 6

The correct answer is d. SLIP is a line protocol that supports only TCP/IP. SLIP is an older protocol that has been replaced by PPP and lacks many features that PPP supports, such as error correction and multi-protocol support. Therefore answer a is incorrect. Answers b and c are incorrect because these do not exist.

Question 7

The correct answer is b. There are several types of DSL technologies within the xDSL family. The two main categories are Asynchronous DSL (ADSL) and Synchronous DSL (SDSL). Answer a is not true; therefore, it is incorrect. Answer c is partially true in that ADSL and SDSL are digital subscriber lines, but they are used over copper wire, not fiber optics; therefore, answer c is incorrect. Answer d is incorrect because ADSL and SDSL have nothing to do with High Definition Television (HDTV).

Question 8

The correct answer is a. PPP is a ubiquitous data-link protocol and is not a tunneling protocol. L2TP, PPTP, and L2F are all Layer 2 tunneling protocols, and IPSec is a Layer 3 tunneling protocol; therefore, answers b, c, d, and e are incorrect.

Question 9

The correct answer is a. The protocol portion of the URL specifies the specific Internet protocol used to access network resources. Most common is the HTTP protocol, which is used to access Web pages, but other Internet protocols are also supported. Both **www** and **comptia.org** are part of the hostname; therefore, answers b and c are incorrect. Answer d is incorrect because index.htm is the file for the hypertext page.

Question 10

The correct answer is e. Use the **file://** protocol to access files located on a local disk. Answers a, b, and c appear to point to a local drive, but these are not valid protocol designators; therefore, they are incorrect. Answer d is incorrect because **http://** is the protocol designator to access documents located on a Web server.

Question 11

The correct answer is c. TCP/IP is the *de facto* standard protocol for use on the Internet. NetBEUI is a non-routable protocol limited to use on local area networks; therefore, answer a is incorrect. IPX/SPX is a set of Novell protocols used on and in-between local area networks; therefore, answer b is incorrect. Novell uses SPX in conjunction with the IPX protocol, which transports packets; therefore, answer d is incorrect.

Question 12

The correct answer is b. A cookie is a small text file transferred between the server and the client. Cookie files provide many benefits, including the ability to provide personalized Web pages. Answer a is incorrect because BinHex is a format for converting binary numbers to hexadecimal numbers. Answer c is incorrect because PING is a protocol and a utility for testing connectivity between systems. Answer d is incorrect because comma-delimited refers to a file in which data fields are separated by commas, making it easy for different database systems to share data.

Question 13

The correct answer is a. To require that a word be included in a search, use a required operator (plus sign) before the word. To exclude a word, use a prohibited operator (minus sign) before the word. Answers b and c are incorrect because they use the required and prohibited operators incorrectly. Answer d is incorrect because this search would not necessarily filter the word "elephant." Answer e is incorrect because this would find pages containing "africa" and "animals" and would also look for pages with the word "only" in all caps.

Question 14

The correct answer is c. The **ALT** attribute is used with images to specify alternate text to display. This attribute is used primarily to provide functionality when a browser does not display graphics. Answers a, b, and d are incorrect because these are valid attributes that are used with both images and tables.

Question 15

The correct answer is d. The <SCRIPT> tag used with the **LANGUAGE** attribute marks the beginning of a script and defines the script to be used in the Web page. To mark the ending of the script, simply use </SCRIPT>. Answers a, b, and c use incorrect syntax; therefore, they are incorrect.

Question 16

The correct answer is d. The <OL> tag is used to create a numbered, ordered list. You will typically want to use an ordered list when your list items are required to be in sequential order. Using the <UL> tag creates a bulleted, unordered list; therefore, answers a, b, c, and e are incorrect.

Question 17

The correct answer is b. To create a hyperlink that launches the client's email program with a preaddressed message, use the **HREF** attribute and the **mailto:** designator with the <A> tag. Answers a, c, and d are incorrect because they use the incorrect format for a hyperlink. The correct format to use is <**A HREF=** "mailto:*email_address*">Text user will click</A>.

Question 18

The correct answer is c. Shockwave content is developed with the Director Shockwave Studio program from Macromedia. Shockwave is popular for interactive games on the Web, as well as for business presentations, interactive Web content, kiosks, and CD-ROM and DVD titles and games. Answer a is incorrect because Flash is best used for designing vector-based animation and effects. Answer b is incorrect because QuickTime VR is used primarily for letting users interact in a virtual 3D environment in which objects can be fully rotated and explored. Answer d is incorrect because RealPlayer is a plug-in, used primarily for streaming media over the Internet.

Question 19

The correct answer is b. PDF (Portable Document Format) is a file format developed by Adobe Systems. PDF files provide a method to view documents in their electronic form exactly as they appear in their original form. Answers a and c are incorrect because these are made-up terms. Answer d is incorrect because Macromedia Flash files use a .swf extension.

Question 20

The correct answers are a, b, and c. Developed by Visa and MasterCard, SET is a protocol that allows for the safe transfer of payment card information and allows the merchant and the consumer to check the validity of each other. Although the primary purpose of SET is to provide mechanisms for the safe transfer of payment card information, SET uses public key encryption, not secret key; therefore, answer d is incorrect.

Question 21

The correct answer is d. By default, a Class A network uses 255.0.0.0 as the subnet mask. A Class B network's default subnet mask is 255.255.0.0; therefore, answer c is incorrect. The default subnet mask for a Class C network is 255.255.255.0; therefore, answer b is incorrect. 255.255.255.255 is not a default subnet mask—it is actually a broadcast address; therefore, answer a is incorrect. A Class A subnet mask is also known as /8. The eight is for the first eight bits, which are controlled by the InterNIC; therefore, a Class B subnet mask is /16, and a Class C is /24.

Question 22

The correct answers are a, b, d, and e. HTTP, FTP, SMTP, and Telnet are common examples of protocols residing at the Application layer. Answers c and f are incorrect because these protocols reside at the Transport layer.

Question 23

The correct answer is c. The decimal value 240 in the third octet equals 11110000 when converted to binary. Each "1" represents a power of 2, thus 2^4 equals 16, and we must always subtract two, which gives us 14 usable subnets. Left over for the host addresses are 12 bits; thus 2^{12}-2 equals 4,094 hosts per subnet. Although this gives us more subnets and hosts than required, if we tried to use 255.255.192.0, this would give us only 2 subnets; therefore, answer b is incorrect. 255.255.0.0 allows for 1 subnet with 65,534 hosts; therefore, answer a is incorrect. 255.255.255.0 allows for 254 subnets with 254 hosts per subnet; therefore, answer d is incorrect.

Question 24

The correct answer is a. Port 21 is used by FTP (File Transfer Protocol). Port 25 is used by SMTP; therefore, answer b is incorrect. Port 80 is used by HTTP; therefore, answer c is incorrect. Port 119 is used by NNTP; therefore, answer d is incorrect.

Question 25

The correct answer is b. The loopback address is 127.0.0.1. Another possible test would be to ping the client IP address; however, determining the client address is not necessary to perform a loopback test; therefore, answer a is incorrect. Answer c is incorrect because this is a broadcast address. Answer d is incorrect because this is a valid Class C network address.

Question 26

The correct answer is d. The Point-to-Point Tunneling Protocol (PPTP) was developed by Microsoft as an extension to PPP, and it is widely implemented as a tunneling protocol for VPNs. Answer a is incorrect because PSTN is the Public Switched Telephone Network. Answer b is incorrect because MS-DOS is a legacy operating system from Microsoft. Answer c is incorrect because L2F is a tunneling protocol developed by Cisco Systems.

Question 27

The correct answer is d. Microsoft Internet Explorer and Netscape Navigator are the two major players in the Web browser market. Both of these programs provide the client functionality needed for browsing the Web. Although many of the latest Web browsers are incorporating added Internet functionality, such as including software for email and news support and built-in FTP functionality, these products are still primarily thought of as Web browsers. Because Web browser is the best choice, answers a, b, and c are incorrect.

Question 28

The correct answer is a. A firewall, which can be hardware or software implemented, monitors incoming and outgoing traffic. A firewall can be used to filter traffic based upon certain criteria and can prevent access across certain ports. Answer b is incorrect because a Certificate Authority is an organization, such as VeriSign, that is in charge of digital certificates. Answer c might sound

good, but such a system does not exist; therefore, answer c is incorrect. Answer
d is incorrect because anti-virus software protects the systems on your network
from becoming infected with computer viruses.

Question 29

The correct answer is c. Temporarily disabling anti-virus software is acceptable
when you're installing software because the installation process may create problems otherwise; therefore, answer a is incorrect. Otherwise, you should always
ensure that you have up-to-date virus protection. Anti-virus software will protect your system from email attachments and from infected files you may
download as long as the anti-virus software is running; therefore, answers b
and d are incorrect.

Question 30

The correct answer is b. UDP is a connectionless protocol, so it does not provide guaranteed delivery as does TCP; therefore, answer a is incorrect. Answer
c is incorrect because a UPS or uninterruptible power supply is a device that
provides power protection to computer systems. Answer d is incorrect because
TAPI is a programming interface for voice services.

Question 31

The correct answer is b. The TCP/IP stack or Department of Defense reference model consists of four layers, and the OSI model is made up of seven
layers; therefore, answers a, c, and d are incorrect.

Question 32

The correct answer is c. Use the **IMG** tag with the **SRC** attribute. Although
the first choice is in the correct format, the file type is GIF; therefore, answer a
is incorrect. Answers b and d use the incorrect attribute; therefore, they are
incorrect.

Question 33

The correct answer is d. When used in the context of computer technology,
biometrics refers to the authentication techniques based upon measurable characteristics used to identify individuals. Answer a is incorrect because bionics is

the study of living organisms, applied to the creation of hardware to simulate the biological system. Answer b is incorrect because cybernetics is the study of control systems. Answer c is incorrect because I made it up.

Question 34

The correct answer is b. An FTP client is not needed to use a Web browser to surf the Internet. An FTP client is needed, however, to use the Internet to transfer files via the File Transfer Protocol. Answer a is incorrect because TCP/IP needs to be configured on the client. For example, the client machine is required to be assigned an IP address. Answer c is incorrect because some sort of connection to the Internet is required. Answer d is incorrect because some sort of device, such as a personal computer, is required.

Question 35

The correct answer is b. An intranet is a private network that utilizes Internet technologies. Intranets are insulated from the Internet. If an intranet provides Internet access, it should be well protected, and all traffic should be directed through a firewall. A Web site on the Internet is susceptible to all types of threats. The owners of even the most secure Web sites must be constantly vigilant in protecting their assets from the open Internet; therefore, answer a is incorrect. An extranet is generally secure because this type of network is formed by joining more than one intranet, usually using VPN technologies. An extranet, however, must contend with those who have access, yet are external to the company, such as vendors, partners, and customers; therefore, answer c is incorrect. Just as a Web site is, an FTP site on the Internet is accessible to the world; therefore, answer d is incorrect.

Question 36

The correct answer is d. JPEG and GIF images are two of the most popular image file formats for displaying graphics in Web pages. Most browsers natively support these two images without the use of a plug-in. TIFF is largely used in desktop publishing applications and requires the use of a plug-in to be viewed from the Internet; therefore, answer a is incorrect. WAV files are sound files, not image files; therefore, answer b is incorrect. A Web browser without a plug-in cannot display BMP images, and this file format is typically confined to Windows operating systems; therefore, answer c is incorrect.

Question 37

The correct answer is c. SMTP uses port 25, by default. The FTP service uses port 21, Telnet uses 23, and LDAP uses 389.

Question 38

The correct answer is c. CGI (Common Gateway Interface) scripts run on the server. Java applets, Java scripts, and ActiveX controls are all examples of client-based solutions.

Question 39

The correct answer is d; **mput** is used to upload multiple files to a remote site in the same way that **put** is used to upload a single file. Similarly, **get** will download a single file, and **mget** will download multiple files from a remote server.

Question 40

The correct answer is a. NSLOOKUP can be used to query a DNS server and find results. TRACERT is used to trace the hops that a packet takes to reach a remote host. PING is used to check connectivity to a remote host. NETSTAT shows networking statistics for the local host.

Question 41

The correct answer is c. The Internet Engineering Task Force (IETF) is charged with the acceptance of all standards as they relate to the Internet. The ISO (International Standards Organization) oversees the creation of standards that work across international boundaries; therefore, answer a is incorrect. ISO's most popular standard was the OSI model, which defines networking; therefore, answer b is incorrect. Answer d is invalid.

Question 42

The correct answer is d. The C language is used to write routines that are compiled into executables. Perl, JavaScript, and Jscript (Microsoft's version) are examples of uncompiled languages.

Question 43

The correct answer is b. ARP (Address Resolution Protocol) is both a protocol used to translate MAC addresses to other addresses, and a utility that can be used to view and interact with the results. The other three choices are all operating-system-specific utilities that display the IP configuration on a local host: Ifconfig works on Unix hosts, Ipconfig works on Windows NT/2000 machines, and Winipcfg works on Windows 95/98 machines.

Question 44

The correct answer is d. The LPR (Line Printer Request) utility is used to submit print jobs on TCP/IP. HTTP is the protocol used for the creation and display of Web sites; therefore, answer a is incorrect. NNTP is used with news, and SMTP is used with mail; therefore, answers b and c are incorrect.

Question 45

The correct answers are a and c. DNS is used on large installations, and HOSTS files can be used on small installations. Unix cannot work with LMHOSTS files and WINS services—both used to translate Microsoft computer names to IP addresses; therefore, answers b and e are incorrect. DHCP is used to issue IP configuration data but not to resolve any entries; therefore, answer d is incorrect.

Question 46

The correct answer is d. POP3, by default, uses port 110. HTTP uses port 80 by default, NNTP uses port 119, and SMTP uses port 25.

Question 47

The correct answer is a. ODBC (Open Database Connectivity) is used to allow SQL servers and Web servers to interact. OSI is a model of networking; therefore, answer b is incorrect. API (application programming interface) allows programmers to write applications to take advantage of operating-system features; therefore, answer c is incorrect. ISAPI is the Internet Service API, used to provide Internet services to the operating system; therefore, answer d is incorrect.

Question 48

The correct answer is b. With push technology, a server sends data to a client without first being asked to do so. The opposite of this is pull technology—which the Internet is built around—wherein a client requests data before it is sent from the server; therefore, answer a is incorrect. Thrust is an invalid option, so answer c is incorrect. XML is a programming language and not a technology pertinent to this question; therefore, answer d is incorrect.

Question 49

The correct answer is c. An extranet—commonly implemented as a Virtual Private Network (VPN)—is used for select access, most commonly by internal employees and outside vendors. Answer a is incorrect because a regional site is an invalid option. Answer b is incorrect because an intranet is used for internal use only. Answer d is incorrect because a Network Access Point (NAP) is used by an Internet Service Provider (ISP) to connect to the Internet backbone.

Question 50

The correct answer is b. A bridge can connect only two subnets into a single network. Answer a is incorrect because a hub is used within a subnet to connect the various hosts. Answer c is incorrect because a router is used to connect numerous subnets and networks. Answer d is incorrect because a brouter is a combination of a bridge and a router and is used with multiple sites.

Question 51

The correct answer is b. XML can be used to specify multiple links from a single location. Answer a is incorrect because SET is used to provide secure credit-card transactions. Answer c is incorrect because Java is a programming language. Answer d is incorrect because VRML is used to create 3D worlds.

Question 52

The correct answer is d. The pound sign (#) is used to signify the beginning of comments within a HOSTS or LMHOSTS file. The other choices presented are invalid for this question.

Question 53

The correct answer is b. The Library of Congress oversees applications for copyright protection, regardless of whether the applications are for work on a Web site, a book, a play, or any other medium. Answers a and c are incorrect because the IETF and IAB are Internet-related organizations and do not dabble with copyrights. Answer d is invalid because there is no such organization—patents and copyrights are protected by separate agencies.

Question 54

The correct answer is a. Copyright owners have exclusive rights to the items they have protected. Fair Use is a loophole that offers specific instances wherein copyright-protected content can be used without first seeking permission. The other choices are invalid terms in this context.

Question 55

The correct answer is d. LDAP uses port 389, by default. The POP3 service uses port 110, HTTP uses 80, and NNTP uses 119.

Question 56

The correct answer is b. The BinHex utility assigns the extension of .hqx to files it encodes. The other choices are invalid extensions.

Question 57

The correct answer is c. SMTP (Simple Mail Transfer Protocol) is used to transfer files between mail servers. Answers a and b are incorrect because POP3 and IMAP are two methods used by clients to view and retrieve mail from servers. Answer d is incorrect because MAPI defines actions to be associated with mail attachments based upon the mail attachments' file extensions.

Question 58

The correct answers are a and b. POP3 and IMAP are two methods used by clients to view and retrieve mail from servers. Answer c is incorrect because SMTP (Simple Mail Transfer Protocol) is used to transfer files between mail servers. Answer d is incorrect because MAPI defines actions to be associated with mail attachments based upon file extensions.

Question 59

The correct answer is a. A T3 connection can transfer data at speeds of 43Mbps. Answer b is incorrect because a T1 connection can transfer data at speeds of 1.544Mbps. Answer c is incorrect because 64Kbps can be the speed of some Frame Relay implementations. Answer d is incorrect because 56Kbps is typically the speed limitation of dial-up modems.

Question 60

The correct answer is b. A gateway is an upper-layer device that can be used to exchange email and other application-specific data between servers. Answer a is incorrect because a bridge is used to connect two and only two subnets. Answer c is incorrect because a router can connect multiple networks. Answer d is incorrect because a hub is used within a subnet to connect devices.

Question 61

The correct answer is c. An Internet Service Provider (ISP) provides Internet access through its Network Access Point (NAP—answer b). Answer a is incorrect because a URL (Uniform Resource Locator) is a means of specifying resource location. Answer d is incorrect because ASP commonly refers to Active Server Pages—HTML pages that incorporate dynamic programming.

Question 62

The correct answer is a. The Internet is used to provide access to the world—usually without restriction. Answer b is incorrect because an intranet is for internal use only. Answer c is incorrect because an extranet is used for internal use and for select outside parties. The most common implementation of an extranet is as a Virtual Private Network (VPN), answer d.

Question 63

The correct answer is b. An E1 connection is the European equivalent of a T1 connection. Answers a and c are incorrect because E3 is the European equivalent of a T3 connection. Answer d is incorrect because a Network Access Point (NAP) allows Internet Service Providers (ISPs) to connect to the Internet.

Question 64

The correct answer is c. Switching allows data to be selectively forwarded to the correct location. Answer a is incorrect because passive hubs have no features at all and send all data received to all ports. Answer b is incorrect because managed hubs offer administrative features that need not have anything to do with switching. Answer d is incorrect because cascading allows multiple hubs to be connected but still sends all data received to all ports.

Question 65

The correct answer is d. ATM uses 53-byte cells and increases response time by never needing to agree upon a cell size. Answer a is incorrect because Frame Relay can work with differing cell sizes. Answers b and c are incorrect because X. standards do not offer switching implementations.

Question 66

The correct answer is b. The resolv.conf file is used to specify the location of the DNS server. Answer a is incorrect because the HOSTS file is an alternative to DNS and is used to resolve addresses locally. Answers c and d are incorrect because the network and services files are used to define feature sets on an individual server.

Question 67

The correct answer is c. The PTR record is used for reverse lookups. Answer a is incorrect because there is no record type with the name REV. Answer b is incorrect because NS records hold name server information for a domain. Answer d is incorrect because SOA signifies the start of a record.

Question 68

The correct answer is d. A mail server is used to send individual messages between individual users. Answer a is incorrect because a news server sends messages to groups of users. Answer b is incorrect because a list server sends a message to all subscribed users. Answer c is incorrect because a terminal server is used for remote access and is not a valid server type for forwarding messages.

Question 69

The correct answer is b. The RCP (Remote Copy) utility exists only on Unix hosts and can be used to copy from a local to a remote host, or vice versa. Answer a is incorrect because Telnet provides remote access but not file-transfer abilities. Answer c is incorrect because SMTP is used to send mail. Answer d is incorrect because BinHex is used to encode data so it can become an attachment.

Question 70

The correct answer is a. Unicode allows each character to be quickly translated into a number of different character sets. Answer b is incorrect because EDI (Electronic Data Interchange) allows data to be translated between applications but not languages. Answer c is incorrect because XML is an enhancement to HTML and not used for language translation. Answer d is incorrect because MAPI defines associations between files and applications based upon extensions.

Question 71

The correct answer is c. The Speech API provides voice and telephony-related services to the operating system. All other choices are invalid in relation to SAPI.

Question 72

The correct answer is a. FTP, by default, runs at port 21. Telnet, by default, is configured for port 23, SMTP runs at port 25, and HTTP runs at port 80.

Index

Bold page numbers indicate sample exam questions.

B

BACKGROUND attribute, 196
BGCOLOR attribute, 196
BinHex, 129–130, **133, 134**, 212, **332**
Biometrics, 248, **328**
Bitmap graphics, 210–211
BMP, 219
Boolean operators, 111–112
BORDER attribute, 194
BRI ISDN, 69, **74, 75**
Bridges, 18, **331**
    advantages of, 15
    described, 14–15
    remote bridges, 15
Brouters, 16, 18, **26**
Browsers, 102, **327**
    antiquated, 281
    caching. *See* client caching.
    compatibility, 178–180
    cookies, controlling, 113–114
    testing, 232
Bulleted lists, 185–186, **205**
Business terms, 271–273
Business-to-business distribution, 272
Business-to-consumer distribution, 272
Bytecode, 161

C

C programming language, 164, 168, **330**
C++ programming language, 164, 168
CA, 249
Cable modems, 22, 71
Caching-only server, 86, **96–97**
Case sensitivity of searches, 109
CELLPADDING attribute, 195
CELLSPACING attribute, 195
Certification Corner, 7
CGI, 159–160, 168–169, **172, 329**
Checksums, 280, **288**
Class A addresses, 42, **56**
    subnet masks, 45, **325–326**
Class B addresses, 43
    subnet masks, 45, **326**
Class C addresses, 43, **53, 55, 56**
    subnet masks, 45
Class D addresses, 43, **54**
Class E addresses, 43
.class extension, 161
Client caching
    described, 107
    settings, 107–108

Client scripting, 169
Client/server model, 100
CNAME, 87, **94–95**
Color
    background, 182–183
    BGCOLOR attribute, 196
COLSPAN attribute, 195–196
Com domain, 85
Comments, adding, 183
CompTIA, 8–9
CompTIA exam software, 5
Concentrators. *See* hubs.
Configuring
    DNS, 48
    gateways, 48
    IP address, 48
    subnet masks, 48
    TCP/IP, 48–50
    WINS, 49
Connection speed, 281
Connectionless protocols, **52**
Connectivity
    ATM, 21
    cable modems, 22, 71
    described, 19
    DSL. *See* DSL.
    E1 connections, 19
    Frame Relay, 20, 23
    ISDN. *See* ISDN.
    multilink technology, 19
    PSTN. *See* PSTN.
    remote. *See* remote connectivity.
    T1 connections, 19–20
    T2 connections, 19–20
    T3 connections, 19–20
    X.25. *See* X.25.
Connectivity problems, 287
Content problems, 280–281
Cookies, 113–114, **118**, 234–235, **239, 324**
Copyright, 268–269, **274–275, 331–332**
Corrupt files, 281
Cram Sheet, 2, 299
Crawlers, 108
Cryptography
    cryptography keys, 250
    described, 250–251
    digital certificates, 251
    digital signatures, 251–252
    PGP, 252
    PKI, 251–254
    private keys, 251
    public key cryptography, 251